Team Leadership in the Game Industry

Seth Spaulding II

Course Technology PTR

A part of Cengage Learning

COURSE TECHNOLOGY
CENGAGE Learning™

Australia • Brazil • Japan • Korea • Mexico • Singapore • Spain • United Kingdom • United States

COURSE TECHNOLOGY
CENGAGE Learning

Team Leadership in the Game Industry
Seth Spaulding II

Publisher and General Manager, Course Technology PTR: Stacy L. Hiquet

Associate Director of Marketing: Sarah Panella

Manager of Editorial Services: Heather Talbot

Marketing Manager: Jordan Casey

Acquisitions Editor: Heather Hurley

Project Editor: Kate Shoup

PTR Editorial Services Coordinator: Jen Blaney

Copy Editor: Kate Shoup

Interior Layout Tech: Macmillan Publishing Solutions

Cover Designer: Mike Tanamachi

Indexer: Larry Sweazy

Proofreader: Melba Hopper

For product information and technology assistance, contact us at **Cengage Learning Customer & Sales Support, 1-800-354-9706**

For permission to use material from this text or product, submit all requests online at **www.cengage.com/permissions**
Further permissions questions can be emailed to **permissionrequest@cengage.com**

"Leadership That Gets Results" by Daniel Goleman, published in *Harvard Business Review* (Mar/Apr 2000) is © Hay Research Group. All other trademarks are the property of their respective owners.

Library of Congress Control Number: 2008929216

ISBN-13: 978-1-59863-572-0

ISBN-10: 1-59863-572-7

Course Technology
25 Thomson Place
Boston, MA 02210
USA

Cengage Learning is a leading provider of customized learning solutions with office locations around the globe, including Singapore, the United Kingdom, Australia, Mexico, Brazil, and Japan. Locate your local office at: **international.cengage.com/region**

Cengage Learning products are represented in Canada by Nelson Education, Ltd.

For your lifelong learning solutions, visit **courseptr.com**

Visit our corporate website at **cengage.com**

Printed in Canada
1 2 3 4 5 6 7 11 10 09

To my wife Stephanie and son Seth Richard.

ACKNOWLEDGMENTS

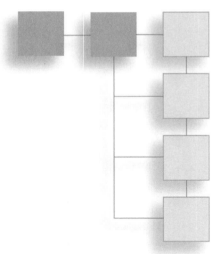

This book would not have been possible without the contributions of a great many individuals who, over the course of my career, taught me a wealth of management and leadership lessons.

At Cengage Learning, thanks go to Heather Hurley, who thought that the book sounded like a good idea and endured my many cover suggestions; my editor, Kate Shoup, who consistently makes me sound a lot smarter than I really am and, in the end, managed to impart to me the proper use of "that" and "which."

This text is far more relevant and engaging for the contributions of the many leaders and game-industry professionals interviewed herein, including Julien Bares, Brenda Brathwaite, John Chowanec, David Fifield, Stephen Martin, Robert Martin, Steve Meyer, Joe Minton, Lasse Seppänen, and David Silverman. Their combined perspectives on leadership and their unique experiences offer real insight to the reader.

At 2K Games, I would like to acknowledge and thank Cindi Buckwalter and Gail Hamrick for providing support and, maybe more importantly, smoothing out the corporate-communications approvals. At Firaxis Games specifically, I would like to additionally thank Barry Caudill, Greg Foertsch, Steve Ogden, and Dorian Newcomb for their feedback and contributions.

I would also like to thank the Harvard Publishing Group and the Hay Group for their generous permissions regarding the notes on their research.

And finally, deepest thanks to my wife, Stephanie, who not only tolerated my weekend and evening writing stretches but provided me with a great deal of support and encouragement.

About the Author

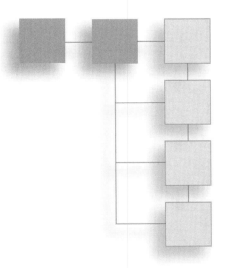

Seth Spaulding is a 14-year veteran of the game industry. After 10 years as art director, senior artist/vice president, and subsequently president of Cyberlore Studios in Massachusetts, Seth moved to Maryland in November 2005 to become art director of the award-winning studio, Firaxis Games, a subsidiary of 2K Games and Take Two Interactive. Prior to moving to Firaxis, Seth worked on titles for SSI, Blizzard, Accolade, Hasbro Interactive, Atari, Microsoft, Ubisoft, and 2K Games, including *Entomorph, WarCraft II: Beyond the Dark Portal, Deadlock II, Majesty: The Fantasy Kingdom Simulator, Risk, MechWarrior4: Mercenaries,* and *Playboy: The Mansion*. Recently published titles include *Sid Meier's Railroads, Civilization IV: Warlords, Civilization IV: Beyond the Sword, Civilization IV: Colonization,* and *Civilization Revolution*.

CONTENTS

INTRODUCTION

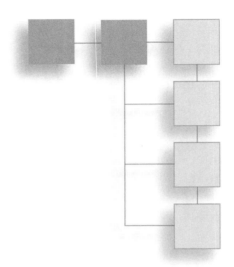

Why Leadership?

I was a grizzled, three-and-a-half-month veteran of the game industry when I became director of an art department consisting of two almost–full-time artists. How very unprepared I was to face the challenges of the next 10 years was not apparent then. At the time, the title and role was basically that of a lead artist with staffing authority and input on company practices.

Looking back, I was fortunate that I had some other related experience from a commercial graphics company to prepare me somewhat for the job—but there was nothing to prepare me or my fellow managers for what our company was to become in the next decade. We were fortunate to catch a few lucky breaks and thrived for many years relying mainly on our talent, our common sense, and the input from each other as we faced the host of challenges endemic to small start-up game developers. One of the toughest problems we faced was finding, supporting, and retaining good team leaders as our project teams grew.

Indeed, the issue of team leadership follows directly out of the growth in scale of the teams who make games. In the 1980s, one or two developers could construct an entire game. By the mid-1990s, the scale of game-development teams was on a steep growth curve, while the industry itself was really still in its infancy. As will be discussed in Chapter 1, "How We Got Here," this has meant that our teams have generally been led by specialists who excel in their specific specializations without a great deal of focus on the interpersonal skills that are required to lead larger teams.

In 2000, I began hosting Art Director/Lead Artist Round Table talks at the annual Game Developers Conference (GDC), partly out of a desire to gain a better grasp on what I was doing as an art director and what we were doing as a company as we—and the industry—grew in scale and complexity. In many ways, this book is as much a result of those discussions as it is my personal experience and the experiences of my colleagues. For that reason, I am indebted to the many Round Table participants over the years who, collectively, have provided a unique window into the game industry. What I—and all the participants—learned through our dialogs was leaders in the industry took many different approaches to solving a set of problems that seemed to be common across all companies, from the Sonys and Microsofts down to the small start-up developers. How do we retain our top talent? How do we define the lead role and organize our project teams? How do we select leads? How do we not blow our schedule? How do we deal with underperformers? And a host of other issues.

French philosopher, journalist, and pacifist Emile Chartier once said, "Nothing is more dangerous than an idea when it's the only one you have." And to that point, I believe very firmly that the best conclusions and deductions are arrived at by considering subject matter from as many valid viewpoints as possible. My experience, while hopefully valuable, is only one perspective of the industry and team management questions and only one opinion on what are sometimes subjective leadership issues. That's why, throughout the book in the form of interviews, I have drawn together the leadership experience of some exceptional individuals—many of whom I've had the pleasure and privilege to work with in the course of my career. I am very much indebted to these leaders and creative people who helped shape my character and allowed me to grow as a leader. The interview subjects are for the most part pretty ordinary people. There are no industry rock-stars (though there is one "legendary designer") or CEOs of publicly traded companies. That said, all have held team-leadership roles, survived some rough patches, and found ways to enable their teams to succeed and maintain a high level of morale during the projects they led. Another factor I used in the selection of the industry interviewees was their record of staff retention following the completion of a project. A company can assemble a talented team and produce a very good game, but if that company cannot retain its talented—and now experienced—people beyond that project, its team or teams will never achieve an efficient cohesive working relationship, and the company will have a much more challenging path to long-term success.

As will be seen, a major cause of people leaving a company is the perceived poor quality of their supervisors and senior management. The game business is a talent-based industry—the stronger and deeper your talent is, the better your chances are of creating a great game. It is very difficult, in any hiring environment, to build the right mix of cross-disciplinary talent who function as a team at a high level; indeed, most companies never manage it. Once you get talented individuals on board, it's critical not to lose them. Finding and nurturing competent leaders who have the trust of the team will generate more retention than any addition of pool tables, movie nights, or verbal commitments to the value of "quality of life."

This book addresses the current state of the games industry, problems of leadership in the industry, and how we choose and support our leaders, illustrated by some case studies. Subsequently, I will discuss some best practices for selecting leads from a pool of internal candidates or making the decision to launch an external search. I'll also discuss classic leadership traits and how they apply to the selection and evaluation of leaders. Exercises are included, covering the essential traits of a lead and a hypothetical lead-selection scenario. Additionally, the book looks at specific roles and responsibilities of leads and directors, and offers some best practices for daily performance of duties based on my decade in the industry and the assembled wisdom of the GDC Round Table attendees. It is my hope that this book will be of value to anyone in a leadership or management position in the game industry, as well as those aspiring to a leadership position. If so, it is my further hope that as a result, the industry as a whole will progress by considering the issue and importance of leadership.

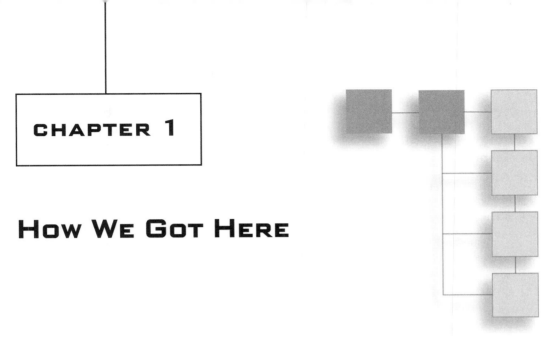

CHAPTER 1

How We Got Here

"How does your company select leads? What are your criteria?"

I posed this question at the Art Directors/Lead Artists Round Table at the 2001 GDC to a group of 30 or so directors and leads, most of whom worked at large, successful, and seemingly well-organized game-development and game-publishing companies. No hands were immediately raised. Indeed, I saw a few sidelong glances and grimaces. It took a few minutes to get the discussion rolling, but once it took off, the group spent the bulk of our one-hour session on this one topic. The dialogue illustrated for me that the industry was going through a transition in the scale of its production teams and was, in many cases, failing to meet the leadership needs of those teams.

Having been a leader in the games industry for 12 years, the industry's appeal is very clear to me—the rapid and constant evolution of our craft, the opportunity to work with incredibly talented and diversely skilled colleagues, and the fact that you can build your professional wardrobe entirely from torn jeans and trade-show t-shirt giveaways. There is no other job like it. However, one of the aspects of the job that I've always found challenging is the scarcity of strong team leaders, the misguided criteria we typically employ to select leads, the lack of support we make available to leads once in place, and the disasters experienced by teams, projects, and companies due to these conditions—hence the reason for this book. If our industry does not begin to employ good leadership practices, game companies will lose staff to competitors who employ better practices and the

1

industry as a whole will experience a drain of talent as employees flee to other businesses.

Team Leadership in the Game Industry is an attempt to identify some tangible and proven practices and common traits that make great team leaders and in doing so present a template for improving team leadership across the industry. What I do not intend here is a discussion of specific production methodologies. Entire volumes of production books expound on the organizational virtues of Scrum versus Waterfall versus Organic, or whatever the buzzwords *du jour* are for a given moment. Although these books are valuable resources, they typically only tangentially touch on what I feel is the most critical issue facing your team— the quality of your leadership. As you will see in Chapter 2, "The Anatomy of a Game-Development Company," there are as many ways to organize your team as there are methodologies to manage your project. In my experience, most companies make decisions for both based on the strengths and weaknesses of their personnel as often as they do based on the assessment of the merit of the idea. Ideally, you will be able to make more merit-based decisions on organization, roles and responsibilities, and production format if you can reach a point where you are less limited by the existing leadership potential of your personnel.

This book focuses on team leadership at the production level, which is not to be confused with the production process or the technical details of a producer's job per se. For our purposes, "team" is defined very broadly. A team can be anything from a specialist lead or sub-lead and one production person, to a team lead who, directly and indirectly, oversees dozens of game developers. In each case, the lead has a set of common responsibilities above and beyond his or her personal production contribution to the project. The lead may in fact, have no production responsibilities at all, as in the case of the large team lead.

Note

As you will see in Chapter 2, many game companies have organized themselves well. Projects are typically headed by leads who establish specialist leads (sometimes called sub-leads) to handle major components like networking, graphics programming, and character animation, to name a few. The leads group usually consists of the art lead, tech lead, design lead, and producer. Each lead, if in a multi-project company, will typically report to a director, who in turn reports to a studio head or president. Note, however, that the terminology varies from company to company quite a bit. For example, programming might be called engineering or tech, or the project art lead might be called an art director and report to a studio art director, and so on. For the purposes of this book, I intend to use the director/lead/specialist lead hierarchy to describe the lead roles, and programming/art/production to describe department roles, regardless of the specific title that some of my examples may have taken.

Problems Facing the Game Industry

Typically, team leaders have been promoted from the development teams, usually by virtue of their production quality and/or quantity, but are now called upon to transition to a different mindset and demonstrate new skills—frequently with little or no preparation time. The game industry is not unique in facing this problem. In the course of my research, many people in other industries have told me that their team leaders are promoted in the same manner, supported in the same way, and therefore experience the same failure rates and negative repercussions. Game-development companies do, however, face some unique challenges, which I think are inherent in the work they do. First, they generally have a very young staff. This population is extremely energetic and driven, but lacking in significant work experience, which translates almost directly to poor or inefficient communication capabilities. Second, the project-cycle length—sometimes three years and longer—requires team leads to maintain the team's focus and morale for an extended time period and through all manner of trials. Finally, the industry is in a state of constant transition, making it difficult to keep pace.

Growth in Scale

The game industry, in the earliest form that this book will discuss, began in the late 1970s with games like *Pong* and, later, text adventure and graphically simple adventure and action games. One person working for a few weeks or months could produce a computer or video game. The massive marketing and retail machines that current game publishers have simply didn't exist. In the 1980s, at companies like Microprose, it was common for everyone to stop work at a certain point when a game was considered finished and start putting disks in plastic baggies for a few days. (This seems bizarre today, given that top-tier games are expected to release simultaneously worldwide, in sync with seemingly abstract fiscal quarters, on multiple first-party platforms, after millions of dollars have been spent in an attempt to raise awareness of the game in a media-saturated audience.)

When I joined the game industry in 1995, developers had already established team and department leads due to the increasing scale of development teams. Unlike games that preceded my entreé into the field, which were often distributed in stacks of floppy disks, my first game was released on a CD. We outsourced our opening pre-rendered movie, we had established—but not codified—job descriptions, and had developed a scheduling system.

In a number of ways, this picture looks similar to development 12 years later—but the real story is in the growth in scale. In 1995, we had an art department consisting of a director (myself) and a 1½ person department as part of a six-person company. We had a lead programmer who supervised a staff of two and a producer who was also a studio director and an HR manager. In the years since, however, development teams have expanded by a factor of 20 or more.

What happened between those early days in the 1970s and 1980s and today, and what did that transition mean in terms of leadership needs for what was now a growing development team? A book of this scope cannot attempt to cover the comprehensive story of the growth of the game industry, but taking a big-picture view of the historical transition in scale of the industry's development teams is an instructive place to begin.

Increased Graphical Depth

Since the industry began, games have gradually taken more graphical depth and have consequently required more complex tools to develop those visuals. Bringing a game to market with dated graphics will greatly hinder its ability to generate any sort of pre-release player interest and even be the direct cause of a game's cancellation late in the development cycle since no publisher wants a sub-par title lingering on shelves and damaging its reputation. Driving this relentless visual content progression has been the combination of audience expectation and market competition, the evolution of display technology, and the rapid growth in media storage capability.

Note

To every rule and global statement, there are always exceptions, of course. Many highly successful games have featured average to poor graphics, but these tend to be sleeper hits or games that are on the forefront of new gaming genres.

Technological developments both push and pull developers into advancing graphical commitments. On the display side, we've witnessed a progression from one-color capability to 16-color to 256-color, to full-color and high-definition. Within the next five or 10 years, there will almost certainly be some new frontier that again raises the bar for market acceptability. With each display advance, new art tools need to be written or purchased for artists to author their assets. For example, if you entered the game industry as an artist in the early 1990s, you needed to master a 2D paint program called D-Paint. D-Paint, short for Deluxe

Paint, had about six tools options from which to select and that was it. Provided that you could navigate DOS and could draw, you were in. Gradually, however, the tools evolved to support the improving display hardware; within 10 years, an artist needed to demonstrate knowledge of, if not mastery in, a 3D program (each of these evolving in complexity with every version), and Photoshop, a comprehensive 2D graphics program. Additionally, there has been a birth and growth of specialized tools for the creation of terrain, trees, effects, and any number of graphical elements. Each of these programs requires dedicated artists to spend significant time gaining mastery of them—usually while developing with them. No longer can one artist produce a game, much less one coder/designer/artist. These tools require some degree of programmer development and support as well as new skill sets for the (growing number of) artists in question.

The expansion of storage media has also had a profound effect on the game industry. Case in point: In 1991, I worked for a graphics company. That year, we purchased our first 1GB hard drive—an impressive behemoth that weighed about as much as a truck battery. When we hooked it into our network, we solemnly declared our file-storage problems over. Exactly two months later, it was full.

Since then, every company I've been associated with has seen storage needs rise dramatically every year. Increased storage capability is a good thing, but it's also an example of how a technological advance can *pull* developers into increasing their graphics commitments. A game-company executive once said to me, "Artists are like gasses. They will expand their assets to fill any given volume." Although he spoke these words in 1996, they remain essentially true today—if perhaps misguided with regard to blame. In fact, almost every member of a development team can think of ways to fill greater storage volume with the goal of bringing a deeper, broader (but not necessarily more fun) experience to the player. Indeed, with CDs being used as storage media in the early '90s, we saw an explosion of pre-rendered opening movies and cinematic cut-scene content, which not only succeeded in filling CD space but also built new specializations within the industry: the cinematic artist and animator. I can still see the lens flare afterglow of these movies—and, I confess, I made a few of them. Beyond the cinematic content, though, increased storage space and increased run-time memory have allowed a steady rise in actual game art content and complexity. We now can create environments that truly beg players to suspend their disbelief and immerse themselves in new worlds.

Note

If someone was asked to fix a date, 1993 was a watershed year for player immersion via game visuals, with the release of *Doom* and *Myst*. These two games probably couldn't be more different in their themes, visuals, and game play, but they both succeeded wildly in creating believable worlds for their audiences at the time, and spawned hundreds of imitators eager to take these visual experiences to the next level.

Expanded Game Requirements and Coding Complexities

A second factor in the overall team-scale increase is found in the increase in programming staff requirements due to the explosion of complexity associated with 3D engine development, the expanded number and complexity of gaming platforms, and increasing performance expectations.

The 3D revolution came to gaming slowly in the early '90s; by the mid to late '90s, it was the rare retail game that made it to market with 2D graphics. Not surprisingly, with the advent of 3D, an expansion of complexity similar to the one on the artistic side of the game occurred on the engineering front. The 3D shift not only required a new set of skills to interpret world and object space onto a 2D screen, but also lighting and eventually physics became highly involved sub-specialties.

Early games running in custom consoles or on specific hardware often had to accomplish comparatively few technical goals. Although even the earliest Atari console games featured single-screen multiplayer gaming, few people in 1981 could have foreseen that the ensuing 15 years would bring a vast array of game-capable PC configurations, consoles, multiplayer needs, voice chat, multi-core systems, and greatly expanded user-interface (UI) and audio capabilities. Now, instead of one programmer (usually also the designer) developing a game, game developers employ programming teams divided into sub-teams of coders dedicated to four or five specialties, totaling in many cases 20–40 personnel, exclusive of middleware development teams. Even when middleware is applied to projects with the goal of reducing development time, the implementation is rarely without need of internal support. With such a growth in complexity of coding teams has come the challenge of managing the coding process to reduce bugs, eliminate redundant work, and ensure that the various aspects of the code are well integrated.

Clearly, these ever-increasingly impressive visuals have not come without a heavy price to the required scale of development teams. Indeed, a developer's resources are strained at every succeeding cycle, as individual asset creation time increases but the overall duration of development cycles—while increasing—has not proportionally followed. Publishers respond to the rising costs by raising the price of games and looking to cut overhead through outsourcing and exploring alternative digital delivery methods like Valve's Steam. Developers respond by adding staff, increasing development time, outsourcing, and implementing better tools—either custom coded or purchased as middleware from a burgeoning industry of specialized toolmakers. This team scale increase has also created growing pressure on game-development team leaders. Not only are their teams larger, but they are more diverse, with more areas of specialized expertise requiring more individuals to take leadership positions on a given team.

Growth in Scale on a Company Level

Most small developers run on very tight margins, with the time between one project ending and the next one starting being the period during which most of them run out of capital and either go out of business or lay off a significant percentage of their staff in order to survive. In the 1980s, when a large development budget was in the low six figures, the negotiation and approval typically happened very rapidly, so the "between project trough" might have been rough, but it was also relatively short. Today, a large development budget may represent tens of millions of dollars for a publisher when development, marketing, and distribution costs are factored in. This requires much more due diligence on the part of all parties and involves a contract negotiation and an internal approval process that can easily take months. An obvious solution is for a small developer to get bigger, taking on two or more projects so that the trough can be covered by overlapping projects' milestone payments.

To handle this increase in projects, the addition of one or more production teams is in order. This simple solution works in a great many cases, but it needs to be understood that the organizational issues and leadership needs of the company have just multiplied. In fact, this expanded company now has to consider issues of departmental as well as project leadership. How do those leaders interact and communicate? Who has approval authority and over what areas in a dual-matrix structure? These and a great many more questions need to be asked and answered, with plans put in place, before any expansion occurs.

The Round Table Answers the Question...

So, how has leadership evolved over time as developer staffs, budgets, and project expectations have increased? My findings from that GDC Art Directors/Lead Artists Round Table discussion in 2001 were not encouraging. The initial stab at an answer to my question, "How does your company select leads? What are your criteria?" came from the art director at one of the most successful developers in the industry, who said, "The art lead needs to be the best artist. It's like cavemen sitting around a fire; the one who can break the biggest bone is the leader." There was a pause in the room while people, including myself, gathered their thoughts. Either everyone was soaking in the wisdom, or no one wanted to contradict the art director of the best-selling games at the time. So I asked the group, "What do you think? Are there any issues with that?" One participant tentatively asked, "Is there a danger in taking your best artist out of production and having them take on management tasks?" Another asked, "What if your best artist is not equipped for that role?" (As I recall, the word "jackass" was used.) A chorus of opinions then began to be voiced—including a few in support of the "best artist" theory.

We used the bulk of the hour to write down some traits of the ideal lead, including passion for the project, effective communicator, capable generalist, visionary, responsible, and so on. Very few of the traits had anything to do with the individual's ability to make great art. We moved toward the idea that instead of being the best artist, the lead should be a capable generalist. That is, the lead should have a solid foundation of knowledge of the art process used by all of his or her specialists. The idea wasn't that the lead should be equipped to jump in to help out unless in a critical situation, but that he or she utilize this understanding when scheduling estimates and giving meaningful critiques. We next decided that the lead needed to be passionate about his or her vision of the project. This is critical to the lead's ability to inspire and lead the team over the course of a two- or three-year development cycle. Frankly, this quality is important for all team members. Next we added a typical (but important) mix of communication and organizational skills. And finally, one word that I remember from the session was "trust." The lead must have—or, if he or she is new hire, must be able to quickly gain—the trust of the team. In addition, the lead must trust his or her team sufficiently to be able to delegate effectively. Without this component, proper communication paths will be ignored, the team will not function properly, and the lead will fail.

Beyond what a lead *embodies* lies what a lead *does* and how he or she does it. At the Round Table, we came up with an exhaustive list that went well beyond what any one individual can possibly do. That was because there are many different management models that game companies employ, and leadership functions are often spread out among a few different individuals. Regardless of title, however, there are certain key functions that leads fulfill whether they are called a lead, sub-lead, specialist lead, director, or manager.

One of the most common—and most commonly cited as needing improvement—is the responsibility for production review of code or assets. I frequently hear a great deal of frustration from artists and programmers regarding how their lead reviews their work—either too rarely, too frequently, incompletely, inconsistently, or incoherently. This issue is covered in greater detail in Chapter 5, "Leadership Types and Traits: Assessment and Development Strategies." As difficult as these problems can be for department or project morale, however, they are among the most easily correctable aspects of a lead's performance. Issues surrounding basic communication and social skills have formed the bulk of the truly intractable lead challenges that I or my colleagues have experienced during my time in the game industry. Sometimes, as you will see later in the book, these issues are resolved only by transferring the lead role to another individual. It's obviously best to avoid such situations altogether, but as awkward and messy as this solution can be, it is usually the lesser evil.

I have repeated this exercise to start every Art Directors/Lead Artists Round Table I have led since. Over time, I have noticed that the answers move closer to that 2001 list. I later formalized and expanded this "Build Your Ideal Lead" exercise for a seminar in 2006 by creating more than 20 cards, each with a single positive leadership trait. I asked seminar attendees to work in groups of three or four and achieve consensus to narrow the traits down to eight and then, after a group discussion and break, narrow it further to five. The exercise was very instructive to all, and is presented in its entirety in Chapter 4, "A Litmus Test for Leads." In the process of running this exercise, personal experience weighs heavily, and the subjectively charged meaning of some of the terms is evened out by the requirement to arrive at a group consensus. (Note that although my background is in art and many examples I cite are from the Art Directors/Lead Artists Round Table, the fundamental leadership and management issues are applicable for all leads and directors regardless of their discipline.)

Note

I have had the great fortune to work with some exceptional leaders during my career. Each had a different approach to the challenges of the job and all had quite different personalities, but there were amongst them a few common traits that are worth consideration for any lead in the game industry. I have yet to meet a team leader who is so well rounded, however, that they function ideally in all situations.

Practical Issues Remain

While the answers may be closer to the list generated at GDC in 2001, in practice, the industry is falling short as a whole due to the adherence to traditional career paths. In business we experience career advancement as the acquisition of more and more responsibility through management and the accompanying higher pay and perks. So it is natural that the best production people will, after a few years, begin to think about how they can climb the ladder at their company. This is why many great production artists and programmers proceed into management—because they need to or feel they need to in order to advance their careers.

This mindset seems broken.

Career Path Management Issues

Fortunately, a few companies in the game industry have recognized this and implemented alternative dual and equivalent career-development solutions, which we will look at in detail later. It is an uphill battle, however. There is no doubt that leads do get more respect; the title looks better on a resumé, and any number of perks are sometimes associated with it. In addition, in trying to implement some other system, we're struggling against accepted societal norms of career progression that are reinforced throughout our culture, media, and calls home to the parents. Consequently, department directors around the industry are frequently faced with the dilemma of having one of their most valued production personnel requesting a lead role and implying that they will consider looking elsewhere for one if the company is not willing to consider their request.

In this environment, it is hard not to promote great production people into lead roles despite their possible lack of suitability for the position and in some cases lack of real desire for the responsibilities that it entails. I have been in many director-level meeting where we've said, "Look, we're going to have this individual be the lead; we know he's got some communication issues, but the producer is really going to keep an eye out for that and help him out...and he's the closest thing to a lead we have" or "He'll walk if he doesn't get it." The first few times this happened in my career, I was keen to accept that rationale and vow to also watch the situation and help out when I could. After all, I got my leadership spot when someone took a chance on me. In my experience, however, promoting an individual to a lead role with known reservations about any key criteria has led to difficulties on the team to some degree *every single time*. Sometimes no one wants to work with the lead again; sometimes the project suffers; sometimes both. Poor support and oversight by the other managers and directors worsen the damage.

The Cost of Poor Leadership

The ultimate victims are your valuable staff members. Most directors of companies I speak with tell me that recruiting and retaining top talent is a major difficulty for them. This seems to be the case regardless of locale. California developers complain about the amount of competition and job hopping among skilled talent, and East Coast and Midwest developers frequently complain that the top talent goes to California and is reluctant to move to a city where there might only be two or three other developers. In every case, given that attracting talent is hard, you don't want your best people to have any reason to leave, let alone over an issue as large as their supervisor being poorly trained, unsupported, or incompetent. According to research from *The 7 Hidden Reasons Employees Leave: How to Recognize the Subtle Signs and Act Before It's Too Late* by Leigh Branham (AMACOM, January 2005), 75 percent of managers believe that the reason they lose staff is because of money, 88 percent of workers say it's other factors, and a full third of these cite their supervisor or senior manager for the reason they left their job. Poor lead assignment immediately calls into question the judgment and overall awareness of upper management by at least a portion of the company. In addition, if a valued production staff member performs poorly in the lead role, that person may well end up leaving anyway or suffering his or her own morale decline.

Leads are like any other valuable employee and they must be supported as such. Your company is in competition with dozens of others not only to attract great employees but to retain them—particularly the ones you have invested time and resources in developing. I've found that in the case of leads, lack of commitment to proper staffing and frustration surrounding resource allocation are the primary reasons that leads cite for leaving an employer.

There are solutions to this uninviting scenario—but most are not simple or quick. The desired role and scope of responsibility needs to be communicated to the company so that everyone is aware of the expectations of the position. Leads can and should be trained and developed over time. Perceptive managers often intuitively know who would make a good lead and, given time, can encourage and develop those skills as needed. Also, great leaders can enter your company by chance. They can be junior production people, QA temps—anything. If you can recognize them and move them into the appropriate roles, the positive effects across your company can be transformative.

Great leads, regardless of their specific role or department, inspire teams, create possibilities, and reinforce a positive culture. I've witnessed cases in which a team was excited about being a part of a project with a great lead without even knowing what that project would be. I've also seen marginal role-players within a team become highly valued problem-solvers by virtue of the fact that they trusted their lead and were inspired by the project.

If you have found your ideal sets of leads, it is important to understand that you are only halfway to having them complete a successful project. Once you've identified a great lead or potential lead, that person needs as much structure within his or her discipline as any other employee. Leads, like all team members, need training, guidance, feedback, and a clear understanding of their roles and responsibilities. It's critical that, at the director level, you work to establish these roles clearly and as completely as you can before the project starts. Having an understood set of responsibilities and expectations for which leads will be held accountable will help marginal leads succeed where otherwise they might falter and require significant management.

The issue of management training is a topic I bring up frequently at the GDC Round Tables; surprisingly, few companies engage in any sort of management training for new or experienced leads. Almost everyone in the room, however, would very much like their companies to invest in such training. I find it odd that a developer would be willing to spend a few thousand dollars to send a lead to GDC but not spend a few hundred for targeted management training. Management training is not a magic potion that will transform someone into a great lead after one seminar, and it won't magically instill potential in someone with no leadership skills, but it will hopefully cause them to begin to shift their thinking to their new role and new set of responsibilities, and ideally, they will come away with many tools to better do their job.

Interview: Lasse Seppänen, Executive Producer, Remedy Entertainment

Lasse Seppänen—currently the executive producer at Remedy Entertainment (best known for its *Max Payne* games) and responsible for the company's organization, recruitment, scheduling, critical processes, and whatever else may lie on the critical path for shipping *Alan Wake*—began his game career as a game designer in 1998. Combining university studies in Industrial Management and New Media Production, Seppänen then earned a Master of Arts in 1999. In the ensuing years, Seppänen founded a start-up studio, worked as a game-industry advisor at Nokia, and served as the studio head at Sumea, the critically acclaimed mobile-games studio in Helsinki. Since 2003, Seppänen has been an active contributor to one of the world's most active IGDA branches, the Finland chapter, of which he is a founding member. In 2006–2007, Seppänen planned and organized an evening and weekend further education course for game industry managers and leads—possibly the first such focused course in the world. Seppänen has worked as a leader and with other leaders as a subordinate, peer, and a leader of leaders. He has also participated in top-level management teams in various roles.

Seth Spaulding: Describe your transition from a production position to a leadership position. What were some unexpected challenges or surprises?

Lasse Seppänen: I started my career as a game designer/storywriter/programmer, first in hobby and student projects, and then in 1998 professionally. The original impulse that got me kicked off in the producer direction was that the company I was working for was so small that they needed people to wear multiple hats, and they lacked enough producers. So I put on that hat as well, and soon enough learnt that being in charge *is* different. Before that point, I admit I had been keen on pointing out problems in our processes and structure but didn't give much focus or thought to presenting solutions. But once in charge, I soon realized it isn't as easy as it seems. You're constantly pressed for time and have to choose to fight only the critical battles.

In this company, producers also had to do some business development—for instance, writing proposals for potential adver-game clients and going on site to pitch the projects to them. Though stressful, this was a valuable period from a learning point of view. You were always expected to come up with something good enough in terms of both creative and production parameters, under very tight time constraints, and to be able to make the whole package easily under-standable and attractive to an outsider.

Then, in 2001, some friends and I founded our own company to work on the Nintendo GBA. Even though my title at the time was creative director, it's fair to say that I ended up being the main driving force behind the whole enterprise, both project managing and pitching the game like in my previous job.

It started to dawn on me that regardless of my intended role, I had nearly always ended up "project managing" even in hobby and student projects, as well as all kinds of private-life activities—e.g., parties, societies, live-action role-playing events, gaming nights, etc. So at this point, I realized that maybe I shouldn't fight it anymore. Who knows? Maybe I could be a decent producer, instead of an unfocused game designer who wears too many hats! Once I took that mental step, I never looked back or wanted to go back.

While I worked at the GBA company, I made contact with Remedy for the first time, and I was immediately converted to their strong branding and positioning thinking. I read a number of books—e.g., *Differentiate or Die: Survival in Our Era of Killer Competition* by Jack Trout—and did my best to apply the theory to the project we were pitching to publishers. But more importantly, this way of thinking about games as products and brands has proved very useful in leading designers and producers later, especially in multi-project environments.

S.S.: Looking back, are there any decisions or practices you would change, and if so, why?

L.S.: I think I have learnt from every step, both from successes and mistakes, so I wouldn't really change anything.

S.S.: What is the most important thing you would tell someone making that transition within their company?

L.S.: The very first question you should ask is if you have a clear definition for what kind of a lead you are expected to be. At Remedy, we divide leadership "hats" in three main categories: HR and recruitment, tasking and scheduling, and expertise and directing. For instance, our art director is focused on applying his expertise and directing others in creative decisions, whereas the art team manager is a combination of HR and tasking.

Then I would say the most important concrete thing is to drop hands-on work, even if you think you could do it better than your subordinates. As a lead or a manager, every hour of your work affects the work of many others, whereas when doing hands-on work, you're only affecting a single person's work. Yes, if you are the new programming lead, it may sometimes make sense for you to do, for example, a quick round of prototype coding that only you can do really fast. However, this should definitely be the exception and not the rule.

Why is that? Soon after becoming a lead, you will notice that you just simply don't have time and mindshare for everything—in fact, these two are your most scarce resources. You have to think carefully where to invest them so that you have the biggest impact on the whole. Sometimes it's hands-on work, but in most cases it shouldn't be. If, after the promotion, you find yourself constantly working hands-on, then you need to consider whether the move to a leadership position was the right one in the first place. Or maybe you should consider recruiting, promoting or training a replacement for the work you seem to constantly end up doing.

Sounds logical enough, right? However, I've noticed that it can be extraordinarily difficult for new leads to give up hands-on work. Sometimes it's simply a case of lacking the replacement, and sometimes the move to a lead position just wasn't that person's calling and he or she needs to return back to production work. Ultimately, only you yourself can tell which way it is.

Also, in a new role, you often have to start with some fire-fighting—solving immediate problems that have become acute in the absence of a lead. It's okay to focus on these for a while, but you should be worried if you are unable, within a few months, to move to looking ahead and preventing problems rather than fighting them after they have exploded on your face. Many studies show that fire-fighting is, in most cases, more expensive than preventive work—and this cost is essentially paid in those precious currencies: your time and mindshare.

Identify your own unique style of leading others and focus on developing it—it's hard to try to do things in someone else's style. Think back about leads whose work you have witnessed in the past—probably some of them worked in ways that seem more "you" than others. There's no single right style of leadership, so you should boldly focus on your own style.

It is important to often take some time to think about the bigger picture—strategy and policies. For instance, as a new programming lead, you may need to simultaneously consider what is the best approach for making sure the current project is completed on the code side within the next six months, while developing a new next-generation technology and, on top of that, recruiting new programmers. It may take some quiet thinking to figure it out—and in the office, it may be hard to find the time to focus on it. Sometimes going off-site to work is a great way to do this, as it removes the daily cycle of interruption after interruption.

From day one, you should start making your continuous presence unnecessary. Eventually, your people should easily be able to work for up to a week or so without you. If that's not the case, your team can't take any chances of you falling ill or being injured in an accident. And you're also unable to take any concentration time for the bigger picture when constantly dealing with day-to-day issues.

You should also regularly take some time to speak in private with each person on your team—not just daily task and problem-solving–oriented talks, but informal chats about how they think the team and the project are doing. This will help you keep your finger on the pulse and give you early warning about problems that may be coming down the road—for instance, if someone is unhappy about something that you could fix if you only knew about it.

Personally, I like to think a leadership position as a "service" occupation—you need to make yourself available to your people whenever they need you. Otherwise, you may easily turn into a bottleneck that is slowing things down. One simple thing to consider is where you are seated after becoming a lead, as it can have a big impact on the project. It may also make sense to change the seating during the project—during concepting and prototyping, you may want to be more in contact with cross-discipline leads, whereas during the production phase, you may want to be closer to your own team.

Finally, the work we as leaders do consists of a lot of problem-solving, and creativity is essential in solving complex problems—but creativity will wither if you only feed similar input all the time. Remember to take some time off as well (weekends, holidays) as these help your mind to see the forest, not just the trees. It's easy to be consumed by work when you are in a new position and driven, but you should care for your own quality of life, too. I have found I do my best thinking and get the most useful ideas when I'm well-rested and possibly doing something other than work.

I'd also recommend reading a good book or two—for instance *First, Break All the Rules: What the World's Greatest Managers Do Differently* by Marcus Buckingham and Curt Coffman.

S.S.: Were there any people who helped, and if so, how?

L.S.: I have to say that I have learnt a lot from every leader I have ever worked for, ranging from some very hands-on pragmatic people, to very theoretical folks, to very high-level business people. Mostly it's been a question of seeing what they do and figuring out what seems to work and what doesn't.

S.S.: What are the most common traits shared by other effective leaders in your experience?

L.S.: I'm a fan of Peter Drucker's writings; he has said "Leadership is defined by results, not attributes." I think he's right in the sense that each leader is different and the ultimate test for leadership is whether or not the goals are met.

Having said that, I think there are several traits that are useful and common in effective leaders I've met:

- Driven and proactive

- Analytical

- Organized

- Energetic

- Has a good sense of time and perspective (on the scale of a day, a month, a year, a decade)

- Has excellent communication skills

- Decisive (often it's better to make a good decision today than a perfect decision in a month)

- Leads consistently to a chosen strategic direction, changes direction only after careful consideration and analysis, and communicates the change clearly

- Thinks about strategy and tactics at the same time

- Gives feedback sooner rather than later so that the connection between cause and effect is clearer

I think it's also important to be empathic, to be able to put oneself in another person's shoes. A keen understanding of the effect your actions will have on people is very important for successful leadership. In the companies where I've worked, understanding of multiple cultures has been rather important—the role and work culture expectations may vary a lot compared to what you may be used to. For instance, people coming from Eastern Europe, the U.S., or Nordic countries may all have a different view of what a leader's role is and may react in a completely different way from what you'd expect. To be effective as a leader, you need to be able to learn the difference in how to deal with different people and different cultures.

I also try to always put people first. Whenever a "people issue"—e.g., someone is not the right person for his or her current position—enters my to-do list, I deal with it as soon as possible. These are usually very fundamental problems that cause the most damage. Once, I had a programmer who agreed in meetings to do one thing, and then at night or over the weekend would do what he wanted with the game—writing features we had specifically agreed not to include. After a rapid intervention and a short mandatory holiday, things worked fine again. Obviously, waiting for a "more convenient time" to handle the situation would have caused great damage and put the credibility of the leadership in the eyes of the whole team in danger.

Another thing I've noticed is that effective leaders make sure to understand the problem before attempting to solve it. That should be obvious, right? But in real life, we often find ourselves addressing a problem that is visible and "easy" to fix rather than finding and tackling the hard problems that are really holding us back. For instance, you create a workaround process to compensate for an incompetent team member instead of confronting the person and moving him or her to a more suitable position. Or, as Peter Drucker puts it: "There is nothing so useless as doing efficiently that which should not be done at all."

S.S.: Which traits do you feel are your strongest, and how does knowledge of these traits affect how you approach leadership challenges?

L.S.: It's hard to see oneself objectively, but I'd say that I always try to be humble and to respect other people's expertise. The one who knows most and has the best vision or solution should influence the decision most, even if it's not the thing I myself thought about first. However, when I have listened to all the relevant people, I know it's my duty to make the call, and stick to it.

I also try to be approachable. In general, I tend to get along very well with everyone, and can find something in common to talk about with almost anyone. I think people tend to come and talk to me quite easily when they have a problem.

Having a varied, colorful background (industrial management, new media studies, game design, programming, and even making music as a hobby) has helped a lot in relating to and leading very diverse types of people.

I also do my best to always have a clear big-picture idea of what we're doing. For instance, from my industrial management background, I see studios that develop new IP more similar to product development laboratories than assembly lines or factories. I then reflect decisions in, for example, designing the organization or recruiting people against that idea.

S.S.: What are the worst traits a leader exhibited in your experience?

L.S.: One bad habit that I've seen is talking to someone but not giving him or her full attention—for instance, reading e-mails or writing text messages. In my view, the team member present in the room should always be more important than someone who is calling, e-mailing, or texting you. If the team members feel they are welcome and get the attention of the lead, they are more likely to come talk to you early when problems are just dots in the horizon and you can still avoid them with smaller efforts.

It can also be a deeply frustrating situation when someone is a bottleneck for all decisions, yet doesn't have enough time to deal with it all. Then everything's held up pending that person's decisions, and the situation is worsened when no other team member is empowered or able to take any responsibility or drive things forward.

S.S.: Are there any leadership traits you admire or perhaps aspire toward but don't feel you embody?

L.S.: I recently read about Pixar's John Lasseter, and someone noted in the book that "If he is talking to you, you are the only person in his world at that moment." I admit that sometimes it's hard to concentrate on the discussion with somebody without thinking forward—maybe about the meeting that is coming up in 15 minutes. Partly it's unavoidable and part of the "normal" fragmentation of a lead's day, but I do try to make a conscious effort to improve focus at times.

(By the way, the book's name is *To Infinity and Beyond! The Story of Pixar Animation Studios* by Karen Paik, Ed Catmull, Steve Jobs, and John Lasseter.)

S.S.: Do you mentor other leaders?

L.S.: I currently have eight leads working under me, and I try to mentor all of them in various ways, depending on what each one's role and background requires. I also organized an evening and weekend course for Finnish game industry managers and leads in 2006–2007. We had about 20 participants, and the lecturers were mainly visiting managers and leads from various game companies in the U.S., U.K., Sweden, Denmark, and Finland.

S.S.: Do you have any training in leadership, either formal or unstructured (e.g., armed forces experience)? If relevant, in what ways do you feel you apply that to challenges in your job?

L.S.: I did my mandatory military service in the Finnish Air Force in 1992–1993 and was trained to lead a small team. It's hard to pinpoint any particular useful item from there, but I still think it may have been useful—though I certainly don't think game companies should be led in the military style.

After the military, I did three years of studies in industrial management and then three years in new media design and production. In the former, I had useful courses like critical chain thinking and work psychology, whereas the latter studies gave a better understanding of dealing with a variety of different personalities and creative backgrounds, as well as how producers work in multimedia.

I have also read a lot of leadership books, and have been considering doing an MBA, but haven't found time for it yet.

S.S.: What do you see as the toughest challenge facing leads during a game-development project cycle or at a game-development company generally?

L.S.: I think this depends a lot on the project and the company, of course. I have mostly worked on original IP, and there I think the balancing between more freeform R&D and a structured schedule-driven production is often one of the trickiest things. How do you create convergence in the product and a reasonable schedule without destroying the creativity? It's always a balancing act.

At best, I've seen systematic prototyping and planning. The fun needs to be proved early; then the rest is mainly execution and iteration.

Some leads push too early straight to production mode before the pre-production is done. This can obviously cause problems and inefficiencies.

Another interesting leadership challenge in games is how to stay market oriented and, for example, take the marketing or sales team's feedback without losing the team's creative ownership of the game. It's yet another balancing act.

S.S.: What are some common mistakes you've seen leads make, be they new or experienced? How could these missteps have been avoided or were there any that were important learning experiences?

L.S.: One peculiar thing I've noticed is that new leads sometimes tend to recruit people who are similar to themselves, whereas diversity might actually be more productive. For instance, if every game designer has a storywriter background, they might not be as good as a team at designing mechanics or pitching their ideas through concept visuals. I know I've made this mistake in the past. If you want to keep the team creative and develop new IP, you really need a mix of people and skills.

Another thing I've noticed is doing recruitment mainly based on a resume and "technical" skills (e.g., experience with a particular software), but not considering other factors like the personality match with the team or other potential. In many cases new tools can be taught if the talent is there. And there are ways to have people do a test to determine if they have certain kinds of talent.

For many new leads, it's hard to let go of the hands-on work and bear the risk that others may make mistakes. Also, some new leads think that now that they are "management," they are supposed to work crazy hours and that when they do, they are automatically doing the right thing. But doing a *lot* of things is not the same as doing the *right* things.

S.S.: How have you seen new leads best get support from directors or executives?

L.S.: There needs to be clear communication to the team about what the new lead is responsible for, and the message has to be reinforced by the executive's actions. I always do my best to strengthen the chain of command. For instance, sometimes people come to talk directly to me about issues that really belong to the new lead. If I comment on whatever they have in their mind, it easily becomes my decision and I'm undermining the new lead. Therefore, it's better to say "So and so makes the call about things like that, please talk to him."

I always try to follow the mantra "Praise in public, criticize in private." If there's negative feedback about the new lead, we need to talk about it in private.

I also try to support the new lead's decisions. I don't want to overanalyze or second-guess their decisions all the time; it's important to let them also make their own calls and stand by them. Keep in mind that people also learn from mistakes. But of course I need to step in if I think it will be a major disaster. People also can surprise you sometimes; you'd think something won't work, but for some reason, they can make it work. Blocking such decisions would prevent them from applying and developing their own style of leading.

The most important thing is to set up the new lead for success one way or another. I recently hired a new producer from outside the company; to get him up to speed as fast as possible, I created an exceptionally exhaustive two-page list of bullet points for a basic briefing that we went through together. Another thing I did was a written briefing with background, goals, expectations, and other useful information for his first "mini-project" to make sure he had a very clear picture of what was expected and a reference he could dig up when he needed to remember some key point. I also sent him links to all the materials he was supposed to read. I made sure he was seated next to me at the office, did my best to coach him daily, and arranged lunches with all the other leads. I'm glad to see that he hit the ground running and is already carrying very important responsibilities in the team after only four months.

S.S.: Do you think good leaders can be trained? Or is the essence of a good leader simply innate ability?

L.S.: Any successful training requires good student material, so yes, potential leaders will gain a lot from training, but it doesn't mean that everyone can become a leader. Skills can be taught, talent not.

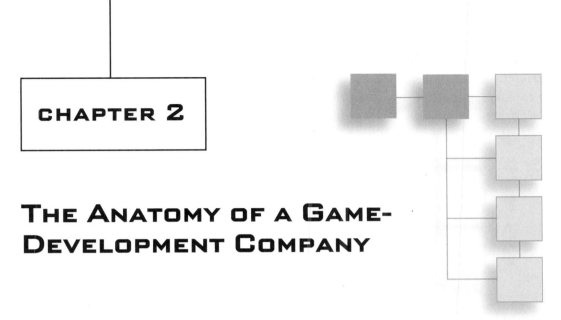

CHAPTER 2

THE ANATOMY OF A GAME-DEVELOPMENT COMPANY

Establishing and communicating the organizational structure of your company is the first step toward ensuring that your people understand their roles and are able to approach development in a reasonable fashion. Managers and leaders can also spot bottlenecks and areas of over- and under-staffing in their company by building an organizational chart like the ones found in this chapter.

There are probably as many ways to organize a game company as there are game companies. This chapter focuses on three models representing three stages of scale, the challenges inherent within each model, and the specific leadership issues that frequently evolve from them. These models do not purport to be any attempt to create an "ideal" company organization; they merely represent common models.

Note

Due to differing corporate structures and simple nomenclature diversity, one company's art director may be another's lead artist or art manager, and so on. This chapter helps to define and clarify the terms used throughout the book.

The organizational charts in this chapter show project and department reporting structures, the number of direct and indirect reports, optimal communication paths, and in larger companies, the need for a dual matrix management. They do not, however, show a key component of a game-development company: the company culture. Establishing an attractive and effective company culture is critical to a developer. It's one of the main things that can make your company stand out in a crowd when recruiting and retaining skilled people. Given that, it is imperative that decisions affecting company culture be considered and deliberate. When the culture turns negative—and it can, for any number of reasons—no organizational wizardry will bring it back.

Small Company Organization Overview

The structure of most start-up game developers looks something like what's shown in Figure 2.1. Typically, managers do a great deal of production work on top of their management duties, which can be quite light depending on the exact number of staff in each department. This leads to a dual communication path

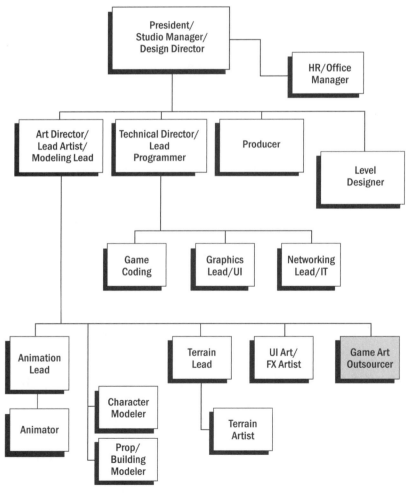

Figure 2.1
Small studio organization chart.

model that is not necessarily evident at first, but by the second or third stage of growth development may become an issue.

Company culture is much more homogenous in smaller companies than in larger structures. That is to say, with such a small group, there is usually one weekend social plan such as movies and parties in which the bulk of the company participates.

Strengths and Weaknesses of the Model

The major strength of the small-developer model is the low ratio of overhead compared to production personnel. The ratio in this model is about 15 to one production versus management and administrative personnel, excluding the possible contribution of outsourcers. The ratio becomes even higher, around 18 to one, when the dual responsibilities of certain positions are considered. This makes the project team very production focused, dynamic, cost effective, and adaptable. Leaders in these models have the relative luxury of a very light management load (in terms of quantity). Assuming that the tech director in this model does bi-annual reviews, he or she need only prepare three reviews, and this activity might occupy only a single day. Departmental issues such as purchase requests, timekeeping, and hiring can usually be handled with one quick meeting, or by simply turning around in one's chair for a speedy ad hoc conversation. Culturally, this small setup encourages a feeling of community across the company, which can make shared burdens, such as extended overtime situations, a time of positive company-wide social bonding.

Within this sense of community, however, there exists a potential inherent weakness: Small companies growing out of this phase into larger structures frequently carry the community feeling to a "family" level, wherein a tightly knit subculture develops among some legacy employees and managers, which can lead to some unprofessional practices. Among the symptoms of this condition is an inclination to retain underperformers and ultimately fail to nurture sustainable, skilled personnel who move the team and the company at pace with the industry.

Note

There are, of course, other weaknesses that the reader familiar with the industry may imagine, such as the danger of being too small to effectively complete a project in the event of a change in scale to project needs, but for our purposes, we will focus only on the weaknesses that directly affect leadership and management.

In this model, we see a potential anomaly at the director level. The producer, a project lead, sits alongside the art director and technical director, who also act as project leads. At this stage, the arrangement is probably going to work fine, but at the next level of growth, the director-level communication paths will diverge from the project-lead paths. Recognizing and discussing this early can prepare the company and the specific individuals affected for potential title and role changes. One way around this is to give the producer the additional title of production director or executive producer. This solution at least approaches the assumed role change upon the growth of the company, but it will strike many as odd to have a director who is not actually currently directing anyone in the entire company.

Physical Organization

There are entire books dealing with the subject of effective office layout. While this book cannot attempt to go into any depth on the subject, there are some very important physical-layout factors to consider that directly affect employee well-being and team and department communication. These issues are explored here to the extent that they apply to leadership and management issues.

The layout of personnel at this stage of growth is usually one of the least-considered aspects of a management team, whose primary concern tends to be getting the least-expensive space and furniture to support the number of staff. But attention should be paid to physical layout as well as office location, preferably early on in the formation of a company. Specifically, you'll want to consider the following: Do you want large team rooms, individual offices, or a mix? Cubicles or open work areas? Pool table or no pool table?

Some of these considerations may seem trivial, but decisions made at this formative time have a great impact on company culture moving forward for years. For example, one developer I know decided early on to use $20 folding tables as desks. These were neither attractive nor wonderfully functional, but they were cost effective and easy to move into different configurations as project and personnel needs dictated. Years later, they were a multi-project company working on top franchises, and trying to attract top-tier industry talent—still working on $20 folding tables. On the positive side, they showed that you can make great games on shoddy folding tables, but one can imagine the impression this office made on experienced interviewees as well as publishers. Quality office furniture is an expense, but it's an expense that directly improves the quality of everyone's workday experience—and that latter factor should be the litmus test for evaluating overhead expenditures.

Challenges for Leaders

Leaders in small companies must set up processes and plans to approach the challenges of this model, with the goal being to prepare to effectively grow into a larger structure. This practice—essentially, establishing a professional company culture—will certainly add overhead in terms of work and perhaps added personnel, but the rewards of that investment will become evident when the company does expand. A balance needs to be struck here; "professional culture" does not mean process heavy and overly formal. No one wants to work at a humorless job with faceless management, especially in an industry that has a reputation for a casual, even fun, culture. Actually doing this can be a daunting task, but it's not something that should be done in a vacuum. It is very important to solicit feedback from the entire company on work issues, particularly those affecting everyone's workspace, the company culture, and your employees' quality of life.

Leaders in companies at this stage also personally need to carefully walk a fine line between being friendly and becoming friends with team members. This is probably one of the most difficult things for a new leader in a small, tight-knit company to do, particularly in such a structure where there are no other examples of professional work relationships to model. When the time does come for growth in the company, leaders may realize that they have become too personally close to their subordinates and need to make sometimes difficult and awkward adjustments in their social activities. Leaders who are promoted from within teams face this challenge at any size of company, but, like in many other areas, the most difficult attitudes to break are those that become a key component of the company culture at an early stage.

Successful communication can be one of the least worrisome features of this model. Team members are usually placed close together with leads and management nearby, making the act of communication easier. However easy communication is at the team level in this model, it can still be ineffective if good practices are not developed and adhered to. Bad habits, such as agenda-less meetings and too many ad hoc meetings in which no note taking occurs, can easily become part of the company culture. Establishing ground rules for communication early enables good practices to become part of the culture. It is important to recognize that multiple roles in this model can create communication confusion. For example, the art director in this model needs to communicate as a lead modeler and as a supervisor to the same people at different times—which can get particularly complicated and odd when the company begins to grow into multiple project teams.

Careful attention needs to be paid to potential bottlenecks developing in studios where departmental-lead and project-lead roles are shared and production work is also required. Figure 2.2 is another look at the same small company, but from the perspective of the project-reporting system.

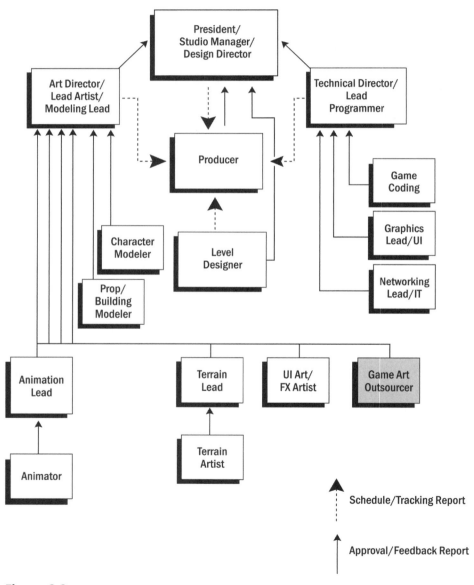

Figure 2.2
Small studio project communication path. Many solid arrows going to one box = bad.

You can see in this view that the art director/lead artist/modeling lead is currently receiving six direct reports as well as doing lead reporting to the design director and schedule reporting to the producer. This will likely produce an overload at this position, and any one of his or her individual duties may suffer as a result. In my experience, project-management responsibilities typically take the forefront and the greater share of attention, followed by personal production work and then departmental duties. Things like technical quality control, schedule management, departmental reviews, and training tend to get less attention than they might otherwise in favor of more important project-related tasks. One way to divest the art director of some reports is to assign another member of the staff the role of the lead modeler. In a small organization, however, this may not be an option depending on the skills available in the company. Where that is the case, it's critical to scale the production expectations of leads based on the number of direct reports.

Leadership transition at the director level, which is always a delicate matter, is magnified in a small company simply due to the fact that the company cannot cover the responsibilities of the departed employee as easily as might happen in a larger organization. A single high-level departure can sometimes have a much larger effect on company culture. In addition, there may potentially be thorny ownership or equity questions to resolve. Needless to say, it is advisable to get all ownership and equity agreements in writing and to ensure that everyone understands and agrees to the exit plan for the studio and for the individual owners.

The final potential weakness of this arrangement that can develop is an overtly dictatorial studio head/design lead at the top of the chart. The design lead is by nature going to lead the team creatively; if that role is combined with the authority of the studio head, you have an unstoppable force. This can be a good thing; history is full of benevolent and effective monarchs. But the model is not very sustainable, particularly during and after periods of transition. In my experience, the separation of these two roles makes for more reliable structures. In this example, the level designer could conceivably work as the design lead, thus removing complete creative control from the studio executive.

Things to consider at this stage:

- Create an employee handbook that includes information on the company's mission and values as well as expected workplace conditions (hours, holidays, etc.), benefit information, and whatever else might be useful. Review and edit it annually at a minimum or as needed by circumstances.

- Set up an employee-review schedule and review form. This does not have to be very complicated at this stage, but a form reassures employees that their contributions will be reviewed objectively and by criteria that they understand in advance.

- Define and write a description of roles and responsibilities within the project and department. As part of this, consider who has approval or recommendation authority in the project structure. See Chapter 6, "The Project Team Leader: Roles and Responsibilities," for some sample "Role" and "Responsibilities" lists.

- Poll employees on topics like benefits, social activities, and physical organization. The more ideas you have to work with, the better your final decisions will be and the more relevant they will be to your company.

- Plan for growth. Consider models of how you want your company to grow and what modifications to the organizational structure and job responsibilities will be required.

- Set clear expectations for managing and recording meetings. This may seem trivial or even annoying at this stage, when your "meetings" may be little more than quick chats between people sitting four feet from each other, but setting and adhering to a few good practices at this stage will set the tone moving forward.

- If your company has a shared ownership, make sure that plans for owner exit and transition are agreed to and are part of the legal structure of the company.

Mid-Size Company Organization Overview

The next stage of growth is illustrated in Figure 2.3. Here you can see that the company has grown to more than 70 people. Typically, managers now do very little, if any, production work. This company supports a dual-matrix management structure, meaning that project and department issues are handled on separate communication paths. This necessitates another level of coordination outside of normal project communication needs, which is typically handled by a weekly director-level meeting run by the studio head or president.

Company culture at this level has the tendency to be more heterogeneous—and that is normal in a structure of this size—but it is important for leaders to be

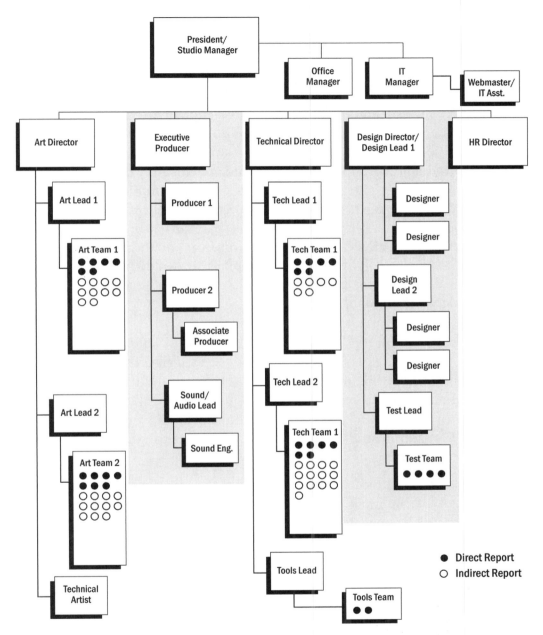

Figure 2.3
Mid-size studio organization chart.

aware of this and to make sure that these social/professional subcultures do not become insular or damaging to the overall mood of the company. It also becomes more critical for leaders to ensure that the social structure and activities are inclusive to as many employees as wish to participate.

At the project level, team sizes are now large enough to require structured meetings and detailed project-reporting systems. In addition to overall growth in existing departments, there is now an audio team, a tools team, and a technical artist in the production group. These groups are not currently tied to a particular team but are resources that float as needed. On the administrative level, the duties of the office manager and human resources (HR) director have been split due to the increasing complexity of their duties, particularly on the HR position. A Webmaster has been added to assist the HR director and the increasingly over-burdened IT manager. A permanent test group has been added and currently sits in the design director's department, but tests can also be managed under the production department along with audio.

Strengths and Weaknesses of the Model

Our developer has had some success and has now expanded to a two-project company. The ratio in this model is about 10 to one production versus management and administrative personnel, excluding the possible contribution of outsourcers. In this model, only the design director and art director occupy a dual production/administrative role; the tech director has no production tasks and no project reporting.

Figure 2.4 shows a detailed breakout chart for the mid-size studio art teams. Representing this structure is more complex; this is an effort to explain this a bit more and help link it conceptually with the previous organization chart. Only the direct reports are shown, but notice that one of the outsourcers reports directly to the modeling lead. This is typically where I recommend the outsourcer feedback loop be managed; for more information about this topic, see Chapter 6.

This company is now fairly well set up to handle the project responsibilities and probably to handle further growth as well. The component to this success is that it has begun to remove performance bottlenecks caused by production-tasked administrative personnel. The tech director and executive producer are now well supported, organizationally speaking, to devote their full time and attention to department-management issues like career management, scheduling, hiring, and training and mentoring new leads.

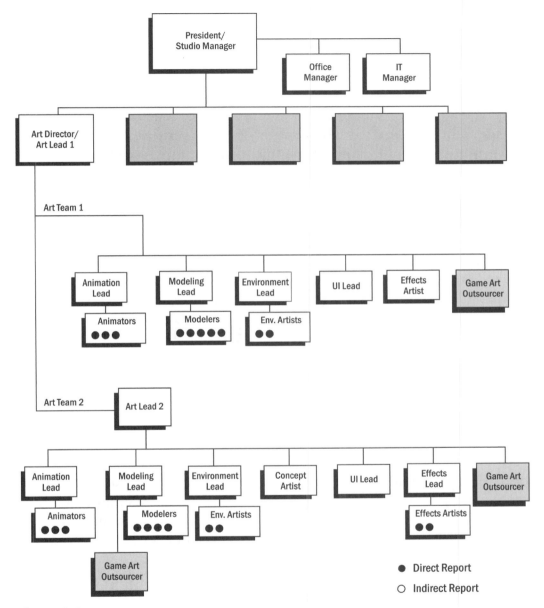

Figure 2.4
Department detail of mid-size studio organization chart.

There are some irregularities in the diagram shown in Figure 2.3, however.

- At the director level, we see an executive producer as the only "non-director" job title. This is entirely a nomenclature oddity. The job description of this title in the game industry is quite different from the same job title in the movie industry. Like most things, this may not be universal; there may well be many production directors, which is a more consistent title, but one that I don't hear used frequently.

- In the mid-size model, I have preserved the design director and the art director as the director positions also tasked in production. There's usually one of these (at least) in every company in my experience. In this example, I chose the design director because this position has a much smaller set of direct reports, which makes the dual role easier to manage. Also, this position and set of responsibilities seems to be not uncommon in the game industry. The art director was chosen to illustrate a few points and because very few companies grow perfectly.

Anomalies like this can arise from the best of intentions gone awry rather than poor decision making or simple inexperience. It's possible that Project 1 in this example started out as a small expansion pack and grew unexpectedly, or it's equally possible that this company, despite its size, had no other artist that had the skills or experience to handle the lead role at the time the project was required to start. There are many reasons why problematic structures exist. The important thing is to recognize them for the potential serious issues they create and to take action to resolve them intelligently.

Physical Organization

A great deal of change has taken place in this company in terms of physical organization as a result of its growth. In all likelihood, there was a period of overcrowding followed by a move to another space or an expansion into other parts of the same office location. In both cases, an opportunity and a need to reorganize the physical layout of the office have presented themselves. The resolution of the problem can take many forms: The company could seat people grouped by department or even by their specialization within their department, by project, near their supervisor, or even completely randomly. The best thing for management to do at this point is to communicate the challenge, frame a range of solutions, and then involve the entire company in a discussion of the relative merits of the proposed solutions. Frequently this will involve education and research and an honest assessment of how your particular products are developed in terms of communication needs of your teams. Other individual factors need to be considered as well such as the desire or need for some people, particularly programmers, to work in an area that has few visual or audible distractions—usually an individual office. Lighting preferences need to be taken into account as well. For example, many artists prefer low-light environments to reduce screen glare.

Most of my better-than-average ideas for office layout have come from visiting other game studios, observing the conditions, and asking managers how their physical arrangement is working. Almost everyone will be happy to tell you about the good and the bad of their situation and what they are planning to do to change it when "the current crunch is over." The biggest cause of office-space frustration is always some combination of "not enough" and "poorly designed for our needs." So, as a cautionary note, get more space than you think you initially need, and allocate money in your move plan to accommodate both office-design costs and actual build-out production costs. Build-out costs can usually be rolled into your monthly rent, but be careful not to do so much semi-permanent work (studs and drywall) that it becomes prohibitively expensive to rethink your structure as your project needs change or your company grows.

A few years ago, I visited a multi-project developer of mobile games in Helsinki who had a very open interior space. Because its teams completed projects and re-formed in different configurations every few months, the company needed a very flexible and attractive office environment. Team areas could be cordoned off with moveable half-wall sections. All the employees' desks were sleek metal—and on wheels. When project teams changed, they could restructure the entire floor in a matter of minutes. In addition, they maintained four large conference rooms located just off the open areas to handle meetings and private conversations easily. The office was surprisingly bright for a software developer, which I found personally refreshing, but I can imagine some of my colleagues wanting for their cave-like lighting solutions. There are two major caveats when considering this plan: The teams' sizes involved must be relatively small (in this case, around six team members), and there must always be a certain amount of flexible space to accommodate the odd situations where a team needs to stay in place longer than expected or the "Office-Tetris" just doesn't work in a given instance.

In contrast to this arrangement are studios that choose to organize into rowed cubicles or individual offices. While there are advantages and disadvantages to any specific organizational implementation, I very much believe certain models are superior in general for a software developer. The first step is to understand how your product is created and then try to arrive at the optimal environment to assist your team or, at the very least, not have the environment become an obstacle to development.

There are two major factors in which space directly affects your team: facilitation of communication and comfort. Communication encompasses two aspects: where you are in relation to whom you need to talk to most and what spaces are available for all the types of communication that happen during the day. With regard to the first part, there is no one answer. Strong arguments can be made for organizing a company by department or job specialization so that job skill support and development may be encouraged. Equally powerfully, one can make the case that team organization is most effective because easy, fast, cross-disciplinary communication is most critical to the efficient creation of the company's product. Having worked within project teams laid out both ways and seen a number of different developers' offices, my personal opinion falls into the latter category. I very much feel that having the team as co-located as possible, particularly ensuring that leads are in close proximity, is the best way to support game production. Programmers, artists, and designers speak very different languages and use very different tools to create a single game, which ideally has a consistent and unified vision. Physical layout can best assist this goal by getting these diverse leads as close as possible and ensuring continual ease of communication. And I think it's obvious that a greater sense of team spirit will be achieved in a shared space.

There are always going to be exceptions. For example, a very successful console and PC studio in the United States organizes its space by specialization, such as character animation or user interface (UI). The studio runs about four products simultaneously, and each sub-group is managed and tasked by project leads who coordinate the production schedule of each specialist group according to the needs of the overall studio project plan. Spatially, then, it makes the most sense to co-locate each group as opposed to a team because moving so many people so many times would become a logistical nightmare.

The reason that the debate remains active is that the single most important part of successful communication lies with the abilities of group doing the communicating. You can implement the Perfect Seating Arrangement of the Gods and provide every voice and e-communication tool available, but in the end, where the people sit and what tools they have are going to be limited by the interpersonal skills and dispositions of the people using them.

Challenges for Leaders

Leaders in mid-size companies must be aware and considerate of new communication paths. More cooks are now in the kitchen, and their interaction needs to be coordinated properly in order to be effective—indeed, not destructive—to the company. In the course of my career, I've found that few things in a company culture are more disconcerting and demoralizing to employees than getting conflicting feedback from a management team that does not function well or seems to be confused about their own roles and the responsibilities of the other leads and directors. An example that happens far too frequently: An art director or executive producer in the course of daily rounds chooses to comment on an image on an artist's screen that contradicts the lead artist's feedback given perhaps 10 minutes prior. For this reason, it is very important to explain roles, bounds of authority, and one's place in any approval/feedback channel. The creation of a role/responsibility chart (shown in Chapter 6) can help clarify this to the company. Beyond that, it is the responsibility of leads and directors to respect and enforce communication channels. Otherwise, dominant personalities on a given team may begin to redefine reporting and approval structures. That said, this is not always a negative thing—as long as the issue gets addressed in some way. For example, suppose an artist on a team has begun to take charge reworking a pipeline outside his or her specific area or leading the push for some greater quality effort on a project. This situation can be resolved by recognizing a new role for that artist, and through this, it may be discovered that there are some inadequacies in the current lead structure or organization. Though some communication behavior may violate the letter of a reporting structure, one should always embrace and encourage any positive energy and results that will make your project and team stronger.

The model in Figure 2.5 shows two potential problem areas. The first and most glaring is the art director/art lead. This individual now has a 20–30 person department to manage as well as a large team with six project direct reports. Additionally, the individual is receiving project and department updates from the technical artist and a feedback/approval report from the lead artist on Project 2. The only constructive change made from the earlier stage of growth is the addition of a modeling lead, who manages four artists directly. In my experience, this art director/lead artist role is destined to fail at both the project and department levels in a multi-project studio.

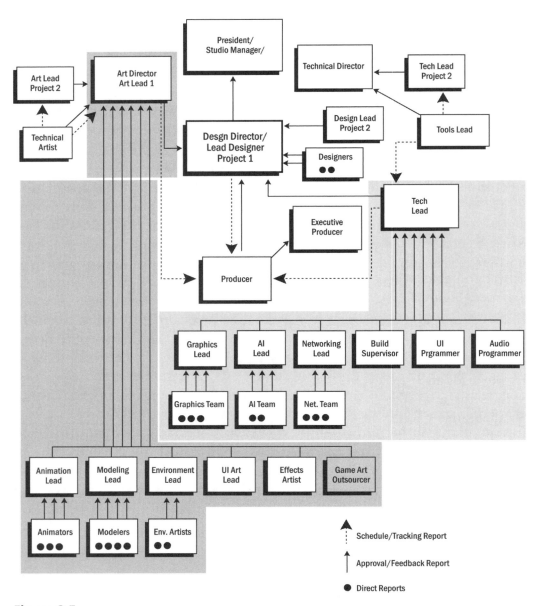

Figure 2.5
Mid-size studio project communication path, prior to a reorganization.

This company desperately needs to hire, or promote from within, a lead artist for Project 1. From a simple resource perspective, I'd propose that person should come from the modeling group. This will weaken the modeling group, but perhaps in non-trivial ways, because the individual chosen would probably be one of the more senior artists. I would also organize the outsourcers in this model to report to the specialist leads for modeling and animation tasks. The reasons for this are twofold: ensuring proper time management for the lead and the availability of direct production experience from the specialist lead or team member. Managing feedback can be a time-consuming endeavor at any stage, and at the beginning of an outsourcer relationship, it is a major time commitment. The lead needs to be freed to work with and for the team as much as possible. Arranging simple communication alone can require a level of coordination and planning when your outsourcer is on the other side of the planet and the language barrier crossing needs assistance. Additionally, the lead will probably need to call on specialist leads or team members anyway to provide detailed technical feedback on assets that they don't have. My preferred method is to have specialist leads manage communication and delegate the bulk of technical feedback generation to team members. This process keeps the lead focused on the bigger picture of the project and able to be maximally available to the entire team for feedback and guidance. Figure 2.6 shows a reorganization of the same company. The only personnel change is the addition of a new art lead.

Note that the art lead now has only five direct reports and no departmental responsibilities. The art director now has just three direct reports, composed of the two leads and the technical artist. This seems light, but keep in mind that the art director and tech director now have departments of 25–30 people. The administrative overhead at the department level has increased along with the amount of director support that should be made available to art leads, each of whom has a group of around 15 individuals in this model. In practice, teams can be anywhere from three to 50 people and frequently fluctuate in size dramatically as needed by the project during the course of development. Management of this ebb and flow of resources over two project teams is another responsibility of the director that requires close coordination and communication with the project leads, producer, and studio executives.

The tech lead still has six direct reports incoming. This situation, while not unusual or worrisome, needs to be carefully managed in order to be successful. The tech lead's personal coding tasks need to be restricted appropriately in order to give him or her the time to properly plan features with the design lead, provide specs and guidance as needed to the artists, coordinate scheduling with the producer and leads, and, probably most importantly, devote time to review the coding done by the other team members. There is no official formula I've found for work/management tasks, but over the years, I have developed an informal guide: For every four direct reports, reduce 30–50 percent of the production

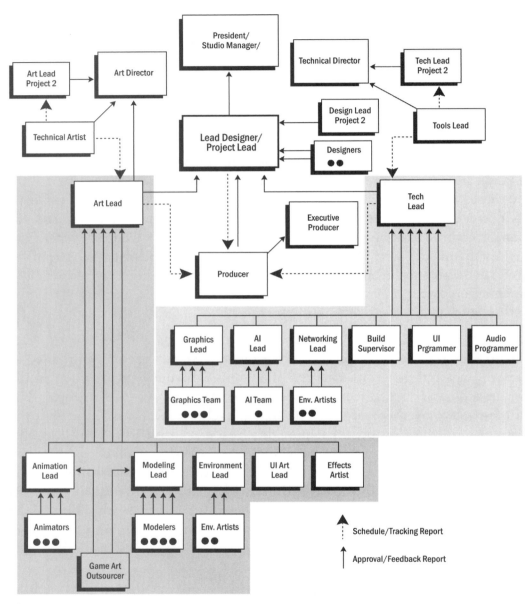

Figure 2.6
Mid-size studio project communication path, after alleviating a bottleneck.

time, depending on the complexity of the tasks done by the direct reports. Using this calculation, a specialist lead with three direct reports should devote approximately 75 percent of his or her time to production tasks; a lead with eight direct reports should be involved in production about 30 percent of the time (at most) and should never be responsible for critical path tasks. In situations where the direct reports are involved in complex or risky tasks, the latter example might well have no production responsibilities.

In the example in Figure 2.6, I'd recommend that the tech lead be tasked at no more than 20 percent for production purposes. A huge variable in this equation is the effectiveness and number of high-functioning specialist leads—people like the graphics lead or the networking lead. The more independent and capable these individuals are, the freer the tech lead is to potentially take on more coding tasks.

On the social front, the growth of antagonistic subcultures within an organization may emerge in companies of this scale and is a particularly destructive element. Where such conditions are discovered to exist or seen developing, leaders in the organization must take immediate steps to turn the situation around. I've see conflicts develop between departments, teams, and groups of diverse employees united behind single charismatic individuals. Sometimes the onset is quiet and unnoticeable; other times it starts as a raging disagreement that never gets properly resolved.

Note

The worst thing a leader can do in these cases is take a hands-off attitude with the thought that a cooling-down period will be productive. Time does not heal all wounds; indeed, in the case of office politics, time usually deepens divides. Honest and direct communication is the only way that a company can properly refocus on its goals and reach some mutual understanding.

Leaders should work to maintain a single company identity and foster an environment of mutual respect, open exchange, and support between projects and departments. One way to do this is to keep people focused on the common goals of the company. One developer I visited posted the goals of each project outside the team room along with a copy of the timeline of the project. The message was clear—this is who we are, what we're about, and, quite publicly, where we are. Leaders who find a negative situation developing despite their efforts need to identify the core issue or issues, find a resolution, and communicate that to all parties.

Sometimes simply being aware of these situations can be a challenge, since you may not even be in a communication channel to hear the details of emerging points of conflict or negative cliques in your company. As a company director, I was once helping test a product, which required me to relocate to the test pit for a few days. At first, the atmosphere was very quiet and professional. After a couple of hours, however, it turned back into a test pit, with the expected amount of noise and chatter. After a day or so, my presence became a non-issue, and I learned a tremendous amount about the atmosphere going around the company just by sitting quietly and listening. The amount of speculation that went on, and the assumption of a beyond-worst-case scenario based on a vacuum of information, was astounding to me and to others with whom I shared the event. One change that was recommended out of this experience was to start publishing the notes from our lead and director meetings to the company (after removing confidential or personnel-related information) and allow anyone in the company to put issues on the lead or director meeting's agendas. At the very least, this action lent some sense of reality to the discussions going around, and the leadership group at the project and department level could stay ahead of a controversial issue before the company grapevine took it to wild extremes. And while it was infrequently used, the idea that anyone could put forward an issue for discussion at the highest level of the company was very empowering to the company as a whole.

Things to consider at this stage:

- Hire a human resources professional. This is a very complex field that gets more so every year. The HR manager should edit the employee handbook and ensure that the company complies with state and federal hiring laws and OSHA requirements.

- Evaluate your employee review schedule and review form. Now that multiple roles have been added to your company, your review form probably needs to be edited to reflect the growing number of individuals involved in development and support.

- Review and edit descriptions of roles and responsibilities within the project and department. Again, more roles means more careful attention to the responsibility chain.

- Continue to involve employees in discussions on topics like benefits, social activities, and the physical organization. The more ideas you have to work with, the better your final decisions will be, and the more relevant they will be to your company.

- Review the results of your growth and plan for further growth if applicable. Consider the transition the company has made in scale, what problems have emerged, and how they were dealt with, and apply these lessons to future plans.

- Enforce clear expectations for managing and recording meetings. Your meetings are more expensive now simply based on the number and seniority of people attending them. Minimize wasted time and tangents, keep a record of decisions made, and communicate those decisions to all relevant parties.

- Make a concerted effort to build a positive company culture. Arrange training sessions, organize social gatherings both on and off site, and promote honest and open communication across projects and departments through cross-project critiques and cross-departmental gatherings.

Large Company Organization Overview

The next stage of growth is illustrated in Figure 2.7. Here you can see the company has grown to more than 150 people. This model is typically found in in-house, publisher-owned studios or extremely successful independents with multiple teams. The management structure has more levels, and the reporting stress falls equally if not more on department heads than team leads. Team leads now do very little if any production work due to their management overhead. Executive-level project review is typically handled by a weekly director-level meeting run by the studio head or president. At this stage, unified company culture is in danger of evaporating in the face of the growth of many subcultures centered around project teams, disciplines, specializations, or charismatic individuals.

Figure 2.7 shows a large studio organization at a very high level. It is assumed, and will be illustrated, that the same lead and specialist lead structures exist within the teams. It should be noted that this is not any actual company of which I am aware; it serves purely as a basis for discussion. Specifically in this case, the top two levels of organization can be extremely varied and are frequently a result of earlier executive organization preference or an expression of executive ability. For example, the position of business development/brand manager probably will not exist as one person. Additionally, it is entirely conceivable that an actual company might not have any owned intellectual property to manage as a brand and in fact may contract its business-development work (such as building new relationships leading to the signing of new projects) to a third-party individual or company who might only report to the president as needed.

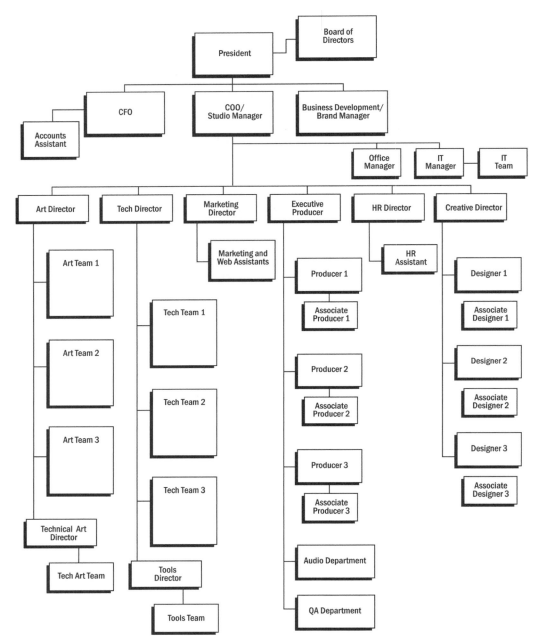

Figure 2.7
Large studio organization chart.

A new addition is the position of the board of directors. This can and should exist at all levels of a company, but at this level, the board may have a role that goes beyond the formal advisory board at smaller companies. The role of the board is to oversee the performance of company executives, advise on business questions, and of course be available to network with associates who might otherwise not be available to company directors. The board traditionally meets quarterly or as needed in times of unusual activity such as the potential sale of the company.

A marketing director has also been added in this model. The lack of a marketing director in the previous model may well have been a weakness in that model. In my own experience, even in a small independent studio, our publishers were very glad to see that we had someone to act as the main point of contact with the marketing department. In the absence of this position, this role would most likely fall to the developer's producer, which could easily overburden him or her at critical stages of a project cycle. Marketing is a very important component to the success of a game and establishing effective developer communication and coordination is one of the biggest hurdles to a smooth relationship with a publisher.

The CFO spot is also new. This spot may be someone who is offsite or part-time, or the entire function may be contracted to another company depending on the needs of the studio. Other positions that might exist in this model include the chief technical officer (CTO), community manager, outsource director, and many others whose functions will be specific to the individual studio's needs.

Strengths and Weaknesses of the Model

Our developer has enjoyed considerable success, perhaps to the point of being purchased by a larger entity, and has expanded to a three-project company. The ratio in this model is roughly eight to one production versus management and administrative personnel, excluding the possible contribution of outsourcers and the members of the board who are traditionally not compensated but may be significant stakeholders. In this model, no director is in any sort of production role, which is necessary due to the size and complexity of each project team.

The studio is probably at its maximum effective size, but even still, inefficiencies due to scale may begin to appear. These inefficiencies are typically a result of too few managers or poor coordination and communication between leads, directors, and senior management. One famous example occurred during a production audit at a large producer of educational software in the late 1990s. This action was performed by representatives of a publisher who had recently bought a smaller publisher, who had in turn bought the developer, all within the span of a year. During the audit, they came upon a row of cubicles on one floor filled with programmers. When asked what they were working on, one of the programmers answered, "Well, nothing. We haven't had a manager or a schedule for about seven or eight months." This extreme example was compounded by a situation involving the removal of the directors, but nonetheless points to the management complexity that simple scale increases represent. John Chowanec, development director at 2K Games and former executive producer at Crystal Dynamics, has this rule of thumb: For every doubling in growth of production staff, management resources need to quadruple.

One of the issues in this model is that the management structure is not very different in size from that of the mid-size studio example. Although the problem of dual roles at the lead/director level has been rectified, another potential bottleneck has emerged based on the team size. Each project has an art and tech lead, producer, and assistant producer, but as you can see in Figure 2.8, the team size has expanded a bit. The project team size is around 50 total, with about six of that number involved purely in oversight roles. QA (testing) and audio are managed in this model by the producer, but other organizations might put audio as a separate department or under art or design, and QA can certainly be organized under the tech department.

Here the reporting stress falls in two areas: the studio manager and the team leads, particularly the art and tech leads. The modeling and animation leads may be overloaded as well, but I recommend that they offload outsourcer technical feedback to a senior member of their respective teams. As a cautionary note, doing so will introduce a level of managerial responsibility to those production personnel and that should be factored into their schedules as appropriate to the amount of incoming assets requiring critique and feedback.

This organization chart, unlike the previous charts, does not show communication flow, but you can tell that the producer in this model is going to be bombarded with more reporting at certain times during development, particularly at later stages as QA and marketing become more involved. Communication flow is fundamentally the same as in the improved mid-size company model.

The changes recommended in Figure 2.9 include two management additions. The first is a project lead. The project lead could be one member of the lead group, but I recommend a separate individual for the position not only for workflow reasons but also because the position calls for a level of detachment

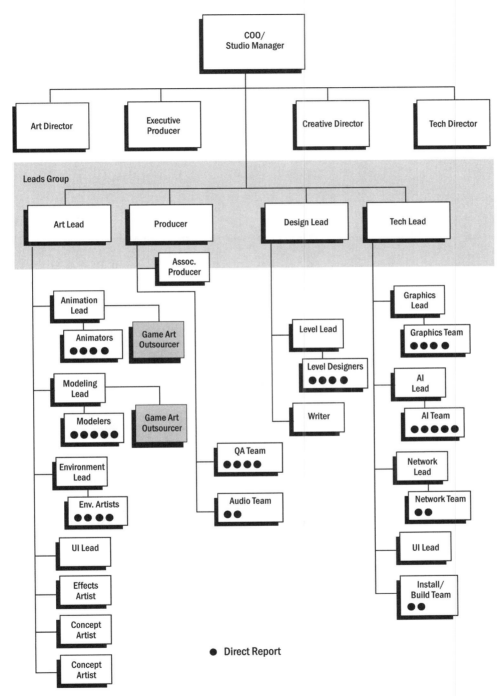

Figure 2.8
Large studio organization chart showing project detail and a potential bottleneck in the leads group.

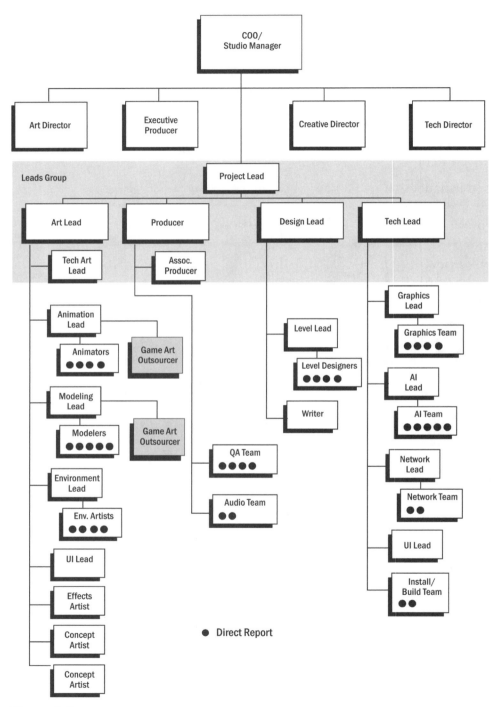

Figure 2.9
Large studio organization chart with a project lead added to the leads group.

from any one discipline associated with development. The project lead role in this model is to oversee the entire game with an eye toward the overall feel of the game and enforcement of the vision. In studios adopting alternative production methodologies such as Scrum or Agile practices, this position might be titled "project owner." Whatever the title, this individual is tasked with being the decision maker on features and any other development decisions as they affect the project budget. The project lead can also act as the arbiter between otherwise intractable differences of opinion held by the other members of the leads group.

The second change is the addition of a tech art lead at the project level and a tech art director outside the project structure. The tech art lead assists the art lead in doing technical reviews of assets in addition to other tasks, which may include automation, scripting, rigging, or shader-development tasks. Automation of technical-review tools is strongly encouraged because once full production starts, the amount of time required to ensure technical correctness of sometimes very complicated assets can become overwhelming for the art lead and/or specialist leads. The danger is not that an asset doesn't work or breaks a build—those are easy issues to spot. The real result of failing to regularly perform a thorough technical review is that poorly performing assets may be introduced that function well enough, but are not optimal for the engine. Over time, as more and more problematic assets become part of the game, performance hits are noticed—but by that point in development, the fix for the issue will be costly in terms of resource time. The tech art director coordinates the scheduling and reviews the work of the tech leads and team as needed. The tech art director also coordinates closely with the tools team on the programming side and provides an additional communication bridge to the tech team.

Some positions not included in the chart but that may be considered are those of an art manager, assistant art director, and outsource manager. The art manager is typically a project-based position responsible for art scheduling and coordination and working in close collaboration with the producer. The art manager may also assist the art director in managing searches and reviewing portfolios for staffing consideration. The assistant art director may do some of these latter functions as well but, as the title suggests, may be more involved at the department level with responsibilities such as assisting with performance reviews. The outsource manager can be at the project or department level; he or she is responsible for maintaining the relationship, tracking progress, ensuring clear and complete communication, and other duties as the general point of contact for the outsource company or companies.

Physical Organization

Many of the physical issues of the mid-size company remain similar at this size because the structure is similar; only the scale has increased. The main concern at this scale should be finding a cost-effective space large enough for each team to be in the same general area and for the company as a whole to be comfortably housed. The need for small to mid-size conference rooms increases as team sizes increase due to the number of smaller specialty-focused meetings that need to occur during the day. The use of large spaces for offices or cubicles is tempting when increasing staff to accommodate project needs, but maintaining a percentage of open private areas is every bit as important as creating comfortable and functional work spaces for your employees. The exact amount of meeting space and private areas varies quite a bit depending on your production needs and methodology. In general, I've found it good practice to have one area that an entire team (or company up to a certain size) can meet comfortably in and roughly one other smaller meeting area for every 15 employees. Companies embracing Scrum or Agile production methods will probably require more quiet meeting areas that are close to development work spaces for teams to gather as needed. I also recommend for companies in open floor plan office environments the addition of smaller private areas for one-on-one meetings such as performance reviews as well as for people needing to make private phone calls. The number of these can also vary a bit, but I think in general the one to 15 ratio feels right.

Challenges for Leaders

The biggest challenge for leaders at this level, in addition to massive planning and coordination efforts, is making sure that enough attention is paid to the individual members of the company—assuming that project-level communication and lead bottlenecks have been resolved. Do the art and tech directors have enough time in their day to make personal contact with and mentor the people in their departments? If so, what form does that take when an art director might be two leads removed from the feedback loop that an artist experiences during the day (the first two being their specialist lead followed by the art lead)? The appropriate communication content needs to be understood by all parties, but in a department of 50 or so artists, is it even possible for an art director to maintain regular contact? One tech director in my experience made it a point to engage in short check-ins with every member of his department once per week. This worked fine until the tech department grew to more than 20 people; at that point, he had to move the one-on-one meetings to once per month. Personal contact, though, is critical. Information content is flowing through the company, departments, and teams from many sources, all of which need to be managed in some fashion to keep people focused on the mission and values of your company.

Communication efficiency has been a recurring topic in each model presented, and at this level, maintaining face-to-face communication is vitally important. Large companies characteristically offer an array of tools to enable people to easily communicate across floors, buildings, or even cities. These include feature-laden phone systems, company-wide instant messaging, and video conferencing. All of these are great, but are usually inferior to personal contact; for this reason, personal contact should be maintained if at all possible. Many times I've seen an e-mail-based communication go completely sour or miss key points, which would have not happened had the communication been verbal. That said, there are also instances in which it is advisable to use e-mail so that a record is made and preserved of the discussion and decisions. When conditions permit, it is preferable to have a personal conversation followed by a confirmation e-mail.

Things to consider at this stage in addition to reviewing and considering applicable issues posed for mid-size companies:

- Maintain personal contact at the director and executive level. Develop a check-in strategy that keeps you as the department director or lead of a large project team personally aware of and involved with your staff.

- Explore ways to improve company information flow, particularly in a publisher-owned studio. Make every effort to stay ahead of the rumor mill by releasing information in a timely fashion to the entire company.

- Always strive to keep current with games, game-development techniques, and emerging production methodologies.

Conclusions

This chapter has provided a working foundation and a language with which leadership issues can be discussed in an industry that lacks cohesion of terminology and job titles and functions. Hopefully there are also some practical tips for new leaders who are just starting out or whose companies are experiencing scale transition or organizational problems. Bottlenecks, or overloading of one manager with too many reports, are the central thing revealed by organization and communication charts. The answers are not always centered around adding staff at key places to divide responsibility; this approach just happens to be the easiest to illustrate. Many times, bottlenecks can be lightened by redefining the roles and responsibilities of leads and specialist leads and even production personnel.

The solution to effective team communication and leadership is not, of course, as simple as making sure all the boxes in the organization chart are lined up correctly and don't have too many arrows pointing to them. If it were, you would be holding a much shorter book in your hands. But as we all know, the crux of great team leadership and successful project teams lies in the leaders themselves and the work environments that they create and support. The reality of the leaders in a given company—the people behind the organization chart—is often unpredictable, irregular, and complex.

Interview: John Chowanec, Development Director, 2K Games

John Chowanec started his career as a tester at Accolade, advanced through the production ranks, and worked for a time as an executive producer at Crystal Dynamics. Currently, John serves as the director of development at 2K Games in Novato. During his 12 years in the industry, Chowanec has worked on top-tier franchises, licenses, and original IP; his current position enables him to view the industry from the publishing side.

Seth Spaulding: Describe your transition from a production position to a leadership position.

John Chowanec: My transition into a leadership position was extremely challenging. Managing people is the hardest thing I've ever done, if for no other reason than the people keep changing, which forces you to change your own management tactics.

I was surprised to find out how much of a difference there is between the "official" chain of command and the "unofficial" chain. As an associate producer, I could get results because I wasn't the authority; the team would respond to me asking because I was in the trenches with them. However, when I made the leap into a full producer and had this newfound and real authority, I found getting results was sometimes harder than it was before. I had to learn all about the concepts of hard versus soft skills and that just because I knew how to use Excel and Project and that I could talk about Gantt charts, it did *not* make me a good producer. Learning how to navigate 30, 40, 50, 60 personal relationships within a team could make up for what you might lack in hard skills every time.

S.S: Do you think developers are unnaturally suspicious of authority figures, regardless of experience?

J.C.: I don't think so. I think I had a hard time transitioning to the lead role. I made bigger deals than I should have over some issues. It took some time to learn that it wasn't about authority, but an opportunity to lead. I've seen projects shipped that were led in an overly authoritarian manner, but it isn't a sustainable strategy for a healthy company.

S.S.: Looking back, are there any decisions or practices you would change, and if so, why?

J.C.: I would have spent more time with the APs I was assigned during my first job as a producer (and even subsequently as a senior producer or executive producer). I think the associate producer has one of the hardest jobs in the building—all the responsibility, but none of the authority. You can always find good producers amongst great associate producers.

And I certainly would have relied less on my hard skills for the answers. Making games is not like building a house. I would get so wrapped up in what the data told me that I sometimes lost sight of the actual game that we were making.

S.S.: How have you best been able to "keep sight on the actual game," both for yourself and your team, when perhaps the game might not be playable or fun yet?

J.C.: Preproduction is the time when you frequently cannot see the game, and that is the hardest time to know whether you are being effective as a project lead. I'd say the most important thing is to learn to listen to and trust your leads. Give them the resources they need and make sure that you are accounting for as many variables as possible. Enable constant communication with stakeholders and make sure each discipline understands how they are affecting each other. As far as presenting information up the chain during this period, I'm a big fan of over-informing. Project information can never be "too clear" when communicating up or out to the team for that matter.

S.S.: What is the most important thing you would tell someone making that transition within a company?

J.C.: It's not about you. The role of a leader is to lead, not necessarily to dictate. If you don't focus your efforts around those you are leading, you might find yourself with no one to lead any longer. You're not always going to be popular, and you're not always going to agree with what you have to do, but it's important to know that there are a lot of people looking to you for strength, looking to you for guidance, and looking to you for answers.

Also, it's okay to say, "I don't know, but I'll find out." As long as you follow up, it is constructive. I used to get stuck on needing to have all the answers before standing in front of the team. It was my leads (thanks guys!) who taught me that it's sometimes better to tell the team as much as you can in a timely manner than to try and wait until you have all the information to answer all the hypothetical questions your brain is cooking up. Most of the time, the team won't ask any of those questions you're scared of. It is totally okay to know what you don't know—people like the humble over the arrogant.

S.S.: Were there any people who helped, and if so, how?

J.C.: Everyone, really. From my father, who taught me the basics of management, to the great managers I've been lucky enough to have during my career, to the teams that have kept me in check, kept me honest, and kept me motivated.

S.S.: What are the most common traits shared by other effective leaders in your experience?

J.C.: I feel weird even answering this, but the most common trait I have seen among effective leaders is honesty. I'm amazed that it isn't more common than it is, but just because you lead doesn't mean you are smarter than those around you. Don't try to fake anything—the team will see right through it.

A few others are

- **Drive, self direction, and motivation:** These are all super-important. Most of the time, in a leadership role, you are going to operate without much direction from on high. The ability to move forward with little direction is key.

- **Decisiveness:** It's better to make any decision than to make no decision. You can fix a bad decision. We're not in an industry where science or prediction is going to always give us the answer. When the research has been done, good leaders make decisions. You have to have a sense of accountability if it goes wrong, but in my experience, I was better served just making decisions rather than being paralyzed, worried that I'd make the "wrong" decision.

- **Good listening skills:** All the great leaders in my past have been great listeners. They have the ability to focus on you when you're talking and to take your problems seriously. They help *you* think of the answer to the problem without making you feel stupid or belittled. People don't bring you the problems they already know how to solve. Regardless of whether or not you have the answer immediately, work through the problem with that person. Help that person come to the conclusion that you are already at—that's how he or she will learn.

S.S.: What are the worst traits a leader exhibited in your experience?

J.C.: The single worst trait in a leader is one of self-absorption. The leaders who view the job as their path to some sort of geek celebrity usually don't have the team behind them for long. The ones that are in it for the money should work in a different industry. The ones that are in it for the power will generally leave a wake behind them and will, more often than not, push away the best people on the team or even at the company.

People who manage through fear manage effectively for only a short period of time. I think it's the worst management tactic in the book and only embitters people in the long run. Support, don't oppress.

S.S.: Do you have any training in leadership, either formal or unstructured (e.g., armed forces experience)? If relevant, in what ways do apply that training to challenges in your job?

J.C.: No formal training, no. I've attended some leadership seminars, but I prefer to learn by doing. I'd recommend reading books to reinforce or tweak what you already are good at. I always try to remember what I hated about management before I became a part of it.

S.S.: What were some of the things you hated?

J.C.: I think the thing I most hated was the non-inclusive nature of it. The notion that managers are infallible, or somehow possess superior subjective opinions. And I think a lot of (poor) managers feel that they cannot be seen to have made a mistake. This is nonsense; we all make mistakes. Some of the most important decisions and moments as a manager in my career have been the ones that exposed flaws—admitting mistakes or having to deliver bad news to the team, and so on. These moments test a manager's maturity and confidence more than any other. Also, inexperienced managers sometimes feel that they have to know everything and have an answer for every question on the spot. As I noted above, "I don't know" is a perfectly acceptable answer.

I also chafe at the notion that people in management are valued more. Games are not made by a management genius in a corner office; they are made by teams of talented, dedicated people. It sounds Utopian, but I want to get to know the people on my team well so when things get stressful, we look at each other as people, not positions. I firmly believe this approach leads to a happier workplace, a more committed team, and, of course, better games.

S.S.: What do you see as the toughest challenge facing leads during a game-development project cycle or at a game-development company generally?

J.C.: The most effective leads group I have ever worked with started with a solid foundation of trust. Each of them knew their discipline incredibly well and realized that they weren't as capable in the other disciplines. That's not to say that we didn't have conflicting agendas between the disciplines, but we always, always trusted that each of us was being honest.

Great leads groups never show a lack of unity in front of the team. Even if we disagreed in a leads meeting, we'd always show a unified front to the team. I'm a big believer that everything trickles down from the top. Great development teams have great leads.

The least effective leads groups I've seen have generally lacked that trust amongst themselves. Next thing you know, the art department hates the designers who hate the programmers who hate the producers. When that happens, you're in trouble.

S.S.: What are some common mistakes you've seen leads make, be they new or experienced?

J.C.: The most common mistake I've made (and seen made countless times) is the idea of promoting your best content creator to your best lead. Sometimes it works great—but remember, you're taking away one of your best team members to place them in a role they might not like and may not utilize the talents you admire and value so much about them.

The important take away is that I started really sitting down with folks who wanted to move into management to explain what the job actually is. It's less about making content for the game and far more about managing people to do so. I've seen excellent content guys make poor leads and mediocre content creators make great leads.

In terms of the leads themselves, the biggest and most common mistake I see is that of an inability to delegate. Just because you can do it faster doesn't mean you should. Just because you know how to do it doesn't mean you should. Remember, there are people around you who *want* to learn—and you have to give them that opportunity.

Oh, and you don't need to be in every single meeting.

S.S.: How have you seen new leads best get support from directors or executives?

J.C.: By something as simple as one-on-one meetings. In my career, the best bosses I've ever had have all let me know that it's okay to make mistakes (as long as I didn't repeat them). If I didn't have those meetings to suss out my options and discuss my mistakes, I might not have learned some of the important lessons I have.

If a lead is only as good as the weakest member of his or her team, an executive is only as good as the weakest lead. Spend time with *that* guy to help him be better at his job. Let the guys who are naturally great do what they do best—and get out of the way. Let folks know that you're there to help them.

S.S.: Do you think good leaders can be trained? Or is the essence of a good leader simply innate ability?

J.C.: Whew—tough question. It depends on so many different things. If I had to pick one or the other, and this sounds so hippie of me, I'd have to say it's innate. In the world of hard skills (Microsoft Project, Excel, Maya, Max, whatever) and soft skills (conflict resolution, morale management, etc.), I have found that you can teach the hard skills, but you oftentimes cannot teach people how to interact with others. And soft skills are something I think we find in people and help promote it rather than teach it directly.

S.S.: What are some issues surrounding growth in scale in a company?

J.C.: Rapid growth is something I've never witnessed a positive outcome from. It's going to happen to you at some point. Either your company will expand (either in an orderly fashion or not) due to a new project team being added or because one project is finishing in two months and you have to double another team's size (or lay off personnel, but that really isn't an option assuming your company will be starting another project at some point), but it's *so* delicate to do properly. I was on a team once where we went from 20 to 40 in two days. We spent two weeks before that getting ready and two weeks after that ensuring that folks landed okay. And this was the entire leads group. We spent a month not looking at the project, but rather bracing for the impact of doubling our size so quickly. And typically, you don't know what failed in that transition until much later in the process.

One of the things we did to combat this was to write a team-based orientation document. The document contained everything from how to get to our team documentation/wiki to the org-chart to the creative hierarchy, core hours, etc. I'm really glad we did it, as it ended up being incredibly useful and made transitions much, much smoother. It was effectively a document of the unwritten rules on the team, so we formalized it and it worked brilliantly.

We started accounting for training time in the schedule as well—where everyone new to the team would get some start-up time—so as to not drop them into the make-assets-right-when-you-start mode. We also assigned them someone on the team to ask questions to so they didn't have to wait around for the leads all the time. This was subtle, but tremendously effective.

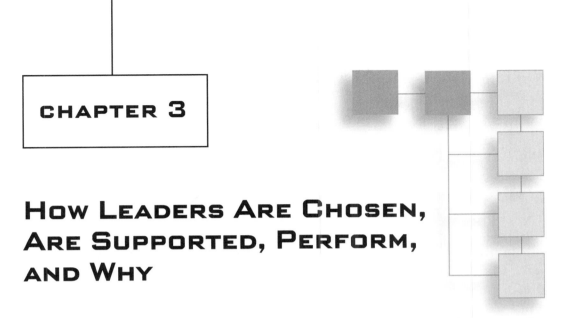

CHAPTER 3

How Leaders Are Chosen, Are Supported, Perform, and Why

So how do companies select leads? In most cases, it's a very rational process. The scenario from the company's perspective involves finding and developing new leaders as the company grows and project teams are added. The company ideally started with strong department leaders with good management skills and a talented and energetic production staff. The need to develop leaders from the production group emerges with the company's growth.

The Ideal and the Real

The goal is always to find the right people and match them to the right role within the company. Assuming an ideally staffed and well-functioning studio, an individual production employee is seen during the course of a development cycle to demonstrate an inclination to work with others and does so effectively, usually through mentoring and in group feedback sessions at early stages. They are recognized for their work ethic and sense of responsibility to (and sometimes beyond) their specific task lists, and as such they are offered a position as a specialist lead or sub-lead at the time these become available. At this level, they work for a project cycle or perhaps two under the supervision and mentorship of experienced art leads, other specialist leads, and the art director, from whom they receive guidance in the duties of their new role. From there, if they prefer to remain at the specialist lead level or return to the role of senior artist, that path is open and ideally just as attractive a career option as the management track.

If instead they continue to show aptitude and desire for greater leadership opportunities, they may continue to move into a greater management role, possibly as an art lead on future projects, inspiring their teams and building morale across the company.

Unfortunately, there are several possible points of failure in this sunny scenario, which seem to occur with regrettable regularity in the games industry. The most prevalent points originate from the first two assumptions—that a studio is fully staffed and well functioning. The sad fact is, no company in my direct experience has ever been ideally staffed. The result is that the candidate pool for leaders in an organization is probably going to be sub-optimal, particularly when a studio moves to multi-project development. Even if your company is staffed with a dream team of talented, experienced, and driven individuals, there is no guarantee that any of them are going to have the aptitude or desire to manage. The possible solutions then amount to selecting a candidate for a lead position with reservations about his or her potential for the role or looking outside the company for a candidate who more closely meets the job description. Either choice can be problematic; indeed, for a small developer, the latter may be impossible. Due to production schedules, it may be highly unlikely that even a mid-size developer would choose to begin a possibly lengthy search when the need of an individual to fill the role is immediate.

The second assumption—often unspoken—is that a studio is well functioning or perhaps rationally functioning. As far as lead selection goes, the issues of favoritism or nepotism and simple inexperience do exist and, in the case of favoritism, can be extremely dangerous even if it is merely perceived to exist. Suppose, for example, the best person to lead a project happens to be the president's best friend. If you find yourself justifying a lead selection by including his or her social relationship as a factor in any way, it may be perceived very poorly by the company. That negative perception should disappear to a large extent if and when the individual demonstrates effective performance in the role to the team. Even still, the idea that favoritism exists in an organization however small or large can be very detrimental. A far worse scenario emerges when this hypothetical individual is not qualified or is perceived to be not performing to expectations and no action is seen to be taken by senior management.

Inexperience, while an innocent and recoverable condition, can lead to many problematic leadership selections. The most common errors based on inexperience involve selecting leads based solely on production art, design, or coding skills. The result is often a lead who is most comfortable doing the job that he or she has always done and trusting that the team will take care of itself from a supervisory perspective. Few if any teams are capable of this; indeed, self-management of this type is impossible for larger groups that require inter-departmental communication coordination.

In many ways, the process of selecting a lead from an internal group of candidates should be looked at as a job interview, with all the positives and negatives that go with that event. If you have ever had the experience of interviewing and failing to get a job, you know what that rejection can feel like. Now consider that a valuable employee has had that ego-damaging rejection and tomorrow they have to go in to work, smile, and do a great job. Managers need to recognize the individual goals of their staff and not let an internal rejection for a lead role spiral into a negative outlook on their prospects for career advancement within the company.

In some instances, the number of hypothetically suitable lead candidates can also cause problems. As we saw in some of the organization charts in Chapter 2, "The Anatomy of a Game-Development Company," there can be three or more specialist leads per project working under each art lead. Presumably, some or all of these specialist leads will want the opportunity to be what I'll call a "full lead" at some point. Typically, not all of these candidates will be suitable or will even want a full lead role for any number of reasons, but the situation can be complex in some instances. The director and other managers must at times make difficult decisions between internal lead candidates based on the criteria they set for the position. These decisions will always disappoint at least one prospective candidate and will disappoint them for a considerable amount of time given the multiyear length of current development cycles for AAA games. In these cases, management needs to provide very clear expectations of the role, honestly assess each candidate, and communicate the decision-making process to all parties. In addition, future commitments for lead roles, if they are made, need to be kept. Instead of telling a rejected candidate, "You'll get the next lead spot that comes up," I recommend something with more flexibility, like "I greatly value your contribution at all levels and as appropriate, I am going to work to make this company match your career goals."

On the opposite side of the spectrum are cases where a potential or proven solid lead needs to be persuaded to take the role for a given project. This is ultimately a no-win situation. In such a case, it would be plainly evident that any sort of passion for the project was missing, and I feel that passion is a key characteristic of a lead. That said, there are occasions when the situation calls for just such action. At the GDC Art Director/Lead Artist Round Table in 2005, I asked attendees what motivated development production personnel to become leads; surprisingly, the answer from a number of participants was "more money." If you find your company in this situation, take a close look at the list of responsibilities on your leads and pay attention to the overtime being logged. These experienced individuals are key to your company's continued success, and they should be supported, and their quality of life considered, every bit as much as every other staff member.

Finally from the Pandora's box of what can go wrong, leads can fail. They can decide that the move to a lead role doesn't appeal to them for any number of reasons, or the team and management can make the determination that they are not performing to expectations. Perhaps they fail to motivate their team, or they lack the skills to cooperate with fellow leads and effectively communicate to the team from a position of power. Management in this event is forced to make a decision to either move them out of the role and find a more suitable lead or support them through the project if the issues are not so severe or circumstances simply dictate this strategy. Obviously, neither of these options is desirable, but at the point that the determination to remove the lead is made, it is vital that management take swift corrective action.

The following case studies of unsuccessful leadership examples represent composites from my own experiences, observations of colleagues around the industry, and tales from others—many coming out of the Art Director/Lead Artist Round Table at GDC. I would like to point out that I have enjoyed a great many successes and worked with a number of talented individuals, many of whom are interviewed throughout this book. However, it has been said that success is a poor teacher—and I can confirm that the most valuable lessons I've learned have come from making painful mistakes on the job. The second most valuable lessons have come from hearing about the painful experiences of other people and taking lessons away. This second tier may be a bit less effective, but they are also a lot safer for your career and gentler on your psyche.

Case Study: Rick
Background: Wrong Person, Wrong Role

Rick was a studio director hired into a mid-size, one-project development studio. He was formerly a high-level project manager at an entertainment giant that was highly respected but outside the game business. Rick had no previous software experience but had managed substantial teams in the film and broadcast industry. The game studio had produced one hit game and was working on its second. Senior management at the developer hoped that his experience would bring some manner of order to what they felt was a production process that was beginning to drift and was losing momentum. Despite having one hit game, they were looking to greatly increase the capabilities of their engine while developing the next game, and the process was floundering. Rick's credibility for the role stemmed entirely from the credentials of the entertainment giant with which he had previously been employed; the studio's senior management also factored in the business connections that Rick could bring to the them.

Once in place at the developer, Rick began to reorganize the staff and brought in two former associates. From his very first days, it was clear to the mid-level managers that he had no idea how to run a game-development project or a studio. The cultural difference between the small development studio and the entertainment giant from which he had come was immense, and he made little effort to find common ground—probably in part due to his complete unfamiliarity with the software-development industry. Rick was in a difficult position; he was expected to come into this struggling developer and make a positive difference, to bring a slice of the success enjoyed by the entertainment giant. The problem was that he had no idea how to translate the skills learned at the entertainment giant to a high-functioning staff at a small game-development studio. He began to create political camps similar to what existed at his previous 1,000-plus employee company. By holding private meetings with staff in which he complained about other leads and employees, he created divisions among the development staff, pitting artists against programmers and even leads against each other.

The result of this cultural chasm and sudden political infighting was a series of poor decisions that eroded the morale of the leads as well as the company. Initially, senior management at the developer was resistant to hearing complaints or seeing any warning signs. Even when they did see these signs in concrete fashion, they were very slow to take corrective action. Indeed, management was slow to take action even when it was apparent that severe problems existed, in part because Rick shielded senior management from the realities of the situation. For example, Rick tasked one of the leads with writing a postmortem on a recently completed project. The lead approached the postmortem in the industry-standard fashion, providing an overview of the project, discussing five things that went well, and discussing five things that went poorly. After reviewing the postmortem write-up, Rick spoke to the lead privately and said that he wanted "the bad stuff" taken out—a comment that sounds laughably naïve to anyone who has been through at least a couple development cycles. There are always at least five issues from any development project I've ever worked on that need attention and improvement from cycle to cycle. These issues occur because we work in an imperfect world and frequently reach for new, never-before-attempted technical, artistic, or design achievements. These are not issues that get people reprimanded or fired; instead, the issues raised in postmortems—and the postmortems themselves—should be considered part of the development process. Rick, not having ever experienced this, made a very bad decision with the intention of protecting himself or others politically speaking. This, of course, resulted in a further lowering of company morale once the story spread around the office.

During Rick's first year as studio director, more than a quarter of the staff at the developer resigned in disgust. Not all of this lack of retention can be blamed on Rick, but his errors and the blind yet unwavering support that senior management gave him changed the atmosphere at the studio for the worse. When employees don't think management is paying attention to the studio and the concerns of their key leaders, bad things are going to happen. The studio lost another third at the end of Rick's second year, at which point management finally requested Rick's resignation. By then, however, the damage had been done. The studio was down to a skeleton of its former self, project development was moving at a crawl, and the money was running out.

Analysis

Could management have spotted the error in bringing Rick on board and corrected it sooner? Even more importantly, could they have made a better hiring decision? Should they have listened more closely to their key production leads? The answer to all these questions is an emphatic, "Yes, of course they could have"—yet the management group did not. Why?

Ego Issues

First, they had committed considerable resources to bringing Rick on board both in terms of his salary and of the corporate cachet they imagined would result from bringing in a person from an entertainment giant. The idea was that Rick could separate himself from the entertainment giant but bring with him that culture, that process, whatever "it" is that the game developer wanted. Attaining otherwise unavailable expertise is a very real and compelling reason to hire a leader from outside the company. The key is to clearly identify your need and match that need with an individual who has a proven record solving just that problem. The studio's senior management team was perhaps dazzled by the title and the corporate glare of the entertainment giant and missed the fact that Rick simply was not qualified to do the job. Rick bears some responsibility in this case as well; he should have spent some amount of time absorbing the studio's practices, learning its culture, and learning about the game-development industry as a whole. The fact that he did not perhaps points to an issue of egotism, which explains many of his actions. Senior management was guilty not of protecting Rick so much as protecting the correctness of their decision to hire Rick and not taking swifter action once the issues with Rick were obvious.

Lack of Open Communication

Beyond the resource commitment and the ego issues, the senior studio managers, assessment of Rick's performance was based on information received from Rick himself, who was in daily contact with them and controlling the message. The only other information sources were senior employees and leads who were courageous and desperate enough to go over Rick's head and warn the senior managers. The problem was that senior management had been listening to desperate complaints about the lack of a studio director for months prior to hiring Rick. Now they had an expensive, experienced studio director from a well respected entertainment giant and their employees were now complaining about the person. Naturally, they felt a certain amount of frustration, however much they may have respected the opinions of some of the staff.

After Effects and Corrective Action

The fact that senior management waited to take action until key staff members left points to a considerable disconnect with their own studio. In this case, the results of an exit interview from a senior designer led to immediate action. This is a great example of an exit interview's usefulness. However, it should be noted that six prior exit interviews produced no similar result. It is possible that the seventh interview produced a tipping point in terms of the weight of evidence, or perhaps the interviewee had been a major contributor and thus was listened to more closely. Another possibility is that none of the other exit interviews mentioned Rick—and herein lies a danger of relying too heavily on exit interviews for honest assessments of what may be wrong in your studio. The game industry is still a rather close-knit group, and prudent employees will very often avoid calling out senior managers or leads in writing in an exit interview. You never know where your career will be in five years, or where the career of a director such as Rick's will wind up. Getting to the core of why an employee is really leaving is not that difficult if you as a management group have effective communication paths with employees at all levels of your company.

Note

A similar situation was discussed at the 2007 Art Directors' Round Table during a segment devoted to the effects of and solutions to problems caused by poor leadership. The participant from a mid-size studio described a senior manager who was legacy, but was incompetent and intractable and causing problems across the team. "What did you do to correct the situation?" I asked. "I quit" was the immediate answer.

Case Study: Victor
Background: Right Person, Wrong Role

Victor was an art director and lead artist at a small, one-project company. The subject of a lead/director split emerged when the company grew to two- and then three-project teams with a corresponding growth in staff. Victor expressed the strong desire to remain director but also keep his hands in production as a lead—an option that was afforded him based on his level within the company, his strong performance to that point in his role, and a miscalculation regarding the amount of management time that would be required to build and maintain a strong department. Along with his director duties, Victor assumed the lead on the largest and most complex project while two other artists were selected for lead roles on the other games. Victor would oversee art development on these projects in the role of art director.

The company expanded very quickly and the management time commitments grew correspondingly. Victor, however, insisted that he maintain some project-level control because he felt that doing otherwise would lead to his production skills eroding and eventually lead to the loss of his ability to work in art direction at the company. Such fears are not uncommon, and are not totally unfounded either. As noted in Chapter 1, "How We Got Here," the game industry's technical advances happen very swiftly. Art-creation tools and methodology, as well as programming for different system architectures, can evolve considerably across the industry within the span of one project cycle. Skills can become obsolete if one is not in a production environment during the transition or acting as a lead or director and involved in management on successive projects for a few years. The willingness to surrender reliance on production skills as a foundation for a professional is a huge psychological hurdle for directors in particular to resolve. These skills usually have been built up for years and have attracted many compliments as well as afforded the individual many professional opportunities. To set those skills on which one has built a career aside and make a commitment to a management track is huge career decision—one that should not be taken lightly. At the lead level, the concern is not perhaps as severe. Leads frequently are involved in production work and can often move in and out of the lead role depending on the project and studio needs. It can be a terrifying step, though, moving to the director level at a multi-project studio where your future power app looks like Microsoft Excel.

Note

The validity of this concern is reflected in the comments of one art director at the GDC Round Table, who noted that "The lead needs to be the one who can break the biggest bone." At some point during the Round Table, I usually say "Please raise your hand if you are an art director at a multi-project studio. Keep your hand raised if you still do a lot of production artwork." I do so in part to show the artists and lead artists in attendance the price of management in terms of production time lost due to time spent developing and maintaining technical skills. Nonetheless, I'm always stunned by the large number of hands that remain raised—typically about 80 percent. Interestingly, but also entirely anecdotally, some attending art directors have also expressed amazement at that high number in private one-on-one talks after the round table has broken up.

In Victor's case, he began managing his project as lead and giving wide latitude to the other art leads. The three leads met together once per week to compare notes and review project status, but Victor was never able to devote enough time to dig into preproduction efforts, art pipeline development, or personnel issues emerging on other teams. Few of these errors are ever apparent in the early stages of production and preproduction because so little is known about the project and early milestones tend to be softer than later ones, which require more game functionality and art polish. In other words, it's easier to get away with stuff in the first third of a project if you don't have active and experienced oversight. Victor was not able to provide either, and chose to put the majority of his time and focus on the art lead duties for what was the largest project at the studio. There's nothing wrong with this arrangement in one-project studios, but

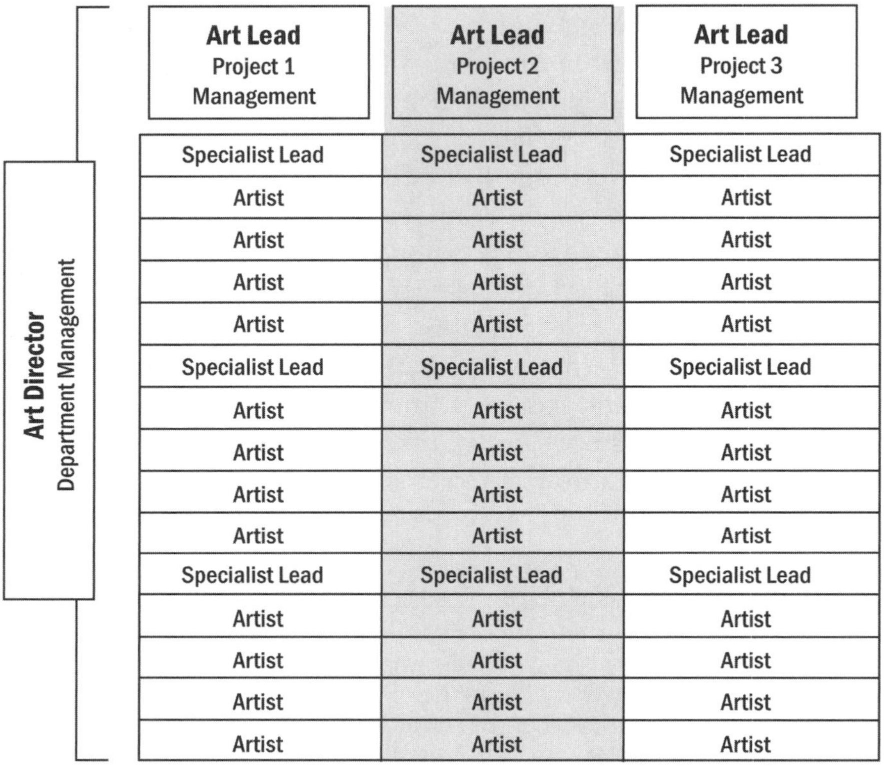

Art Director Department Management	Art Lead Project 1 Management	Art Lead Project 2 Management	Art Lead Project 3 Management
	Specialist Lead	Specialist Lead	Specialist Lead
	Artist	Artist	Artist
	Artist	Artist	Artist
	Artist	Artist	Artist
	Artist	Artist	Artist
	Specialist Lead	Specialist Lead	Specialist Lead
	Artist	Artist	Artist
	Artist	Artist	Artist
	Artist	Artist	Artist
	Artist	Artist	Artist
	Specialist Lead	Specialist Lead	Specialist Lead
	Artist	Artist	Artist
	Artist	Artist	Artist
	Artist	Artist	Artist
	Artist	Artist	Artist

Figure 3.1
A dual-matrix management structure representing a 48-person art department in a three-project company.

in a multi-project studio, the director level exists primarily to supervise and support the department staff and project leads. As evidenced in Figure 3.1, the departmental-supervision role is not insignificant. Ultimately, a few of the company's projects were cancelled over the years. These cancellations weren't necessarily related to the issues around Victor; some were due to the vagaries of the industry. Nonetheless, some were related to situations like his, which were found across all departments of the company.

Analysis

Inexperience

The leadership failure in Victor's case is one of him and his fellow directors not having the experience of running a larger company or an understanding of the associated organizational needs. Victor was simply unable to manage the role of art director after the company reached a certain size. It was difficult to see the tipping point where project duties became so time consuming that departmental issues were suffering because the departmental growth occurred gradually, over a period of a few years. During this time, both project complexity and Victor's department size expanded rapidly. By the time the company had been running between two and three projects simultaneously for a few years, Victor and the other senior managers had begun to sense the problem; subsequently, they and Victor decided that it was not in the best interests of the company for him to continue to devote time to both jobs. He ultimately chose the role of lead artist over director because he felt that he gained more professional satisfaction from facing project-level challenges. He was also able to address his concern regarding the loss of his professional skills by this decision. A new director was promoted from within the art department, who immediately began making very positive and overdue adjustments to the department both in personnel and practices.

An ironic downside of Victor choosing to focus on the art lead role was that while his production skills had not declined very much, his ability to stay current with new practices and software had suffered. As a result, the succeeding projects at that developer did have quality issues that might not have existed had management recommended that he simply move into the director role, where his greater strengths may have been.

Founder's Syndrome

The practice of senior managers clinging to roles is particularly thorny because there are simply fewer people to tell them the honest truth about the effect of their dual focus. The term "founder's syndrome" describes the condition that develops when founders or long-term legacy employees make decisions based on things as they were, not as they are. The hope is that based on the level of their experience and maturity, they are more capable of grasping the situation and taking self-directed action to change it, but the causes of inefficiency, poor project results, and poor retention are not always so clear as to point to a single problem that needs to be addressed. Self-awareness and awareness of project- and organization-level needs are also not given traits, regardless of level of talent and skill sets.

After Effects and Corrective Action

The company moved to clearly define the scope of responsibilities for all employees all the way up to the executive group. Some other directors shifted titles and responsibilities, in addition to Victor finding a more appropriate role. What emerged was a more focused leadership group that was able to effectively lead a growing company without project needs distracting half of the directors.

Case Study: Xavier
Background: The Best of What's Available at the Moment

Xavier was the lead programmer (and tech director by default, since there was only one other programmer) in an eight-person startup that experienced a two-fold growth after one year. He was a very friendly person whose contribution to the social fabric of the small company was considerable. He frequently led and organized movie nights, dinners, and other out-of-office events. After the completion of the first project, however, questions arose about Xavier's ability to lead a growing tech department. These questions centered around an inconsistent work ethic, insufficient technical skills, and at times insufficient communication skills. Specifically, although Xavier received feedback on his coding, he showed resistance to actually implementing the feedback directives and multiple iterations were frequently required to achieve a desired result. At around the same time, and prior to any message from management about poor performance, Xavier expressed a desire to move into more of an audio role. This was something the studio needed, and Xavier had been a musician at one point in his career, so it was decided to move him over to a programmer/audio engineer. Xavier completed one project in this role, after which it was determined that Xavier, while a good musician, did not have the skills to be a game audio engineer. At this point, management was distracted to a degree by studio growth and the potential building of a second and then third project team.

Because the company was about to expand into a multi-project studio, this serious issue of what role to find for Xavier was seen in one light as a happy opportunity to solve two problems—where do we find a producer for the new projects and what do we do with Xavier? Xavier also recognized the need for production work on the coming projects and suggested a move to a producer role.

The move was made, and Xavier began to learn the skill set of a producer, mostly centered around MS Project. He produced one project successfully, although there were inefficiencies and friction from some team members; this friction centered around his aforementioned communication issues. Xavier seemed to perform well enough on the second project, although the project experienced a difficult development cycle and arrived a few weeks late. In postmortem comments from the team gathered a month after the project shipped, the art lead expressed his unhappiness with Xavier as well as his unwillingness to work with him on a future project. Now the problem of what to do with Xavier became more intractable; at that point, six years into his tenure, management decided to terminate his employment.

Analysis

Failure to Address Negative Performance and Take Effective Action

The prominent leadership failure in this study has more to do with senior management's behavior than with Xavier's possibly sub-par leadership skills. In fact, we know very little, based on the information here, about exactly what the roots of his professional leadership inadequacies are. Regarding his difficulty implementing feedback directives, we should consider that perhaps the directives were not clearly given or perhaps phrased as suggestions. We don't know. There is usually not one person at total fault in cases of communication problems. Most of the performance criticism that Xavier experienced could be subjective; without more explanation and examination of the specific occurrences, we cannot make any judgments. What we do know is that upper management did very little to support and mentor him, or to really get to the source of his difficulties. Instead, management chose to not directly address these issues, to focus on his positive contributions, and to try to "find the right role" for him in the organization. The opportunity to accommodate this mode of thinking occurred because the company was growing and roles were quickly expanding.

There is nothing wrong—in fact, I view it as a positive—with trying to find more appropriate roles for people in an organization and working with employees' career goals to that end, provided that the role is truly needed and the individual is capable of performing well in that position. The negative issue here is that management seems to have addressed recurring perceived negative performance in one position by transitioning Xavier to another role in the company. I've gathered that this seems to be a more common occurrence than one might suspect in talking to others in the industry over the years. Indeed, I've heard of similar transfer practices in almost every discipline from participants in GDC Round Table discussions of problematic employees.

Why do this? Why not confront the employee? Why burden another department with what you know, or strongly suspect, will be a recurring problem? And, most of all, why promote them? These are all the questions that the top performers in your company will be asking when they see no action or inappropriate action taken regarding perceived inadequate performance. I would preface the answer to these questions by maintaining that there are very few dumb people who are in business. Everyone does things for at least what seems to them to be good, logical reasons based on the information and conditions at a certain point in time. It is sometimes only in hindsight that we can examine and evaluate questionable decisions, but it is vital that that examination and evaluation take place.

In this case, the project needed a producer quickly, and management may have, generally speaking, truly valued Xavier's contribution to the company and felt that, initially, the path of least resistance—transferring him to that position—was preferable insofar as it kept his morale up. Besides, and maybe more likely, it may have been that no one wanted or had the skills themselves to intervene in an effective way. This is not uncommon in a small or even mid-size company. Xavier was chosen as lead because he was in a very small sample group that required people to function well in multiple roles. If we look back on Figure 2.1 in Chapter 2, we see that almost every individual in a small company is fulfilling duties in more than one capacity. It is normal and expected that not everyone will excel at every spot all the time. As a company grows, then, management must have the discipline to evaluate staff based on their performance in every area and make appropriate decisions when growth does occur and roles need to be clearly defined.

Failure to Provide Support

Once in a leadership role, Xavier was getting very little support in terms of developing new skills or correcting perceived problems. This follows directly from the fact that to begin with, no one directly confronted him on his performance issues. Management also failed to provide leadership or management training to anyone at this time. Now in the role, all the directors could do was hope that professional growth and competence would occur spontaneously. It should be noted that although we know very few of the details of Xavier's troubles, the fact that he experienced the same sorts of general problems in three different roles indicates that he did probably have some genuine issues to which he was at least somewhat obvious. In this case, lacking consistent and timely feedback, he felt only that certain people in management were difficult, or saw him as difficult, and that for the most part, the team was very happy.

After Effects and Corrective Action

After Xavier's employment was terminated, the management group recognized its own failures in the process. Members in the group came to few conclusions regarding leaders in general moving forward, but they did acknowledge that there was no clear message of performance dissatisfaction being delivered to the employee in a useful, consistent manner, with expectations for improvement stated, and that a general lack confrontation on issues surrounding poor performance was a company-wide management issue. As a result, a more diligent review form and process were created, and a clearer description of the producer role, among others, was developed. Management realized that they acted in the fashion they did because they felt that the producer position was needed quickly and, ultimately, they were over-accommodating what had become a difficult, legacy employee. In the end, choosing not to start a search for a skilled producer led to a reduction in office morale over the course of a project, a messy termination, regret over the situation among some, and, of course, a need to hire a skilled producer. The positive effects that came out of it were a better understanding of roles and responsibilities and clearer communication of role expectations generally across the company.

Case Study: Yvette
Background: There Is No "I" in Delegate

Yvette was promoted to art lead on a project of 10 artists after two years as an artist in a mid-size company. She was an especially active artist, contributing assets and ideas above and beyond her specific responsibilities. In concept meetings, she was very vocal regarding creative ideas and best practices for the art pipeline. Moreover, she enjoyed a very effective collaborative relationship with the lead designer, who many considered to be exacting and sometimes disengaged with the team. At about the one-third point in development, the original art lead was removed to kick off another project, leaving a vacancy for Yvette, who was approached about the possibility. Yvette accepted the role and the team was very supportive regarding the transition.

The project's art production was just getting underway, and Yvette threw herself into almost every aspect of the art-asset pipeline—updating practices and personally editing or requesting re-dos on a number of art assets. The net effect after a few months was a considerable improvement in the graphical look of the game.

The high degree of rework was seen as a minor negative by the art director, but he trusted Yvette to manage the overall schedule appropriately. Yvette had also wanted to redo the opening movie, done by a contractor, and see it expanded in scope and completed by an internal team. The art director vetoed that idea in favor of having the same contractor rehired to make edits to the original piece.

As the project proceeded, Yvette continued the practice of editing or, in some cases, redoing sub-par assets. She also assigned herself the task of completing the user interface (UI) alongside her management duties. This was a huge undertaking whose true scope was not fully appreciated until it was too late. The UI component of this, as well as many other games, is a fluid asset that can change substantially up to the last minutes of development time. In this particular game, the UI was also more complex and robust in terms of features. At this point, an art director should have intervened, asked for a time estimate on the task, and suggested strongly that the UI be delegated to a team member. In this case, however, the art director was also the art lead on another project, and was not fully aware of the specifics of the task assignments on Yvette's project. The result was that Yvette's time was increasingly devoted to production tasks and less focused on overall team performance and team contribution.

As an example of the negative effect of this focus, an artist on the project at one point deviated from the set pipeline and created a complex asset with an unproven and, it turned out, buggy plug-in for the 3D application used for asset creation. The result was a piece of art that caused headaches for months until the problem was diagnosed and a fix could be made. The fix required the asset to be rebuilt almost from scratch. Proper attention to timely asset reviews would have spotted the error in early development and perhaps prevented the loss of production time associated with it.

As the project reached completion, Yvette was staying roughly on schedule, but regularly working 80-hour weeks. The art director had been pulled into production to help finish the user-interface tasks and was also unable to keep attention on the team and the department as a whole.

The resulting game was attractive and commercially successful, and the company was proud of their effort, but morale in the art department had suffered in noticeable ways. During the project, individual artists didn't put the same level of care into their own contributions, feeling that the art lead was just going to change it herself if she didn't like it anyway. Prospective leaders in the department were now wary of the time commitment involved in accepting a lead position. And most damaging, Yvette was now completely burned out. She resigned from the company a few months after the game released. The result was that the art department was missing a senior artist, and an experienced lead, and had a department full of artists who needed coaxing—of the financial and emotional variety—to consider a lead artist role.

Analysis

Inexperience

Yvette was a dedicated and accomplished senior artist who may have made a great lead on the project—if she'd had experienced support available to her. Some of Yvette's performance issues, such as her taking over sub-par assets, shows a commendable commitment to the quality of the product; properly channeled, that energy could be an extremely positive force on a project. As the energy was applied, however, it led to a disassociated team and a burned-out lead. The management team, especially the producer and art director, should have enforced a limit to production-schedule commitments. The art director in particular should have been more involved in mentoring Yvette, and should have required her to delegate asset edits to the artists who created them. That they did not is probably a case of simple inexperience.

The assumption of the user-interface element of the game by the lead also contributed to the problems late in the game's development, but the blame for that does not rest on Yvette's shoulders. Rather, it rests on those of the management team. No lead should be tasked for production code or assets more than a certain percentage based on the number of direct reports; moreover, no lead—art or technical—should assign themselves any task that involves major dependencies for other team members. An example of this might be developing an animation pipeline or leading visual-effects creation.

Understanding and Supporting the Role

The lead's primary job is to make sure that everyone on the team is working at peak efficiency, and that they have no resource needs or obstacles preventing them from completing their tasks. Critical management and review work can far too easily take a backseat when the lead is tasked in the production schedule—and that eventually makes the entire team work at less than peak performance. It is vital that this shift of mindset, from production to management, take place for a leader to be effective. In the case of Yvette, she went from 100 percent production one week to being named the art lead the next, without any real adjustment in work practices or scheduled tasks. As a compounding factor, there was never an opportunity for Yvette to explore the role of the lead or to learn leadership skills as a specialist lead on a project before diving into the full lead role. This situation is sometimes unavoidable in small or mid-size companies that do not have great staffing flexibility or resources, but the absence of this step should not be overlooked as a reason for Yvette's problems. Given that Yvette was a new lead, she should have been mentored and monitored much more closely by the art director.

Note

> By "mentoring" and "monitoring," I mean meeting one-on-one with the lead as opposed to hovering over the lead's shoulder. The new lead must be given the opportunity and latitude to truly lead the team on his or her own; having the director physically there undermines the lead's authority, and usually causes the lead to simply defer decisions to the director if present. Mentoring and monitoring should be done away from the team for this reason.

After Effects and Corrective Action

Following the completion of the project, and for many years afterward, the company in question was forced to offer a "lead bonus" to candidates in order to get staff to consider lead roles. While many companies follow this practice, I consider it to be a bad idea; instead, I try to foster an environment where a senior artist or programmer is every bit as valued, appreciated, and compensated as a lead with comparable experience and contribution levels. It's bad enough that the lead on the organization chart gets a bigger box—and is at the top of the credits—but if one side of that equation is also getting a salary bonus, even a temporary one, it further erodes any attempt to equate their importance to a project. And besides, sometimes even the money wasn't enough of an incentive. Some of the most accomplished artists at the company refused to consider lead roles due to the perceived lack of support for the position, the associated personnel-management headaches, and the amount of overtime that was required. Over the course of a few years as the company modified its practices, that perception did change, but it was certainly a challenge that the management team could have done without.

Other practice changes that the company adopted in part because of this experience included external management training, role and responsibility clarification, and weekly one-on-one art director asset reviews.

The management training was made available to every new lead and director in the company. An external leadership forum focusing on new managers and leaders was selected for the first try. While it wasn't an overnight success, it did lead to a more professional approach to management in the company, gave managers a heightened awareness of their new responsibilities, encouraged further education (mostly through the reading of management books), and gave new managers a starting vocabulary and skill set with which to do their job.

The clarification of lead responsibilities included a different approach to personnel management. Hereafter, the lead was responsible for basically as much personnel review or performance critique as he or she wanted. Typically, this took the form of the lead giving an initial performance talk to the employee when warranted due to underperformance in some area. The director would then take the situation over if further corrective or disciplinary action was needed. This was more or less the way it worked before, but communicating that to prospective leads turned out to be very helpful. One of the most difficult things for new leads to figure out is how to give feedback from a position of authority to people who were formerly peers. With the potential personnel-management aspect removed, senior management found new leads felt much more comfortable.

The art director reviews began immediately, but were only truly successful and productive when the art director stopped also being a lead artist and could devote his or her full attention to the needs of the other projects Unfortunately, this development did not occur until there was a personnel transition at the art director position, some four years after Yvette's departure.

Case Study: Zeke and Alan
Background: A Tale of Two Leads

Zeke was a skilled designer who was new to a mid-size development studio. He brought newer game genre experience to the team and was very energetic and aggressive regarding schedules and abilities. His first assignment was the lead on a prototype project in which he was the primary designer of two on the project. The project was extremely successful and his efforts on the project were lauded by all, to the notice of senior management, who pegged him as a potential future lead designer.

One issue for senior management was Zeke's relatively low level of job experience and his newness to the company. To answer these critiques, senior management decided to pair Zeke up in the lead role with Alan—also a new designer but with a bit more industry experience and a slightly longer tenure with the company.

Alan, it was felt, had a more traditional approach to working in a team and had demonstrated his ability to do so; the thought was that his more even, mature presence would balance out Zeke's exuberance and allay management's concerns in this area. The goal was that the two would work as dual leads on the project with a clearly defined split of job responsibilities, and neither having authority over the other.

Once the project was underway, the relationship and communication between Alan and Zeke began to deteriorate. Most of the disagreements centered around the basic approach to the design, and there was purposely no chain of decision-making authority between the leads. Alan doubted Zeke's general approach, and Zeke responded to the situation by quietly taking on more and more design features to the implementation level. Senior management appealed to a senior design director for advice on which approach was truly best; unfortunately, the director could only equivocate, saying it was too early to tell whether Zeke's approach was too aggressive or Alan's was too conservative. After a couple of months of this quagmire, Alan and Zeke both expressed their frustrations with the situation to the producer and to senior management. The odd thing as far as senior management was concerned was that the project itself was outwardly on track; milestones were being met, and features were being implemented. If there was really a problem, then it was at a level that was deep within design philosophy and methodology and dependent on significant senior designer analysis, which was inconclusive. For their part, the tech lead and the art lead were both reasonably satisfied with progress but wary of the growing rift between their two lead designers.

Matters came to a head when Zeke and Alan separately asked management for a resolution that eliminated the dual design lead spot. Zeke, for his part, felt that he should be the lead. He argued that he had, to this point, done most of the design work in the game, and it was logical to select him as sole lead based on this fact. Alan was so worn out by the situation that he consented to the arrangement—as long as there was no credited title change. Management expressed concerns about Zeke's perceived divisiveness on the team and in the company but ultimately consented.

Now fully in charge of game design, Zeke threw himself into the development of the game and very rapidly brought it to a playable state—not a fun state, but a playable one. As the project entered the alpha stage of development, more questions were asked about why the game was still not yet ready, and why there were still significant design problems. Zeke was seen to be working diligently for long hours but reacted very defensively in response to questions and negative feedback, dodging responsibility and, ultimately, resigning from the company, and leaving considerable ill will on both sides. The game design was then overhauled and missions and levels completed by a senior designer, who was pulled from another project, and by Alan, whose opinion of Zeke's design work had now found more favor.

Analysis

When Two Heads Are Not Better Than One

There is a very good reason that we elect a president and a vice president as opposed to two presidents, and that throughout all of human history you rarely see dual kings: It simply does not work very well. I've seen it tried a few times and heard anecdotally from some GDC Round Table attendees of its effectiveness, but only in very specific cases with individuals whose workflow and nature lend themselves to operate effectively in that arrangement. The vast majority of stories I hear are tales of woe—some ending in a whimper, and others with a spectacular cataclysm. And this is not a secret. It's not something that has never happened before. Anyone who has ever worked on a group project at school where no leader who has any authority is appointed can probably tell you a funny story about how excruciating the process was and how awful things would have turned out had they not done the whole thing themselves at the end. At the project-leadership level, it's the same story—except one person can't do everything, and it's not at all funny.

So why would management, a rational and intelligent group, consent to this? Why didn't they change it the moment they saw it going awry? Why did they ultimately make the wrong decision?

The Project Staffing Trap

An unusual staffing arrangement like this comes into being because there is no ideal candidate in whatever discipline to put into the needed position. This is a bad situation for a company to be in—so bad, in fact, that one of the only ways to make it worse is to put *two* non-ideal candidates into the position, with neither having final decision-making authority. The obvious rationale behind the decision is that a weakness in one lead will be compensated by a strength in the other and vice versa. It's a great theory, but it just doesn't seem to work.

The solution is simple and equally obvious: Hire the right lead designer—someone who has a proven track record of making great games and being a solid team leader. The problem is that great lead candidates, design or otherwise, are not easily found. The process can be time consuming and expensive for the developer. Let's assume that a developer is pitching a game to a publisher that would require them to hire a programmer with some advanced ability on a new console system. They cannot hire a candidate or even realistically start a search without a signed contract. Doing so would not only be expensive, but they could potentially lose an ideal candidate if the pitch or contract negotiations were extended for a significant period of time. It's worth noting also that the period immediately preceding a new project starting is one of the most fiscally dangerous times for an independent developer. Cash reserves are usually at a low point, and the idea of extending into a line of credit with no signed deal on the table to back the loan up is not something that the principals of the developer or their bankers are all that happy about. Another factor to consider is the new hire himself or herself. Does the company feel comfortable hiring and relocating an individual only to have to fire that person immediately if the project deal collapses for some reason? The ethical answer (for me at least) is no.

Now, weeks or months later, the developer has the executed contract in hand and is ready to find and bring in their console expert. The problem is, they now must also start preproduction if they haven't already—and the search itself, if not immediately successful, could take several months depending on the job market and the location and reputation of the developer. This situation is what makes many small and mid-size developers look internally whenever possible for senior and lead positions on projects.

Management must now ask themselves, do we wait who knows how long to find our great hire, or do we look internally to a quantity that is known but questionable for whatever reason? It's a tough call. That iffy internal candidate might be great. I've certainly seen many examples of individuals who successfully grew into their role, despite the fact that many had questions regarding their suitability at the start. There is a tipping point at which an internal candidate is regarded as a potential lead who needs development and is worth the risk or is regarded as a great senior-level contributor who needs to hear an honest assessment of why he will not be considered for a lead spot (and, if applicable, what steps he or she would need to take to be so considered in the future). It needs to be recognized that it is a very subjective judgment, and senior management may not be able to reach unanimous consensus in some cases.

While there may not have been conclusive evidence that a qualified lead designer needed to be hired externally at the time in this example, there were a number of stakeholders involved in the decision who had serious reservations about the dual-lead plan from its conception—including both Alan and Zeke.

After Effects and Corrective Action

Alan was promoted to the lead role following the completion of the project and vowed never again to attempt a dual-lead arrangement. Zeke left on a sour note toward the close of the project; by then, the design department as a whole was convinced that a change had to be made and that the removal of Zeke was the correct decision.

Lessons Learned

These case studies predominantly illustrate the problems inherent in how we select and develop leads as opposed to issues of leadership quality. The major reason sub-par leads get selected from an internal pool is we don't really think about defining the responsibilities of the lead the way we would if we were launching an external search for the best candidate. This attitude almost ensures that a less than optimal candidate will find himself or herself in a lead role. It might be assumed also that if management developed and adhered to a set of responsibilities that defined the lead role, we would see less promotion from within and more of an emphasis on bringing in external expertise. Possibly, but I would counter that defining the role, communicating expectations to the company, and demonstrably supporting existing leads will encourage internal staff to realistically assess the position and determine whether they want to pursue it. If so, the company will quickly see their internal lead candidate pool grow in ability and number.

If an individual understands and meets those leadership qualifications and is enthused about the leadership aspect, then senior management has done a good job. If, however, no candidate is deemed appropriate for the role, or a qualified candidate needs an amount of cajoling deemed extreme to consider the role, I strongly recommend if at all possible that an external search be performed. The cost will be high to find such an individual in terms of time lost for the search, but the cost of putting a poor leader in place will be far higher in a year's time—not to mention by the end of your development cycle. As seen in these examples, the cost is not just felt by the lead, but by the entire team or company.

The subject of hiring an external person into a leadership role comes up occasionally. This can be a delicate situation with regard to senior staff who are looking to advance their careers and who feel closed out when senior management resorts to an extensive external search to fill a lead position. Where appropriate and possible, hiring from within is almost always preferable to bringing in a new hire to lead a team. There are notable exceptions, however, such as instances in which some specific technical or creative ability does not exist within the company. Such cases can exist in any department—a specific platform expertise in programming, game genre, in design or art. The team will respect and probably strongly encourage seeking outside hires in such instances.

Interview: Joe Minton, President of Digital Development Management (DDM)

As president of DDM, Joe runs the Support Services division, which assists clients with contract negotiations, overcoming development hurdles, working with the project's stakeholders, and aligning their corporate structure for long-term success. He also oversees the process of making DDM into the model agency for the video-game business.

As president of the development studio Cyberlore, Joe was responsible for overseeing the day-to-day operations of the company, setting the corporate direction, building a management team, and generally maintaining a tight ship in a competitive industry. Joe was responsible for all business development, from securing millions of dollars in console and PC development deals to fostering major brand relationships with international companies like Hasbro and Playboy. Joe focused on becoming an expert on studio organization, personnel management, and communication systems, and has lectured on those subjects domestically and internationally.

Seth Spaulding: Describe your transition from a production position to a leadership position. What were some unexpected challenges or surprises?

Joe Minton: The transition was easier than I had expected as far as working with people in the company was concerned. Being an executive producer requires a lot of the same skills and internal relationships as does the president position.

What was a surprise was realizing that the buck really did now stop with me. I could get advice and seek input, but at the end of the day, I was the buffer between the company and the board, between the business realities and the hopes and dreams of the studio employees, and between the practical needs of the company and the actual resources at hand. The job felt like a non-stop balancing act.

The way I approached the challenge was to be as open and candid as possible to both the board and the employees of the company. For the company, we instituted an "open book" policy regarding the financial aspects of the business so every employee could see the effects of things like missed milestone payments on the company's overall financial picture. Some in management thought this would be too much information for the average employee to handle effectively, and that it might upset them or cause undo concern. In some cases, it required additional discussions to allay concerns; however, overall the effect on the company was very positive and built a lot of commitment and trust among the employees. We usually presented the financials at the end of every quarter, and we also included projections looking out about a year. The projections included Best Case, Most Likely Case, and Worst Case scenarios.

Communication to the board was handled with the same candor, openness—and even bluntness where appropriate to accurately describe and highlight key issues and in particular challenges in the coming quarter or year.

S.S.: Looking back, are there any decisions or practices you would change, and if so, why?

J.M.: I would insist on a clear written agreement between all significant shareholders on how key aspects of the ownership role would be handled, such as exit plans, personal guarantees, level of acceptable risk, short-term goals, and long-term goals. If the owners are not in perfect alignment, the business never can be.

The people who are in leadership seats at a twelve-person company are not likely to be the same people you want in those seats when the company grows larger. But they remain in those seats at a lot of companies to the detriment of the company and, ultimately, the careers of those individuals. The people in roles need to change to make sure their skills and contributions are best aligned with what the company needs from them to be successful.

S.S.: What is the most important thing you would tell someone making that transition within their company?

J.M.: You can (and I believe should) be friendly with people, but you cannot retain close friendships with people who you need to lead. You can pretend that you are able to, but when you control their livelihood, it simply is not a workable dynamic. It is best to embrace your new role fully or not to enter it at all. A company leader has to be able to make very tough decisions that have very large ramifications on the lives of individuals. If you are not willing to do this with clear eyes on what will make the company stronger (thus ultimately helping the most people), you will not succeed as a leader. This doesn't mean you need to be cold, or that you should hide your agendas—just that there is a difference between "friendly" and "friendship," and it is important to realize the distinction early.

S.S.: Were there any people who helped, and if so how?

J.M.: Other leaders in the company helped. Otherwise, finding people in similar roles in other companies—even ones in vastly different fields—was beneficial simply to understand what most everyone had to deal with and what was more specific to my situation. I found it very helpful to just have a safe and confidential environment where I could bounce ideas, vent, whatever, and not worry at all about the effect on the company.

S.S.: What are the most common traits shared by other effective leaders in your experience?

J.M.: Openness, communication, trustworthiness, integrity, ability to motivate, willingness to take measured risks, not procrastinating, understanding that being in charge doesn't mean being the expert.

S.S.: Which traits do you feel are your strongest and how does knowledge of these traits affect how you approach leadership challenges?

J.M.: Getting people to work in a common direction, and openness. I prefer employing everyone to help move the company in a particular direction instead of trying to do it all myself.

S.S.: What are the worst traits a leader has exhibited in your experience?

J.M.: Randomness, thinking one is the expert on everything, being wishy-washy, weak willed, easily overwhelmed, operating from fear, pretending to be a celebrity.

S.S.: How did these traits manifest themselves, and what was the result of their involvement in terms of the team, project, and/or company?

J.M.: Having a leader who is not consistent and who does not articulate where the company is going causes constant problems with direction and morale. People will not do their best because they have no clear goal in front of them, or, worse yet, will look to leave.

S.S.: Are there any leadership traits you admire or perhaps aspire toward but don't feel you embody? If so, how do you feel embodying these traits would make you a better leader? Do you consciously try to develop these traits? Do you mentor other leaders?

J.M.: Greater sense of being proactive on the large scale decisions that can dramatically affect the success of the company. I am attempting to develop this. I do mentor other leaders, usually by modeling behavior.

S.S.: Do you have any training in leadership, either formal or unstructured (e.g., armed forces experience)? If relevant, in what ways do you apply that training to challenges in your job?

J.M.: No.

S.S.: What do you see as the toughest challenge facing leads during a game-development project cycle or at a game-development company generally? How have you seen this handled most and least effectively?

J.M.: Leads generally are great at their discipline, and very often people who are great at their discipline are not great at leading people. They are two very different skill sets, and it is simply random as to whether someone has both—having one is not a predilection toward the other. In the worst case, new leads are thrown onto a team and expected to know how to communicate, how to run meetings, how to motivate, how to effectively discipline, how to appropriately filter information from a publisher, etc. It can work well to make them a sub-lead first, or a lead on a small project with experienced leads as mentors.

S.S.: What are some common mistakes you've seen leads make, be they new or experienced?

J.M.: Most commonly, it is speaking for the people on their team without getting input. For example, deciding on schedules without talking to the people actually doing the work. This destroys morale and breeds friction as each party will blame the other when the project runs late, but the lead may not hear it publicly due to the employee's concern for his or her job. The very most important thing for a new lead to learn is how to communicate, listen, and to make informed decisions that build teams and do not destroy them.

Many new leads struggle with how much they need to command versus listen, communicate, collaborate, and guide. New leads sometimes need a lot of mentoring on this point from more experienced managers. It is common for a lead to think that this means "telling people what to do" when in fact it is a lot more about listening.

S.S.: How have you seen new leads best get support from directors or executives?

J.M.: Mentoring. Sometimes skill seminars, but I'm not sure how well these work.

S.S.: Do you think good leaders can be trained? Or is the essence of a good leader simply innate ability?

J.M.: It is innate, but can be trained from there. Some people are not leaders and will never be leaders. A slim few are innately good right away. More commonly, people have the ability but it has to be developed, trained, and practiced—like pretty much every other skill you can think of.

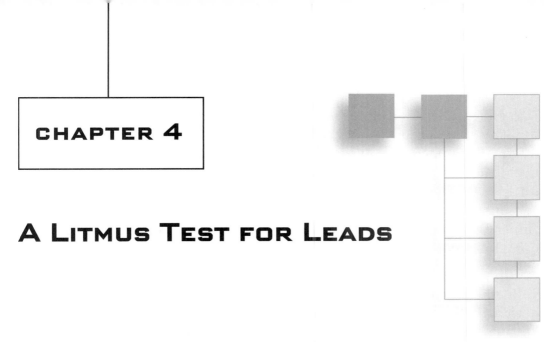

CHAPTER 4

A Litmus Test for Leads

It is first important to identify what the roles and responsibilities of a lead are before we can determine what to look for in a leader. Following that, we need to recognize what motivates someone to want to lead in the first place, as well as what structures, if any, can help properly encourage good leaders to emerge.

The Traits, Practices, and Motivation of the Ideal Lead

A lead's core skills should encompass an ability to motivate his or her team, an ability to be responsible for his or her section of the project but have the capacity to take a broader view, and an ability to communicate effectively at and across multiple levels.

This qualifying skill list, while brief, does not come cheaply or commonly amongst the population of an average development company. These experienced personnel will command some of the highest salaries in your company. Ideally, specialist leads will have two to four years experience, and leads anywhere from four to six years. The lead should have, by weight of his or her experience, earned the trust and respect of the team, or if a new hire, have a positive track record and be able to earn their trust swiftly. For the internal candidate, this trust and respect initially is based primarily on the lead's production effort. The critical thing for a new lead is to be able to make the managerial transition successfully and in doing so earn the same level of trust and respect from the team in the new role.

As management responsibilities increase, the need for soft skills—that is, interpersonal skills and personality traits such as personal leadership style, ability to motivate and inspire, and the ability to communicate and effectively present information—increases. At the same time, the need for hard skills—defined as quantifiable abilities such as coding-language proficiencies, expertise in specific software packages, business acumen, or artistic ability, or alternatively defined as traits such as aggressiveness, decisiveness, and follow-through—decrease, although leads do obviously need a mix of these traits and skills, particularly using this latter definition.

New leaders undergo a transition period during which they rely on their soft skills more than at any other time in their careers. Internally promoted leads must make the transition from contributor and colleague to manager and leader. Externally hired leads and directors must work to gain the trust of their new staff as their leader. In either case, it is important to build that new relationship successfully and as quickly as possible.

The Cheerleader-General

A lead needs to embrace the goals of his or her project to such a degree that he or she becomes a sort of "cheerleader-general." On the "cheerleader" side, the lead must serve as the project's champion both to the team and to those outside the team and even outside the company. The lead needs to be able to communicate this vision and enthusiasm in a natural and forthright manner without seeming forced in any way. Instead of drinking the Kool-Aid, the lead needs to be making it. The lead needs to have as much passion for the project as anyone else on the team. Additionally, the lead needs to embrace and encourage positive approaches to challenges posed by the project. A lead cannot be the chief complainer on a project; indeed, the more the lead promotes a positive attitude across the team, the more success that team will achieve. This does not mean that problems are not addressed or should be brushed aside, simply that they are confronted directly and solutions recommended, agreed upon by all relevant parties, and enacted always with the goals of the project foremost in mind.

The "general" aspect reflects the need for the lead to be decisive and goal oriented. The best approaches into the unknown are frequently fraught with worry and second guessing; the lead needs to find a path for his or her team after as much research as is allowed and recommend a course of action. Projects can sometimes seem to swim in chaos at times, and the lead needs to stay above that, or at least appear so, and set a sensible course. Once a decision has been made and directives given, the lead should remain flexible. World War I German Field Marshal Helmuth von Moltke once said, "No battle plan ever survives first contact with the enemy." These words apply just as well to a software-development plan encountering the realities of the software-development process. Leads need to juggle flexibility of action with a firm goal-driven message and know when and how to balance the weight of the plan's fixed budget or delivery date with the difficult realities that sometimes exist on a project.

The "general" theme also is an acknowledgement that the lead is someone who has been given power on the project. How a new lead responds to this power is crucial to his or her success, as well as that of the team. It should be noted that the lead's power does not give him or her license to dictate everything in his or her area of the project. Even in the case of a studio director this should not occur. The best leaders empower team members to make good decisions and use their position to support them.

Accountability

The lead is ultimately responsible for the area of the project that he or she has been assigned to direct. This represents a considerable shift in mentality from the role of the senior artist, who is technically responsible only for his or her direct tasks. This aspect of the lead role is measurable mainly by senior management, the producer, and fellow leads. The new lead will have to adapt to giving accurate information and estimates to another level in the reporting structure, be it an art lead, art manager, producer, art director, or studio director. The level of complexity in this reporting and documentation will increase depending on the level of the manager receiving the report and the number of direct and indirect reports that the lead must track. Given that, the root of the issue of accountability is the level of personal responsibility toward that project that the individual demonstrates.

As noted, good leads make informed and decisive decisions. These decisions will be dead wrong about half the time, judging from the industry's printed postmortems and my own experience. Sometimes the errors are correctable in production; sometimes it is only in hindsight that the team realizes its inefficiencies and errors. One of the best things that good leads can do is accept this reality and freely admit and diagnose their own failures in full view of the team and their superiors. Finding fault with other team members or blaming the process is detrimental to the team's morale and it sends a bad message to senior management.

Main Model List

Project Y Soldiers and Monsters	Concept	Proxy Mesh to Animation	Hi-Res/Normal Maps	LOD 1 (Cinematics)	LOD 2 (Game)	Textures	Final Mesh to Animation
MODERN SOLDIER							
Modern Medium Male	Done	Done	WIP - John	WIP - John	WIP - John	WIP - John	WIP - John
Modern Medium Female	First Pass	First Pass	First Pass	First Pass	First Pass	First Pass	First Pass
NEAR FUTURE SOLDIER							
Near Future Light Male	Done	WIP - John	WIP - John	WIP - John		WIP - John	
Near Future Light Female	WIP - PM						
Near Future Medium Male	Done						
Near Future Medium Female	WIP - PM						
Near Future Heavy Male	Done						
Near Future Heavy Female	WIP - PM						
FUTURE SOLDIER							
Future Light Male	Done	WIP - Jane	WIP - Jane				
Future Light Female							
Future Medium Male	WIP - EE						
Future Medium Female							
Future Heavy Male	WIP - EE						
Future Heavy Female							
Future Sniper Male	First Pass						
Future Sniper Female	First Pass						
FUTURE POWERED SOLDIER							
Stealth Male							
Stealth Female							
Jump Male							
Jump Female							
Mech Female							
Mech Male							
Monster							
Small Monster	Done	Old Model	Old Model	Old Model	Old Model	Old Model	Old Model
Small Monster Commander							
Med. Monster Soldier	First Pass						
Med. Monster Commander							
Med. Monster Boss							
Heavy Monster Soldier	First Pass						
Heavy Monster Commander	First Pass						
Heavy Monster Boss	First Pass						
Heavy Monster Elite Guard	First Pass						

Figure 4.1

A sample asset tracking sheet, built in Microsoft Excel that might be prepared and used by a modeling or art lead. Note that no time budgets or deadlines are included.

Expertise with some new tools is needed by many leaders at different reporting stages. For most needs of specialist leads and leads for task estimation and perhaps task tracking as well, Microsoft Excel will usually suffice. There is also Microsoft Project and a growing number of task-tracking tools designed specifically for software project tracking; these are typically employed by producers, but other leads may also need to build proficiency in them. Figure 4.1 shows a simple task-tracking Excel sheet that a specialist lead might use for personal organization and reporting to a producer or art lead. Figure 4.2 shows a more robust task-tracking method: Test Track.

Communication

Few skills in management are more inscrutable and yet vital than solid communication skills. These encompass an ability to give clear instructions and effective feedback to your team, coordinate well with your fellow leads, and provide clear, concise, and complete reporting to higher management. All these skills boil down to understanding the needs and status of your team or task and

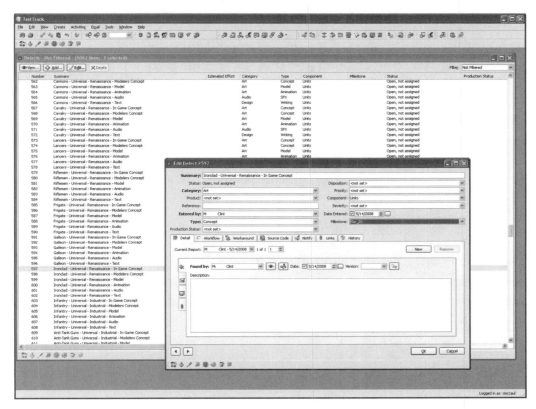

Figure 4.2
Test Track used as a task-tracking tool. Each entry may be expanded to a window and can include a variety of customizable data fields.

understanding the needs of your audience. An effective communicator is able to and is comfortable with bridging these gaps.

In addition, a good communicator understands that different audiences require different approaches to grasp similar messages. For example, many individual employees respond well to blunt, challenging feedback such as, "Hmm, this hit animation just isn't snappy enough. Take a look at some of the other similar assets and make sure this matches the pace at the strike. Nice work, though, overall—particularly on the follow-through motion." Others might require a softer pitch, such as, "Hey, I really like what you did here in the lead up and follow through—good secondary motion! Now to make this hit the mark, the strike itself needs to match the other assets in terms of pace. Take another look at the reference video and make sure the strike is really dramatic. Nice work overall."

The feedback presented in these two approaches is exactly the same, but the delivery is slightly different. The first example might be directed at a more seasoned animator, who I don't feel I need to remind to look at reference video and who needs a bit less overt stroking. The second example I imagine to involve a more junior animator who may need a bit more guidance to get the specific result I need. They may also need to hear what they are doing right a bit more than a veteran (although it is vital to pass along praise for good work to all employees as appropriate). Other factors influence this communication, as well: What is my body language? How many times have I reviewed and commented on this artist's work? Did the artist come to me or did I come to the artist?

I sometimes ask my GDC Round Table groups, "Have you ever had to tell someone they have bad communication skills?" When I do, I see a lot of grimaces and nodding heads. The difficulty is that although poor communication skills are the crux of the problem with some individuals, it is all but useless to offer this as constructive feedback. The recipient is simply unable to do anything concrete with that information, however correct it may be. The problem, frequently, is that that feedback does not address any work-related issue. The manager might as well say, "It's not me, it's you."

Building Soft Skills

A great lead possesses a certain amount of soft skills, which are simply inherent to their personality. They tend to be people persons, extroverts, and generally engaging to be around. These skills can and should be developed continually because these will be the attributes on which the lead will increasingly rely as his or her career advances. It's rare to find a software developer with a staff rich in these skills, however. Indeed, if you were called upon to paint a picture of the personnel makeup of software-development studios with one stroke, the broad brush would have to be nerd colored.

Nerds' strong suits do not classically include suave social ability, high self-esteem, or natural leadership talent. They are typically very intelligent, good at creative problem solving, and have knowledge-based skills such as programming, modeling, animation, and spreadsheets. Nerds *love* the spreadsheets. So in this population in particular, it is vital to find those people who do have these skills or inherent traits and encourage their development. It is equally important to make some sort of soft-skill training opportunities available to all employees. The more your company is made up of people who can work effectively as a team, engage in constructive dialog, and listen well, the more successful your development will be. Following is a list of a few valuable soft-skills. It is not a complete list, but it will give you a general idea of what these skills are.

- The ability to talk and listen effectively

- Empathy, awareness, and observation

- Self-awareness

- Self-confidence

- Cooperation and the ability to resolve conflicts

- Outgoing personality

Model the Behavior You Want

Building hard skills, such as Excel expertise or coding knowledge, is straightforward enough. It's not easy by any means, but the path to mastery is clear. But how do you teach listening or self-awareness or any of the other so-called soft skills, or traits defined as hard such as aggressiveness or decisiveness? The answer is—not easily. The best way to do so is to model the behaviors you want and expect to see from new leaders. If new leads see management backbiting, yelling, and cursing up and down the halls, that's probably what they will do. If they see senior leads vacillating on important decisions and avoiding challenging issues, then that's what they will do. Senior management, team leads, and senior production personnel are mentoring every day, whether they know it or not. Better leads and better staff in general will be the result of awareness of this fact and responsibility regarding it.

Formal and Informal Training for Soft-Skill Development

Certain leadership-training courses focus on personal traits and raising self awareness as it applies to leadership traits. 360 reviews and Meyers Briggs assessments can offer perspective for leaders; we will examine these more closely in Chapter 5, "Leadership Types and Traits: Assessment and Development Strategies." Additionally, participating in public-speaking classes will build confidence (or at least a degree of comfort) for the many instances in which leads must address groups. Even involvement in local theater or volunteer work in your community can be helpful in making people more comfortable and effective in team environments. Of course, it takes a certain mindset to want to do things like this in the first place. It is perhaps a given that there are inherent personality traits that make some people more disposed to pursuing activities like these, which enhance and develop what may already be a strong skill set, but nevertheless these same opportunities exist for everyone to put into practice.

Build Your Ideal Leader: An Exercise

The "Build Your Ideal Leader" exercise in this section was designed for a 2005 game industry leadership seminar I led focusing on art direction in which participants identified from a list the eight most important leadership traits and two most important professional skills or experience. They would then discuss them, from there narrowing the list to four ranked traits and one skill. (Note that the list contains no right or wrong answers; in fact, almost all these traits are desirable to some degree for a leader or manager.)

This exercise is fairly easy and quick if you attempt to do it on your own; it is much harder for most groups of three or more to come to a consensus. Indeed, most groups are involved in passionate discussion when time is called for the first session after half an hour. The second session typically proceeds a bit more quickly because by that point, most of the tougher choices have been made and most of the definitions have been agreed upon by the participants. That said, the second cull really focuses the traits in a more tangible manner. You can frequently discover almost as much about the other members of your group as you can about what you find most valuable in a leader.

Note

The exercise can be streamlined by making one selection pass instead of two, and can take only about 15 minutes.

Personal Traits:

- Honest

- Intelligent

- Wise

- Has a sense of humor

- Outgoing

- Persistent

- Passionate about the product

- Compassionate

- Decisive

- Generous

- Trustworthy

- Ambitious

- Humble

- Spirited, upbeat

- Calm under pressure

- Is a good mentor

- Patient

- Logical

- Contemplative/able to see all sides of an issue

- Fair/equitable

- Ethical

- Is a consensus builder

- Charismatic

- Consistent

- Responsible

Professional Traits:
- Prior game-production experience

- Prior game-management experience

- Familiarity with current game-production practices

- Adept at office politics

- Great speaking and writing skills

- Expertise with project-planning tools and concepts

Personal Trait Pros and Cons

Following is a summary of the pros and cons of the various personal traits listed above. This information is a helpful foundation for anyone running this exercise. Many of the comments come directly from participant feedback and the group discussions.

Honest

Pros: Honesty is the foundation of trust. People want their leader to give them forthright assessments of their own work and the state of the company and project.

Cons: Not many. Honesty is a great trait in a leader and in the staff in general. The phrase "Honest to a fault" comes to mind, however; the leader needs to be a firewall to outside distractions. Sticking resolutely to a policy of 100-percent honesty is probably going to let through some distracting information at some point.

Intelligent

Pros: Intelligent leaders naturally make more intelligent decisions, which will benefit the project.

Cons: Intelligence is rarely chosen by the group as among the most critical traits because, taken by itself, it isn't critical to leadership. Additionally, we can all think of highly intelligent people who would make or have made terrible team leaders.

Wise

Pros: The correct lessons have been learned from experience.

Cons: None. This trait makes my top five.

Has a Sense of Humor

Pros: Being able to maintain a positive and balanced outlook requires a sense of humor in many instances. Additionally, people with good senses of humor tend to be very people-oriented and confident.

Note

This trait does not imply that the individual is or should be a great joke-teller or the life of the party, simply that he or she has the ability to see the lighter side of things and approach business situations with that outlook when appropriate.

Cons: This trait doesn't impart any leadership ability in and of itself but can be a good supporting trait.

Outgoing

Pros: Extroverts make good speakers and tend to be charismatic as well. It takes an outgoing personality to lead a meeting and make a successful presentation.

Cons: There are many examples of difficult people who are also outgoing.

Persistent

Pros: Games take years to make. Persistent people stick with problems until solutions are developed.

Cons: There is a fine line between doggedly persistent and annoyingly stubborn.

Passionate About the Product

Pros: A leader cannot build an enthused team unless he or she is genuinely passionate about the product.

Cons: Very few. This is one of my top five. Others have argued, however, that this is not strictly necessary, observing that as professionals, we should be able to do a great job regardless of the specific title.

Compassionate

Pros: A good leader cares about his or her team members. Leaders demonstrating this trait can build tight-knit teams.

Cons: This is rarely chosen. I think that many would consider this most valuable in an HR director as opposed to a team leader.

Decisive

Pros: A team looks to a leader to make firm decisions. One of the worst things a leader can do is vacillate or defer decisions. The team will feel rudderless and begin to make assumptions in the absence of clear direction.

Cons: Not many. Some may interpret this word in a more authoritarian sense and reject the trait, but I feel that this is a core attribute of a good leader.

Generous

Pros: Generous leaders share the praise and the credit with their team. Generous senior managers also share the wealth more equitably with the team.

Cons: This is also rarely chosen, I think because most groups associate generosity with charitable giving as opposed to sharing of praise and credit.

Trustworthy

Pros: This is obviously critically important. Leaders who are not trusted do not remain leaders for long.

Cons: None. This is new word for the exercise, but would be one of my top five.

Ambitious

Pros: I want a leader who is going for the brass ring 100 percent of the time.

Cons: The word "ambition" can have negative connotations, particularly in a team structure.

Humble

Pros: Humility can be seen as a variation on the word "generous." It is valuable to have humility in a leader. The opposite, arrogance, is an extreme negative.

Cons: The word "humble" can be perceived as being confrontation-averse or malleable.

Spirited, Upbeat

Pros: Leaders must be able to bring energy to the team. This doesn't mean being sunny and bright even when there are serious issues, but it does mean that a leader needs to be positive in his or her approach to challenges.

Cons: Some may read this as needing to be falsely upbeat at times. This is a trait that has never been chosen, but I leave on the list because I think it is valid in the right combination of other traits and it provides good fuel for discussion.

Calm Under Pressure

Pros: Leaders need to have a steady presence in the team regardless of the chaos swirling around.

Cons: The ability to stay calm under pressure is a rare trait. Interestingly, this trait is rarely chosen, but is usually regretfully cast aside by teams.

Is a Good Mentor

Pros: Leaders should consider themselves mentors not only for skills but for modeling desired behavior for team members and other leads.

Cons: Being a good mentor is never an undesirable thing, but some consider that a good leader can coordinate mentoring on his or her team without being directly involved.

Patient

Pros: Patience is a great personal trait, although it is yet another trait that has never been chosen. I leave it on the list because I think it's valuable for discussion.

Cons: Sometimes being impatient is preferable to being patient.

Logical

Pros: This trait has been picked exactly once; indeed, the group that chose it placed it at the top of the list. (I have a feeling that group might have been heavy on programmers.) In all seriousness, making logical decisions is in many ways synonymous with making intelligent decisions.

Cons: Logical may sound cold to some people. "Wise" gets picked far more often.

Contemplative/Able to See All Sides of an Issue

Pros: We want leaders who take all information into account before making a decision. This is an effective companion trait to "decisive."

Cons: Some may read "contemplative" as having the potential to equivocate or overly ponder decisions.

Fair/Equitable

Pros: Although fairness is a great personal trait, it has never been chosen. I leave it on the list because I think it is valid in the right combination of other traits and it provides good fuel for discussion, particularly with the next trait, "ethical."

Cons: Life is not fair, and neither is business.

Ethical

Pros: Ethical has been selected once, usually as an alternate for "honest."

Cons: I cannot see many negatives to having an ethical leader, but I can't argue with the fact that it has not been chosen often. I have had to curtail debate on this point when running this exercise in the past.

Is a Consensus Builder

Pros: This is what a lead is doing many times prior to making a decision, and the ability to do so well is an important trait that can keep a team centered on a unified project vision.

Cons: Some participants have seen this as antithetical to "decisive" and use "contemplative" as an alternative.

Charismatic

Pros: Natural leaders have an abundance of charisma and use it, usually subconsciously, to motivate and advocate for their team.

Cons: Oddly, "charisma" is not chosen often, despite the fact that the best team leaders in my experience have exhibited an abundance of the trait.

Consistent

Pros: Good leaders display consistent behavior to their team. That is not to say they are always happy or sad, but that they communicate and respond to needs and concerns of the team in a consistent manner.

Cons: None. This is frequently chosen and one of my top five.

Responsible

Pros: Leaders must be responsible and accountable, almost by definition.

Cons: None. This is frequently chosen and one of my top five. Some participants have rejected it by using two other attributes that they feel equate to responsibility and have the bonus of having other connotations.

Professional Trait Pros and Cons

Prior Game-Production Experience

Pros: Knows the business from the trenches of production.

Cons: Very few. It's nice to know that the generals leading a team have been in combat themselves.

Prior Game-Management Experience

Pros: The leader is presumed to have successful prior management experience.

Cons: This assumes no production experience, and many find that reason enough to prefer the preceding trait.

Familiarity with Current Game-Production Practices

Pros: A leader's knowledge of current production practices should be current. No one wants to work with a leader who "did it different back in the day" or with experience exclusively outside the game industry.

Cons: The leader may feel more compelled at times to dive into production in the discipline from which his or her experience was gained.

Adept at Office Politics

Pros: The leader can work well within sometimes complex office social/political structures.

Cons: Few traits have inspired more debate, in defense and condemnation of, and yet never been chosen.

Great Speaking and Writing Skills

Pros: Team leaders need to run effective meetings, deliver compelling presentations, write documentation, and engage in other written communication.

Cons: None. Some participants argue that prior game-management experience assumes this skill.

Expertise with Project-Planning Tools and Concepts

Pros: Managers and leaders need to be very familiar with the tools of their trade as well as current project-planning methodologies.

Cons: None. Some participants argue that prior game-management experience assumes these skills and knowledge base.

Additional Questions

At the end of the exercise, the groups are asked to select a work-experience factor: Would they prefer a lead that has shipped one game that was ranked in the 95th percentile or six games that had an average ranking in the 75th percentile? This has caused a lot of follow-up questions attempting to detail what the role of the person was on the projects and so on. I have found it useful to deflect those questions and force participants to make judgments based on just that information.

I finish the exercise by having each group pick a spokesperson and present their selections, writing them on a whiteboard. Each group is also asked to name a single trait they debated over and was one of the last to get cut and to explain why they chose to cut it. This sometimes has produced the most interesting discussions; many participants really wanted their ideal manager to have the fifth of four or sixth of five allowed traits to complete their picture, and without the choice that was cut, they felt that the composite was not viable.

When all groups have presented, we look over all the selections and analyze the results. The debates are always lively. The last question I ask participants is to name a few words they rejected immediately and to name a few words they wish had been on the list. In the most recent exercise, I added "trustworthy" and "ambitious" and changed "dedicated" to "persistent." As is evident, this exercise changes a little bit every time it is run.

Traits that typically make it to the final five among many groups include (in no particular order):

- Calm under pressure

- Wise

- Decisive

- Contemplative/able to see all sides of an issue

- Ethical

- Consistent

- Responsible

Traits that are rarely selected but have been chosen at least once (in no particular order):

- Logical

- Compassionate

- Is a consensus builder

- Charismatic

Where Do We Find Our Leads: External Hires Versus Internal Promotion

There is a strong case to be made for promoting from within based on team and company culture. Hopefully, if your company is an established one, a strong and successful collaborative culture has emerged. Hiring strong individual contributors who can assimilate into this culture and develop into leaders is a great way to grow or maintain your organization. Hiring leaders from outside the company, however qualified they might be, can cause cultural problems within a team or department if that new leader cannot absorb, appreciate, and adopt the positive elements of the company culture and work effectively within an existing system and with existing key personnel.

There are occasions, however, when an external hire into a leadership position is preferable to promoting an existing staff member. One such occasion is if there is no one appropriate for the role internally, or no one available due to other project needs such as one would expect to find in a studio-expansion scenario. Another such occasion is when an external hire can bring about some desired change in the company culture. Particularly in this latter case, it is very important for senior management to listen to the needs and preferences of the most valued team members when formulating their hiring decision. Once the decision has been made to hire externally, it is then vital that the new leader understand his or her role and the desired results and that the goals and the new lead's decisions relating to those goals are well supported by senior management.

It is necessary for a leader moving into a position of authority in a new company to set an appropriate tone. The new leader will want to clarify the scope of his or her role and responsibilities to the project team or department and actively solicit feedback on the strengths, weaknesses, and general workings of the department from all team members. The ability of a new leader to listen effectively is critical in the early stages of a new situation. For a new leader, this is the time when humility can be a most valuable trait. Delivering an opening message to a successful but unfamiliar team can be a challenging task for anyone, but doing so from a humble (but not self-deprecating) position can be very effective.

The humble approach is probably the best course for leads who have been promoted from within, as well. It is helpful in these cases for the lead to hold a meeting with the new team, deliver a message praising the team and its talents, and put into words the honor that the lead feels being named to guide them. Instead of needing to introduce himself or herself and earn the respect of the team, the promoted leader needs to redefine his or her role in the company and earn the respect of the team in that new capacity.

Note

It's good practice to hold a team or department meeting to announce a leadership transition regardless of the circumstances or specific content of the message. The meeting not only gives the new leader an opportunity to introduce himself or herself to the team, but it also serves as a turning-point moment for the lead. This type of milestone can help the new lead begin to shift his or her own mindset as he or she moves into the different role.

I have very often heard the refrain, "He or she's a great (programmer/artist), but not a great lead" from team members referring to a long-time, and even well-liked, colleague in a new lead role. This is almost always due to the fact that the lead has not made the mental transition to management and leadership, instead continuing to rely on his or her strengths as an individual contributor. This is where directors and other senior leads need to step in to provide guidance to the new lead. The result of inaction in this instance will be a frustrated group of valuable employees, a project in need of intervention, and ultimately an unhappy lead.

A newly promoted leader from an existing team may also have difficulty maintaining existing friendships within the workplace. This problem is frequently as awkward as it sounds. The potential exists that the new leader will be perceived as favoring those who were and remain in his or her social circle, and likewise that others on the team who are outside that social circle feel unjustly treated. There is no swift solution to this issue, but it will be overcome by the team seeing the lead treat all team members fairly in public and private over the course of time. I've witnessed a veteran lead simply deciding at a certain point to cease or greatly curtail socializing with friends who were subordinates at their company. This usually occurs after some difficult work situation has arisen. In this specific case, however socially awkward the decision was, the leader soon became more effective at his job and the issue of perceived favoritism was greatly diminished. To be clear, I think leaders should socialize with their teams. Social activities, particularly those occurring off-hours, promote camaraderie and generally improve everyone's enjoyment of the workplace. The key is to be sure that when a lead does socialize, it is with as inclusive a group as possible if not the entire team.

Why Do Leaders Want to Lead?

I have asked lead candidates many times during my career why they want to be a lead. The answers I get most frequently are, "I think I have a strong vision for the game and while it sounds egotistical, I think I'm the best person to do the job." Or, "I feel like it's the right time in my career; I've been feeling not dissatisfied, but ready for other challenges." All sorts of things come out when this question is asked, including answers like, "We botched up the last project with poor leads, and I don't want to see that repeated."

The question posed in the section header, in its theoretical form, is simple enough: People who are good at leading and have a strong base of soft skills will naturally want to do what they are good at and presumably enjoy, namely being a lead. The problems occur when people not suited to the lead role for whatever reason want to lead.

The Right Reasons

Many leaders and successful leadership candidates choose to take on greater responsibility because they believe they have something unique and valuable to bring to the project and the team as leaders. This attitude can be regarded as egotistical, but I think it is actually an essential mindset for a lead when taken in moderation. Hopefully, these leaders also enjoy mentoring and guiding a project team as much, if not more than, performing well as an individual contributor. The downside of this attitude is that it can easily be perceived as a negative trait. It is important, therefore, that leaders understand that the role is ideally a selfless one. The lead should be able to give credit to his or her team for successes and be prepared to personally shoulder the blame for difficulties.

In the best of all worlds, a qualified lead candidate will recognize that he or she possesses the skills and traits needed to do the job, is enthusiastic about the project, and has the full trust of the team and senior management.

Note

Some lead candidates are surprised by the fact that they are being considered for or have been asked to consider a lead role. This can be a bad sign, since either they have not noticed these positive traits and abilities in themselves or you have misread them or have fooled yourself about them. If they are unaware of their positive traits, it could be a sign that they simply don't know themselves well enough to be a consistent leader.

The Wrong Reasons

We want our staff members to choose to take on leadership roles for the right reasons. Poor reasons include requesting a lead role for more money, prestige, power, or even the idea that it will advance the career of the individual. The latter reason is the most pervasive and difficult to combat. Most of these reasons could be rendered irrelevant if we as an industry were to promote and implement dual and equivalent career paths for our employees.

The non-career or compensation-based reasons for wanting the lead mantle typically center on the desire for power in and over a team. Individuals displaying such behavior will be relatively easy to spot and deal with appropriately. These individuals tend to make poor leads because they approach all issues in a dictatorial fashion and are resistant to constructive criticism from above and below. There is the rare case of the power-loving individual who also happens to be really good. I confess, I convinced one such person to take on a lead role by asking him if he really wanted a certain team member telling him what to do for the next year and a half. Surprisingly, even leads who I did not think deeply considered the power aspect of the role have commented to me that they never realized how *little* power they actually felt they had or ended up overtly wielding. They found the job to be much more about successfully motivating, delegating, guiding, and coordinating the team.

The career and compensation motivations for wanting the lead role are harder to handle. I still see great senior production staff members approaching management with the message "Well, it's that time in my career when I feel like I should be moving into a lead spot." The use of the word *should* is a great tipoff that this person does not really want to be a lead or at best does not fully understand the expectations of the role. What he or she seeks is a feeling of progression in his or her career.

This can put a manager in a difficult spot. On the one hand, management wants to satisfy the career objectives of a valued senior team member; on the other, they don't want to place that person in a role for which he or she is not well suited. Additionally, management certainly doesn't want to subject an entire team to an ineffective leader, which will create retention problems and ultimately risk project or company failure as a result. One way to approach the problem is to try the requesting individual out in a specialist lead role, where he or she can get an idea of the amount of delegation and soft skills that go into a managerial position. Sometimes it can be beneficial for such a person to be exposed to the reality of the job early in a more limited scope. I've had leads tell me, for example, that they simply weren't enjoying their job as much now that they were an animation lead. In a way, they felt trapped by the title; they didn't like their job as much anymore, but they were reluctant to give up the perceived status of "lead." The fact of the matter is, like anything else, that the perceived status of the title is only a benefit if you are effective in the role.

Dual and Equivalent Career Paths

One way to codify the dual career path is to develop a dual and equivalent skill ladder that is tailored to the expertise needed by your organization. "Dual and equivalent" means that there are two advancement paths, or tracks—production and management—and that career advancement in title, compensation, and bonus payments is equivalent between paths. This means that there is no inherent compensation incentive for employees to pursue a management path for which they may or may not be well suited in terms of skills or personal traits. This does not mean that everyone at the same level gets paid the same amount. Each rung of the skill ladder represents a range of pay based on experience, skills, and performance.

The key to making the dual career path model work is convincing your company and team that it is a viable way to handle their career advancement. Unfortunately, in attempting this, you as the manager are flying into the face of societal and cultural norms, which tell us that at a certain point in our careers we should stop doing the things that we enjoy and at which we presumably excel and start managing other people. This is simply unnecessary; it is a hindrance to building great teams and elevating great leaders. But conquering these societal expectations remains an uphill battle. It will only become easier when and if more companies, both inside and outside the game industry, adopt this approach.

N o t e

Leaders need to have experience in the trenches of production in order to do their jobs well. Experience by itself, however, does not make someone wise or a good leader; if it did, all older people would be great and wise leaders. Wisdom develops from learning the correct lessons from experiences. The effective implementation of wisdom derives from being able to successfully transform these collected lessons into appropriate actions.

What we need to do as managers and leaders is ensure that our companies and/or projects have the right people in the right roles with sufficient resources to do their job. Adopting a dual and equivalent model for career advancement will help us ensure that the right people are able to enjoy their jobs, find the right fit for themselves, and feel their careers are healthy, progressing in the right direction and at a satisfactory pace. This system also helps from the company and project perspective by ensuring that the most talented individual contributors, vital to the success of any team, do what they most enjoy and what is most beneficial for the project.

Sample Skill Ladder

Following is a sample from an art-department skill ladder that I have employed in the past. (I must credit an ex-Microsoft manager for passing the concept and structure on to me.)

Level 35: Artist IV

Is eligible and may be called upon for art lead or specialist lead positions. (Not a requirement for Artist IV, but a marker for consideration.)

Qualifications:

All of Level 30, plus:

- Approximately five years of industry experience or two to three development cycles

- Displays solid general skills in 3DS Max and has developed at least one area of focus or specialization

- Has working knowledge of the games industry and keeps up with innovative games and games that set high visual bars

- Possesses skills, creativity, and proven performance traits that are consistently in demand by project teams

- Concept artist: Able to produce high-quality preproduction concept work, given minimal direction by team leads. May be considered for storyboard-creation tasks if applicable.

Responsibilities:

All of Level 30 plus:

- Is recognized by the team as being a strong contributor to the project

- Is absolutely reliable for the timely creation of 100-percent technically solid art

- Can be relied upon to quickly learn new processes and software as dictated by project needs

- Is considered a problem solver

- Motivates peers toward excellence

- Can be considered to lead art workshops

Figure 4.3 shows a very general overview of the concept. On the left are sample compensation ranges. These are not based on any industry or geographical data but simply show the concept of overlapping pay ranges and note a wider range at the top levels to accommodate exceptional individuals. The middle columns show the concept of levels and credited titles that might accompany the ranges.

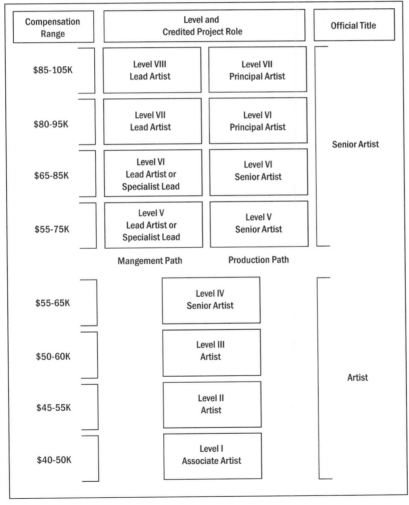

Figure 4.3
A sample dual-career ladder showing equivalent levels between management and production paths.

On the right are the actual titles that might appear on business cards and personnel information. This ladder is meant only as an example, but when fully realized customized to your particular needs and studio focus, it can give your department staff a clear idea of where they stand currently in your estimation and where they can potentially go in the future. Strive to make the ladder as flexible and realistic as possible if you attempt to create and implement such a system for your own organization. It is very important that the company deviate from the ladder only in rare instances, if at all. In the Artist IV example, the employee is eligible for a lead spot even though he or she is not a senior artist. Some may find that unusual, but it is sometimes useful to plan for case in which a less experienced but highly qualified employee could be considered for a lead spot without violating the letter of the job description.

This arrangement removes any de facto financial motivation for assuming leadership responsibility. That said, if you are a great leader, greater rewards will follow; the ladder supports that by monetarily rewarding experience, performance, and overall project contribution. That this is true regardless of path using the salary ranges within each level should not dissuade someone who wants the lead role for the right reasons. And I'd stress again that the scope of lead duties needs to be evaluated if potential leads are requesting greater compensation as a condition for accepting the role.

Note

Wanting more money in the form of salary or bonuses may cause someone to pursue the lead role, but it does not mean they meet the requirements for the role. It sends the message to the company that you advance your career by managing, which I don't think is an ideal motivation tool—even for qualified lead candidates. One problem that emerges is that eventually, a successful lead will need to leave the post due to a lack of lead roles in cases of overlapping project schedules. The resulting dip in salary and/or bonus is not a great reward for a job well done.

One question that comes up is whether it is viable to implement this system in an older company, where many employees may not be able to map correctly without extreme salary adjustments, either up or down, depending on the individual. This is a very tough case. The answer is yes, but it may take some time to balance out lower-paid employees and mentor legacy employees whose job skills may not map appropriately with their compensation level or title. While it may take longer to become truly reflective of the department, the top performers in the company will appreciate the clarity and accountability that comes with a skill-driven, transparent system such as this right away.

Interview: Julien Bares, Studio Director, 2K Shanghai

After working for eight years at Ubisoft Paris as a producer on such games as *Formula One, XIII, Splinter Cell Pandora*, and several others, Julien Bares joined Take 2 to open and run the 2K Shanghai Studio.

Seth Spaulding: Describe your transition from a production position to a leadership position.

Julien Bares: I must admit that I have never been in a pure production position. At first, I was a junior producer whose role was to assist the producer of the game. I was in charge of helping the producer with the task lists and some other related responsibilities.

When I was asked to move to a leadership position, I felt a bit lost at the beginning because I was producing nothing—I had to tell people to do things. I did not feel that confident because I wondered why on Earth I should be the one who tells people what to do. Then I remembered a book I had read about sailing a few years earlier that talked about how important it is to have a captain on a boat, and everything came together. I had also the chance talk with our studio manager a lot, who helped me by asking me to speak freely about the issues I was facing.

To me, the most important thing you should know when you are given a leadership position is to understand that your first goal is to guide, and therefore you must make sure you have a map, a plan, a schedule, etc. to guide people. The plan may be wrong, but if you do not have one, you are stuck. Always ask yourself what your map should be, how you can build it, and then the transition will be easier.

S.S.: What are the most common traits shared by other effective leaders in your experience?

J.B.: I would say first, speaking ability and writing ability, because the biggest leadership challenge is communicating and sharing your vision by any means, not hesitating to repeat time after time to make sure that everybody on the team understands where you want to go. I also tend to believe that a sense of humor is a trait that counts a lot, because if you cannot laugh, you cannot connect and therefore share your vision.

I think the capacity to come up with a lot of solutions is another very useful trait. People will come to you with problems, and you have to be the one who comes up with a solution—or, even better, helps them to find the solutions on their own.

Being solid under pressure is another valuable trait; one should always be able to stay calm even when the project may be in a very bad stage.

S.S.: Which traits do you feel are your strongest and how does knowledge of these traits affect how you approach leadership challenges?

J.B.: I think I can develop a number of different solutions to any given set of challenges. In addition, I never give up. I always try to find new answers or try new angles.

S.S.: What are the worst traits a leader exhibited in your experience? How did these traits manifest themselves and what was the result of their involvement in terms of the team, project, and/or company?

J.B.: I think the worst leaders I have met did not know where they were going. They were not clear about their goals, and they were driving their teams nowhere. They were pretending but they did not know. It destroys the team around them, and this is the worst thing that can happen.

S.S.: Are there any leadership traits you admire or perhaps aspire toward but don't feel you embody?

J.B.: There are a lot of traits I admire in others that I don't have right now, and perhaps I will never have. Some people are very good at convincing others of something, even when they are not fully convinced themselves. Some have a very clear vision of the evolution of our industry and are already working to change their working methods. Some have an incredible way of speaking, etc.; there are so many things.

I am always trying to analyze what those people are doing, how they are behaving, and I try to copy the positive things. For example, I had a boss who only took notes on a very small piece of paper because he believed that in a meeting you need to listen more than you need to write, so I have adopted this practice, and I find it does help. I also believe that we have to be open to other industries and other fields—like the army, the church, or a theater company—looking at how they develop leaders and using whatever we believe can work in our own industry with our projects and with the people we employ.

As a studio manager, I train producers and leaders in a country whose culture is very different from mine, and I try to teach them good habits and good methods.

However, I do not want to force them to adopt my exact leadership style. They have to develop their own techniques and their own balance of skills and tricks.

S.S.: Do you have any training in leadership, either formal or unstructured (e.g., armed forces experience)?

J.B.: I did some specialized training on time and task management, but it was not really useful. I must say I have learned much more directing a theater play at school and sailing or doing any sports that required a team to work together. I have also learned a lot being in China, because you need to be very clear in communicating with people. Not being a native speaker of English, and using English as a common language, requires a lot of patience and clarifications.

S.S.: What do you see as the toughest challenge facing leads during a game-development project cycle or at a game-development company generally?

J.B.: I think the toughest challenge is to describe your game precisely, completely, and early enough to make sure that your team is going in the right direction. With increasing team size, development time, and budget, you have to make sure you are on the right path. I think the industry now tends to have more frequent milestones; you can have regular status checks to determine whether your project is on the right track, and this is good.

S.S.: What are some common mistakes you've seen leads make, be they new or experienced?

J.B.: The most common mistake I have seen is a leader believing that he or she can change people and have them behave their way. It never works. I believe a leader should work with what he or she has been given and should not try to change people, because they never change. They evolve, they grow older, but it is too late to change them. Besides, changing people is not the point. Trying to change people diverts you from your real objective and is a waste of time for everybody.

S.S.: How have you seen new leads best get support from directors or executives?

J.B.: The best support that senior management can give a leader is to give enough power and trust from the beginning. The worst is when somebody is *almost* in charge. If people on the team know that the leader is not making his or her own decisions, there will be no trust from the team. The lead will then not be followed, and the project will go nowhere. The lead must be given the credit and trust from senior management in order to function well.

S.S.: Do you think good leaders can be trained? Or is the essence of a good leader simply innate ability?

J.B.: I think you can train a leader, but there are a few things that cannot be taught because they are part of one's personality or upbringing. Among these is the capacity to listen to, talk to, and respect people, and to give effective feedback. You cannot teach fairness, but you can teach a new leader how to apply equitable practices on the job.

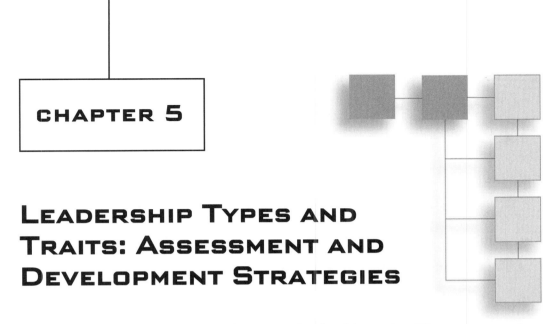

CHAPTER 5

LEADERSHIP TYPES AND TRAITS: ASSESSMENT AND DEVELOPMENT STRATEGIES

All leaders have one or more dominant leadership traits. They may excel at motivating a team, empowering the team members, involving them in decisions, or effectively leading in a directive or even authoritarian manner (note that "effectively" does not mean "popularly"). Great leaders demonstrate the ability to successfully use a greater number of distinct leadership techniques, depending on the situation and the needs of the team.

But while the dominant trait of great leaders may vary, *all* great leaders can cite self-awareness in their list of soft skills. Indeed, self-awareness is a vital attribute of any successful leader. All great—and even good—leaders I have known have had the ability to be introspective and critical about their own job performance and their attitudes toward that performance.

Not surprisingly, these leaders frequently use language like, "I'm really not at my best in situations like..." or, "I know that my perception of this situation is colored by my personal feelings regarding...." Some might interpret statements such as these as acknowledgement of weakness and perceive that as a negative. On the contrary, this deeper understanding of their own motivations, desires, and competencies allows these leaders to make much better decisions and enables them to be more forthright in their dealings with everyone on their team.

This chapter explores various leadership types and traits, as well as tools you can use to assess your own leadership skills. It also discusses various resources for obtaining training in this area.

Leadership Versus Management

It is said that projects require managers and people require leaders. This statement, while interesting, also exposes one of the problems of team leadership—namely, that in most cases, leaders need to do a bit of both. Adding to this confusion is the fact that these terms—leader and manager—are frequently used interchangeably. Although I have not seen an authoritative definition of either term that completely clarifies the difference between them, I do have a few thoughts on the matter:

Leadership:

- Presents and champions a vision to a team

- Is people-focused

- Inspires team members to perform to the best of their abilities

- Defines an ultimate goal

Management:

- Turns vision into reality

- Is project-focused

- Makes it possible for the team to work at maximum efficiency, including scheduling, performing reviews, and tracking efforts

- Develops strategies to accomplish goals

Senior management can use guidelines such as these when determining what skills are needed for a given position. These definitions can also be helpful when used as reference in performance reviews and considerations for career goals. For instance, it may not be necessary for a strong manager to have the inspirational qualities if his or her role is primarily focused on task scheduling and tracking.

Note

In this book, I use the term "senior management" to describe the executive-level positions at a given company. These fictional people may also be viewed as leaders, but this is not implicit in their job title—hence my choice of the word "management."

Leadership Styles

Leadership terminology across the business world is even less consistent than game company–organization terminology. The subtle distinctions between "directive" and "authoritarian" and "dictatorial" or between "democratic" and "participative" become lost when the words are used as terms to describe specific leadership types by a variety of authors and academics. Nevertheless, in order to begin to examine any issue, a common language and set of terminology does need to be established.

Through its research, the Hay Group, Inc., a global management consulting company, has identified six basic leadership styles that cover a breadth of business-leadership experiences. These traits are adapted from "Leadership That Gets Results" by Daniel Goleman, published in *Harvard Business Review*, Mar/Apr 2000. While there are clearly as many different leadership styles as there are leaders, Goleman's and Hay's six basic styles are as follows:

- **Directive.** The goal of the directive style is immediate compliance. This style is best employed in crisis situations. It is considered a negative motivation style.

Caution

I have known a few leaders who have relied primarily on the directive style, and they have not been successful over the long term. They might have produced a great game or two, but their companies tended to suffer from poor morale and, as a result, a poor retention rate.

- **Visionary.** The visionary-style leader mobilizes people toward a goal. This style is best employed in situations where a change of vision or clear direction is required. It is considered a positive motivation style.

- **Affiliative.** The affiliative-style leader promotes team harmony and focuses on conflict resolution. This style is best employed to heal divisions within a team, especially during stressful points in projects. It is considered a positive motivation style.

- **Participative.** The participative-style leader involves the team in decision making and fosters commitment through team participation. This style is best employed to promote an emotional commitment by highly valuable team members. It is considered a positive motivation style.

Note

The participative trait is one that I think all leaders in the game industry should develop. Doing so can help keep teams committed, focused, and motivated through long project cycles.

- **Pacesetting.** The pacesetting-style leader personally demonstrates excellence and expects others, through self-direction, to meet the modeled expectations. This style is best employed in shorter-term projects with staff who need little guidance with respect to quality or pace. It is considered a negative motivation style.

- **Coaching.** The coaching leadership style focuses on mentorship and on the long-term career development of team members. This style is best employed in long-term projects. It is considered a positive motivation style.

Note

It is critical that leaders who employ a variety of techniques use only those that come naturally to them. A very affiliative and visionary leader might be familiar with more directive styles of leadership in theory but uncomfortable employing them in situations that call for such delivery. In such a case, any attempted interactions employing a directive style will be perceived as hollow or artificial unless delivered with sincerity and conviction by a more directive-inclined leader.

Control Versus Influence

In most aspects of team leadership, control is an illusion. Many leaders I've spoken to say they rarely if ever dictate to the team, nor do they feel that they are—or should be—in complete control of the decision-making process. The fact is, even if a leader attempts to control a situation, he or she must still work with other individuals—at which point actual control becomes, in reality, a process of collaboration.

At the best of times, when working in a lead role, I have felt only that I was guiding a project, allowing my leads, specialist leads, and senior production personnel to solve problems and achieve goals. This is a positive process that builds team involvement and commitment, but can take new leaders—who may have misconceptions about their role, either due to inexperience or exposure to poor examples during the course of their careers—by surprise.

Rather than emphasizing control, the effective team leader strives simply to have influence over his or her team. This ability to influence stems from the establishment of strong relationships with peers, team members, and managers—further highlighting the need for leaders and managers to work together to build strong interpersonal connections.

Internal Training

Internal leadership training can take a few different forms, but it is by its very nature tailored to the specifics of the industry. It is also usually focused on the practical aspects of team leadership as opposed to theoretical concepts. Successful internal training involves a blend of one-on-one mentoring and more formal training through presentations, tutorials, or documentation. It should be noted that of these, personal mentoring and presentations are generally far more effective, because most people fail to fully read or absorb information in purely written form—particularly any sort of wiki or online documentation (with this book being a notable exception, of course).

Note

Lead support in the form of internal training is every bit as valuable as external leadership training, if not more so. Mentoring from fellow leads is going to be more effective because the training is, by definition, fully relevant. You'll learn more about external training in a moment.

Formal Internal Training

Following is a sample agenda from a one-hour tutorial session for leads. As is evident, the issues raised are diverse, covering a broad range of responsibilities and skills needed to do the job. The idea is to discuss a smattering of topics to provide leads with some tangible leadership and management tools. You'll likely find that many points in the agenda will lead to pertinent questions and valuable discussions during the course of the session.

Note

This agenda targets specific, practical issues at a particular studio. Every group and studio will probably require a different topics list.

A tutorial session such as this offers an opportunity to reinforce the scope of responsibility of each position in the company, as well as the fact that lead performance evaluations will be based on the use of these "new" skills as opposed to the production skills assessed in the past.

Agenda for Leadership Workshop

Lead Role and Responsibilities

Lead Job Description: Motivator, Communicator, Organizer

Motivation

Positive approach

Passion for the project and quality results

Communication

Instruction and expectations

Feedback: clear, complete, consistent

Honest, respectful, flexible

Two-way street: team responsibility

Organization

Broader view of project

Accountable/responsible

Role and Responsibility Overview:

Senior artist: self-management/mentoring

Specialist lead: front-line asset technical and aesthetic review

Art lead: project art review and project visual style leadership; front-line personnel management

Art director in a multi-project studio: milestone asset review; project visual style review and resource support; departmental budget and personnel management

Production/Management Split:

For every three to four direct reports, reduce 30–40% production time. Using this calculation, a specialist lead with three direct reports should devote approximately 70–75% of his or her time to production tasks; in contrast, a lead with eight direct reports should be involved in production about 20% of the time, and should never be responsible for critical-path tasks.

Dual and Equivalent Career Paths

Why this practice is essential to ensuring that the right people pursue lead roles for the right reasons.

Practically speaking, what does this look like?

Lead Pitfalls:

Spending too much time on production work

Not delegating critical-path tasks

Shutting down team input and creative contributions

Not mentoring or facilitating mentoring

Venting to the team

Poor meeting management

Effective Meeting Management:

Have a written agenda sent with the meeting request.

Invite all relevant parties; no more, no less.

Start on time.

Designate a note taker.

During the meeting, stick to the agenda.

End the meeting on time.

Send meeting notes to all relevant parties, including any stakeholder not present.

Make sure that any meeting decisions are recorded.

A deeper treatment of these topics is best accomplished by creating and maintaining a lead training document, the goal being to clarify and codify the roles and responsibilities of a lead, as well as address the many issues relating to the role that will arise going forward. This document should be looked at as a living document—much like an employee manual for leads crossed with an ongoing post mortem, but focused on departmental and companywide issues as opposed to project-based ones.

Note

This idea for the lead training document was first presented by David Silverman, who was, at the time, art director at Cyberlore Studios, and is one of this book's interview subjects.

Following is a partial table of contents from a lead training document; it should give you an idea of the general themes discussed. This list represents only a sampling of possible topics; indeed, every company will have a different perspective on leadership and managerial responsibilities, which will require the editing or expanding of the document accordingly.

Lead Training Document

Job Descriptions

    Lead

    Specialist Lead

    Senior Artist

    Artist

Traits of Great Leads

FAQs

    Is a lead expected to have top skills in his or her discipline?

    Why should I become a lead?

    If I never become a lead, is that bad for my career?

    Does the lead role mean more work than the senior artist role?

    Why isn't there a compensation bonus?

    What are some common misconceptions about the lead role?

    Where have leads faltered in the past?

Lead Skills

    Delegation

        Using specialist leads

        Using senior artists

Communication

Team communication

Peer communication

Upper-management communication

Outsourcer Communication

Project planning

Developing initial estimates

Task tracking

Direction

Guiding the initial vision

Providing clear, complete, and consistent feedback

Practical Situations

Meeting management

Time management

Conflict resolution

Problem employees

Fostering teamwork

Encouraging innovation/creativity

Training Through Mentoring

Personal mentoring is another great way to instill leadership—in this case, by modeling desired traits and actions. Where possible and appropriate, it is beneficial to pair up new leads or specialist leads with more experienced personnel on a project. The more experienced lead should engage and supervise the new specialist lead in schedule building, task estimation, and asset review, both aesthetic and technical, as frequently as needed.

During asset reviews, the mentoring lead should be as silent and unobtrusive as possible. This is important; the new lead needs to be the point person in the asset feedback loop, or there isn't much point in including a specialist lead in the structure. Additionally, the new lead must be seen as the authority in the room to the extent it is possible. Whatever feedback or critiques the mentoring leader has should be delivered later and in private.

Note

It can be difficult for some leads to let the specialist lead function as independently as they are capable of. This is an area where the art director or a fellow lead needs to step in, calling attention to the lead's micro-management. Otherwise, the lead can swiftly become a bottleneck, even though he or she may not be doing any actual production work in the form of coding or creating art assets. Additionally, this situation can be a serious morale drain for the specialist lead, and create the perception of a confusing reporting structure for the team.

Every so often, I hear about a terrible interaction between a lead and a team member or members that occurred days or weeks earlier. This delay makes presenting any critique to the lead far less effective. Worse, who knows how many other damaging interactions may have occurred around this individual in the intervening time? Successful internal mentoring requires that directors and/or senior management supply regular structured feedback as well as informal advice as appropriate. Performing team evaluations of leaders—both formal and informal—is a key component of that. Otherwise, a communication gap—an organizational blind spot, if you will—may develop between directors and senior management and the project leads and specialist leads who are communicating with their teams on a day-to-day basis. The effect of this gap is that senior management frequently cannot provide timely feedback on a manager's performance. It is essential that senior managers be approachable to everyone in the company; this ensures that informal communication paths are open and effective for the guidance of new leaders as well as for the overall health of the company.

Note

Some senior managers at the president or CEO level institute schedule (usually monthly) but informal breakfasts or lunches with employees at all levels, the idea being to get feedback on the company's practices and development efforts and to answer any questions that employees may have. Such meetings enable the manager to personally express and reinforce goals and visions and have the added effect of personalizing management, hopefully, making them more approachable by anyone in the company.

External Training

The need for external training—that is, training occurring outside the company—in the game industry is self-evident. For one thing, in any given company, much of the internal expertise—a very valuable resource that should be tapped—is self-taught. Secondly, the industry's employee population is very young. At my first studio, the average of employees ranged from the mid to upper 20s; at my current studio, the average is around 33 years. Although, as an established studio, we probably have more industry veterans than most, no one has obtained any management or leadership training outside of what the studio itself has sponsored in recent years.

External training can take a few different forms. One route is individually driven, involving online research, reading books like this one, and the like; another involves participation in formal leadership and management seminars and classes. These offer the advantage of being interactive and targeted to your particular situation—with the disadvantage being you can't read them in bed (and they cost a bit more).

Online Resources

The management-related Web sites, blogs, and forums available online are too numerous to mention, but following are two I've found useful. These should provide you with a good start for further research:

- http://www.manager-tools.com

- http://www.managementblog.org

These sites are not game industry focused per se, but they are searchable by topic or keyword, and can provide some helpful language and scenario examples—with the managementblog.org site including many real-life case studies.

Another useful site is Gamasutra (http://www.gamasutra.com), a comprehensive game-industry site with features including industry news, employment information, and frequent articles on project management from industry veterans.

Books

I admit I haven't read too many "management" books in their entirety. I frequently find that in these books, the authors make one or two valid points, and then hammer them repeatedly until they feel like they've typed enough. That's not to say that the information is not valuable, just that it would be better conveyed by a 10-page article than a 120-page book.

There are, however, a few exceptions including *Good to Great: Why Some Companies Make the Leap. . .and Others Don't* by Jim Collins and *Know-How: The 8 Skills That Separate People Who Perform from Those Who Don't* by Ram Charan.

Although these books are very different thematically speaking, I find them valuable for their tangible and research-based approach to leadership and management issues—not to mention their lack of jargon-laden business-speak.

I've also discovered many useful leadership examples by reading works outside the business category. Examples include exploration tales such as *Endurance: Shackleton's Incredible Voyage* by Alfred Lansing and books about scientific endeavor, military history or politics. These types of books can be every bit as enlightening as business-focused management books.

Industry-Focused Conferences

Industry-focused conferences can be a great option for external training. In particular, the Game Developer's Conference (GDC), an annual five-day gathering of game professionals from all over the world, has been a significant component of my development as a leader and manager in the game industry. While it does not, of course, provide as targeted an experience as a customized leadership/management program that a consultant might present, GDC does offer hundreds of industry-specific sessions and dozens related to project-management and leadership topics. In addition, leading Round Table sessions—in which directors and leads from around the industry discuss emerging issues relating to management, tools, and production processes—I have, through GDC, had the opportunity to attend an incredibly broad range of management presentations, Round Tables, and panels featuring highly experienced veterans from all facets of the game business.

In this environment, most speakers, panelists, and even audience members are eager to share experiences, ask questions, and offer counsel—a unique prospect in an industry that famously guards its expertise, technology, personnel, and practices during the other 360 days of the year.

Here is a small sample of the management- and leadership-related topics presented at the 2008 GDC. These sessions are led by seasoned professional from Sony, Red Storm, Cryptic, as well as business professionals and academic researchers.

- Building and maintaining an art department
- Client-focused management

- Lessons from the front lines: Startup CEOs share their insider stories

- Production: basics and beyond

- Training as a productivity multiplier

Other opportunities for industry-focused career development include SIG-GRAPH, held annually in different cities around the country. It tends to present more technical material, and is less focused on the game industry specifically. Additionally, there are spin-offs from the original GDC (which is itself usually held in San Francisco) including GDC Austin and GDC Paris.

Assessment Tools

I always tell prospective game artists to put only their best work in their portfolio presentations. And immediately following that, I tell them they are not in a position to determine, by themselves, what is their best work. That's because they are simply too close to their work—in some cases, emotionally attached to pieces that degrade their presentation. It's vital, instead, to gather a set of opinions on the portfolio from honest people who are trustworthy and knowledgeable about the game industry. A more successful portfolio will result from these assessments—assuming that the recommendations are considered and acted upon in some fashion.

Leaders need the same kind of assessment of their soft skills—but obtaining it is more complex and, as with game artists, requires the support of a third party. There are numerous leadership-training and assessment tools, including business publications and periodicals, such as *Business Week* or *The Economist,* as well as management and leadership consultants—many offering Myers-Briggs personality assessments and 360 assessments as well as other tools. These assessments, and the analysis that accompanies them, are vital to new leaders who must use soft skills—and who will be evaluated on their use of soft skills—as a primary job tool, probably for the first time in their careers. It is particularly important for new leads to make the transition to a leadership mentality; an organized training session can help do that.

Feedback on job performance can and should be provided by senior management, but leadership assessment should also be made by the individual, the leader's peers, and the leader's team or department. This may sound obvious, but the task of actually performing the assessment—generating the metrics and the format and organizing the assessment—can be quite daunting depending on the size of the team in question. For this reason, employing a leadership consultant to moderate the process and gather and analyze the feedback data (which can be entirely anonymous) is probably the best approach; the consultant can then review the findings with the subject on an individual and confidential basis, help set individual goals, and recommend a course of action. In this way, the assessment results can be more readily used by the subject as a personal coaching tool.

Note

Of course, just as it can be difficult for people to handle negative but constructive feedback on an asset or game feature that they have created, it is likewise difficult—often more so—for people to process negative feedback concerning soft skills or personality issues. Frequently, there is no painless way to do it—and sometimes, there really isn't a constructive outcome.

Myers-Briggs

The Myers-Briggs personality assessment was developed in the 1940s as a means of quantifying differing personality types and identifying dominant traits. The eight traits used for Myers-Briggs assessments represent four dichotomies:

- Extraversion (E) and Introversion (I)

- Sensing (S) and Intuition (N)

- Thinking (T) and Feeling (F)

- Judging (J) and Perceiving (P)

The assessment results are represented by one of 16 possible four-letter combinations, such as ESFJ or INTP, derived from these eight traits. This code equates to a certain profile for each individual. There are no correct answers to this assessment, and no one combination of letters is necessarily "better" than any others.

There are many ways to take an assessment of this type, the simplest being right off the Internet while sitting at your desk. I believe, however, that a far better approach is to take the test with several colleagues with the help of a professional moderator. The resulting discussions can be every bit as valuable as the assessment itself. One of the benefits of this approach for new leaders is that they start thinking about their personalities from a more objective point of view. Also, the assessment provides new leaders with a starting vocabulary for analyzing their personality traits, and can highlight areas for soft-skill development.

360 Assessments

A 360 assessment analyzes a leader's performance based on feedback from the teams they lead, the senior managers they report to, and others who occupy the same level in the business structure. The 360 assessment usually begins with a self assessment as a benchmark, which is very valuable—if not vital—because it objectively highlights disconnects between how a person perceives his or her leadership style and what his or her leadership style is in reality. Being exposed to these contradictions can heighten the leader's self-awareness.

Note

It is important to research different assessment tools and their appraisal categories before you implement them to ensure that they are applicable to your organization. For example, applying a 360 assessment tool designed for customer-service personnel or medical professionals probably won't reveal much helpful information if applied to a leader in a game-development company.

Figure 5.1 shows the result of a 360 self assessment I performed in 2007. Despite having been a leader in the game industry for the vast majority of my career, I had never been exposed to a such an exercise; the results showed not only the degree to which I needed this feedback, but also the degree to which my job had changed over the years—due primarily to the growth in scale of my team and the complexity of our projects. While I saw myself as a pacesetting leader, in fact I was not; due to the size of my department and the complexity of our projects, I was actually doing almost no "pacesetting" work—nor should I have been. The danger for me, then, was that I would fail to develop other leadership styles that were more appropriate and necessary given my current role in the company. When you compare my self-assessment with the collected feedback from my team, my peers, and my supervisor (see Figure 5.2), the differences—and, by extension, the disconnect between my view of my leadership styles as compared to how others saw me—are obvious.

The result of the 360 assessment should be to identify your major leadership style or styles, identify supporting styles (that is, styles you employ but are not seen as being as strong, or used as often, as your dominant styles), and pinpoint styles that are not perceived as strengths and perhaps need development. Again, the

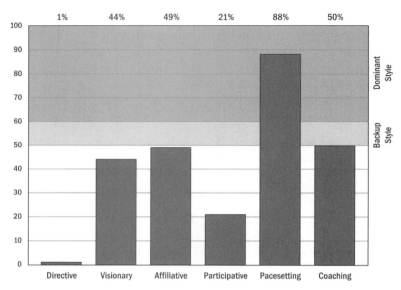

Figure 5.1
360 report detail: self-assessment section.

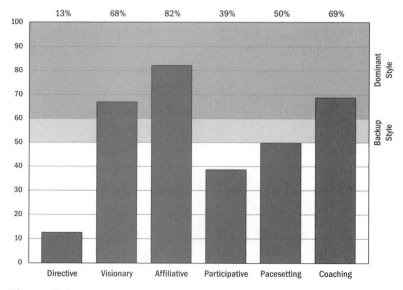

Figure 5.2
360 report detail: team-assessment section.

ultimate goal is to increase your self-awareness and your ability to objectively assess your performance.

Tip

While I don't believe it is necessary to repeat the 360 assessment very often, it is important to review the results of the assessment every six months or so and consider how you have progressed.

Interview: Robert Martin, Management and Leadership Consultant

Robert Martin has more than 35 years of experience as a business leader and organizational consultant. He is the founder of his own consulting company, RM3 Enterprises. For almost 20 years prior to his consulting role, Robert held leadership positions of increasing size, scope, and responsibility in the field of information technology. He was responsible for leading design and implementation of medium- to larger-scale projects in finance and operations. He has presented at two major conferences: on employee inclusion at the Center for the Study of Work Teams and on leadership at a diversity symposium.

Seth Spaulding: Describe your transition from a production position to a leadership position.

Robert Martin: I moved from programmer to manager and ultimately to director in the telecommunications business over the course of about 15 years. In the last several years, I have run my own consulting business.

S.S.: Looking back, are there any decisions or practices you would change, and if so, why? What is the most important thing you would tell someone making that transition within their company?

R.M.: Focus on letting go of the "doing"—it is easy for new leaders to get hooked into that. To be successful as a leader, you must focus your time and energy on leading.

Get into some type of formal leadership development program within six months. Six months is a good time frame to have had a few management or leadership challenges presented to you that you realize you may need help with. I think prior to that time, you frequently don't know what you don't know and consequently the questions that you have would be less valuable and the investment in the value of leadership training is perhaps less than it could be. At six months or so, a new leader is primed to listen to advice and hopefully has some good questions to bring to the table. Delaying any sort of training beyond six months runs the risk of doing some damage or simply having the leader develop bad habits.

Additionally, I think it is important to limit the duration of any training session for new leaders. Something like a one-day seminar with targeted focus gets things rolling and gets the leader starting to think of himself or herself in a different capacity. After doing the job for a while, it can then be more valuable to engage in a more comprehensive training program.

Find a mentor. Mentors within your company can be completely informal or set up in a more formal structure. Informally, you as a new leader or manager should feel free to approach those in your organization who you see to be successful and solicit their feedback and advice as you face challenges that may be unfamiliar.

S.S.: Were there any people who helped and if so how?

R.M.: Yes—I had a boss who was very open about what I needed to improve on.

S.S.: What are the most common traits shared by other effective leaders in your experience?

R.M.:

- Good leaders are flexible. They are able to adapt their style of leadership to the situation and person they are dealing with in the moment. Situations and conditions change during the course of a development cycle and leaders needs to adapt their styles accordingly.

- Good leaders offer clarity in their communication. They do what they need to do to ensure their message is received. Leaders need to engage in a dialogue and really listen to see how the message is received and clarify where appropriate.

- Good leaders provide regular feedback—appreciative and constructive.

- Good leaders work to understand themselves—what makes them do what they do and their strengths and weaknesses.

S.S.: Are there any leadership traits you admire or perhaps aspire toward but don't feel you embody?

R.M.: I'd like to have better self-discipline—to bear down when necessary and focus on what's most important. Too often I allow myself to get distracted and waste time on "busy work."

S.S.: In the course of your job, how do you mentor other leaders?

R.M.: I do lots of coaching using self-discovery through asking appropriate questions to stimulate thinking. These are frequently very simple questions designed to get the participant to really think about the effect of his or her words and actions, such as "What was the result of that?" or "How have you reacted to that in the past?"

S.S.: How do you "train" someone who is interested in developing soft skills?

R.M.: First, you have to work to understand yourself. In fact, before that, you have to have the desire to develop these skills and traits. It sounds like an obvious thing but it isn't. A lot of times I see people in positions of leadership who want the position for whatever reason but are resistant or have little interest in developing the skills that will make them effective in the role.

So how do you work to understand yourself? There are two sides to it—what I'll call the "soft" and "hard" side. The soft side is more "spiritual," if you will. This is probably the area of leadership traits that people would describe as innate to one's personality. You have to develop the ability to be self-reflective, to spend some time just "being" and, as objectively as possible, reflecting on your experiences and asking "What was my role?" or "What was my impact on a given situation or conversation?" And beyond those questions, asking, "How am I engaging others?" "Could I be more effective?" "Was I being defensive then?" And so on. I'd stress that the key is taking the time to do this, and it is not a trivial thing. Leaders and managers are usually very busy people who have lots of folks who demand their time and attention, but this ability is key to understanding yourself and improving your interactions with others.

S.S.: What do you see as the toughest challenge facing leads during a game-development project cycle or at a game-development company generally?

R.M.: Managing personal time to ensure they're focused on the right things for themselves and their teams. This is most successful when people regularly use a time-management system like a daily planner and find ways to stick to the schedule each day. This can be tricky, again due to the many ad-hoc project and personnel needs the managers and team leaders confront each day.

S.S.: What are some common mistakes you've seen leads make, be they new or experienced?

R.M.: Resisting creation of a team environment where expectations are clear and are developed in a participative manner, and people know what they're expected to deliver. Also, meeting management may be a challenge for some.

S.S.: Describe some of the results of the mistakes as well if possible and how recovery was achieved if applicable. How could these missteps have been avoided or were there any that were important learning experiences?

R.M.: Provide training in some basic meeting-management tools. Also ensure they are being provided clear expectations of their role from management.

S.S.: Do you think good leaders can be trained? Or is the essence of a good leader simply innate ability?

R.M.: I feel strongly that leadership is developed and anyone with a desire can be a strong leader. Innate leadership "talent" versus learned skills is probably a 25/75 split with the "innate" portion being the 25 percent. Desire is the key here. Like any other innate talent, be it in the field of art, music, or athletics, leadership requires time and effort to build the necessary skills on top of whatever natural talent an individual might possess. No innate ability is ever developed fully without practice, training, and experience.

Interview: Stephen Martin—Studio Head, Firaxis Games

Stephen Martin is currently the studio head of Firaxis Games, a subsidiary of Take-Two Interactive, whose games are published under the 2K label. Firaxis is the home of legendary game designer Sid Meier, and has been the successful developer of 24 titles in 12 years. The studio is known for the *Civilization* series as well as for *Railroads!*, *Pirates!*, *Alpha Centauri*, *Gettysburg*, and *SimGolf*.

Mr. Martin was academically trained as an accountant and financial planner with a BBA, MBA, and CPA. He has also proudly served in the U.S. Army as a first lieutenant and remains on inactive reserve. He began his professional career as a certified public accountant, working in both the public and private sectors for seven years. He had the good fortune to be associated with a client who was involved in the game industry, MicroProse. It is there that he began a 15-year-and-counting career in the game industry.

His first experiences in the industry were as MicroProse's divisional controller as the company was at that time a subsidiary of Spectrum Holobyte. He became controller and director of human resources and administration. He moved on from there to start his own company with four colleagues.

That company was Absolute Quality, whose mission was to provide testing and customer service to the gaming industry; there, Mr. Martin served as chief financial and administrative officer. This gave him great exposure to developing funding options and expanding internationally to include opening an office in Scotland. As this company transitioned to being predominantly a customer-service provider, he was invited to join the Firaxis team by two former Micro-Prose colleagues, Jeff Briggs and Sid Meier.

Stephen joined Firaxis Games as its chief financial officer and become chief financial and operating officer as the company began to grow in team size and number of teams. When the partners chose to sell the company to Take-Two Interactive, Mr. Martin had the great fortune to be offered the opportunity to run the studio.

As the studio head, he is responsible for 95 employees, with three full-scale teams, one expansion team, and one prototype team. His role requires continued relationship building and communication with the publishing label as well as coordinating the resources and budgets of the team to deliver high-quality projects in a timely manner.

Seth Spaulding: Describe your transition from a production position to a leadership position. What were some unexpected challenges or surprises?

Stephen Martin: I have had the good fortune to have developed "production-like" exposure through senior financial roles in the accounting field so that when I entered the games industry I had the opportunity to be in leadership roles from the outset. These leadership roles increased in of responsibility up to and including being studio head.

Having entered the industry in a less-traditional manner, my leadership roles were not a transition from production roles that were directly involved with product development.

S.S.: Looking back, are there any decisions or practices you would change?

S.M.: Amazingly, after reflecting upon 15 years in the games industry, there is nothing of singular significance that I can point to as a decision or practice that I would change.

I believe taking such a position is a result of having the conviction in the choices you make and adjusting to the imperfections of those decisions in real time so that in the end, change does not occur after the fact but during the moment if you are an effective leader.

S.S.: What is the most important thing you would tell someone making that transition within their company?

S.M.: The most important advice I can give to someone transitioning into a leadership role is that the person making the transition has to want to be in charge. There is nothing worse than to have someone in a leadership position because they think they are suppose to be there rather than because they want to be there.

Once making that commitment, the leader must remain knowledgeable in the areas for which they are responsible. They should always be accessible and visible by getting up out of their seat and walking around. Communicating not just within but across departments and projects is vital.

S.S.: Were there any people who helped and, if so, how?

S.M.: In my opinion, successful leaders are a product of developing attitudes and methods from successful experiences with others. There are many who stand out.

A CEO I had the pleasure to work for was a turnaround specialist. He had an uncanny knack for storytelling. He could capture an audience immediately with interesting stories, tidbits, and personal experiences, always with a sense of humor. These stories gave people something to relate to or imagine rather than listening to some inane management-speak or philosophy.

A captain who mentored me through my commission in the U.S. Army was another. This particular instructor helped me gain perspective on three core problems a first lieutenant would encounter: one, moving into a significant leadership role right out of college; two, understanding how fraternization with enlisted personnel is a balancing act; three, creating a fun environment in a highly monotonous, highly routine military lifestyle. These same three problems are as relevant in corporate life as in the military. He made me address these issues head on at an early age.

Another impactful leader was a studio head I worked for who was simply a person of great principle. He held strong in his convictions about how a studio should be run, and when compromised not on style but on principle, he chose to move on rather than question his own values.

S.S.: What are the most common traits shared by other effective leaders in your experience?

S.M.: The fundamental imperative of a leader is character. By character, I mean moral and ethical strength. Individuals who do the right thing, at the right time, for the right people more often than not will inspire their followers to do what they need to be done. If a leader embodies a strong character, all other important traits flow naturally.

After character, knowledge is most important. Knowledge builds confidence and decisiveness.

Other common traits that flow from a strength of character are

- Trust in subordinates
- Selflessness
- Aversion to yes men
- Mentorship: guidance, counseling, advice, teaching, and door opening
- Consideration
- Delegation
- The inclination to take risks
- The will to take full responsibility for decision
- The readiness to share rewards with subordinates

S.S.: Which traits do you feel are your strongest and how does knowledge of these traits affect how you approach leadership challenges?

S.M.: I would say my strongest trait is trusting in my subordinates. I would like to think I exhibit very little ego in my position and my decision making; therefore I am willing and able to delegate with little to no influence.

I also like to take the attitude that in all situations, no one is making an effort to fail. This perspective allows me to be more constructive and objective in evaluating difficult or messed-up situations.

Lastly, I like to lead, not manage. Therefore, I make an effort to focus on creating an atmosphere for success, not on the particulars of getting a job done.

S.S.: What are the worst traits a leader has exhibited in your experience?

S.M.: Observations on horrible leadership traits:

- **BlackBerry syndrome:** Checking, responding to, and answering BlackBerry messages in meetings.
- **Not sharing information:** If readily available information is not shared, it indicates a simple lack of trust.
- **Bottleneck:** Needing to be in on every meeting and approve every decision.

S.S.: Are there any leadership traits you admire or perhaps aspire toward but don't feel you embody? If so, how do you feel embodying these traits would make you a better leader? Do you consciously try to develop these traits?

S.M.: The #1 trait that I would love to possess is the ability to tell a good story. I believe that this trait allows a leader to capture an audience and develop a sense of belonging. A former boss called this being "rolled out in the bear suit to perform."

S.S.: Do you mentor other leaders?

S.M.: I have never actively mentored other leaders. However, I expect that I am on stage at all times and my words and actions are being taken to heart by each and every member of the studio. I would like those words and actions to be respected; if I had a positive influence on someone, that would be really cool.

S.S.: Do you have any training in leadership either formal or unstructured (e.g., armed forces experience)?

S.M.: Personally I think most leadership classes suck. I feel this way because they tend to create artificial situations that impose a fabricated response by the participant. I do believe in reading about successful leadership styles, techniques, or successes, however. This can provide useful approaches for those in leadership situations.

A couple of experiences have contributed to successful leadership training for me. One is being active in the military; the other is coaching youth sports.

The military provides very practical considerations. The structured environment lends itself to good training. Once, while on training maneuvers, our platoon was attacked by opposing forces. Our referee pronounced the platoon leader "dead," smacked my helmet while I was in the foxhole, and said "You're in charge. Save your troops!" This is stressful but amazingly effective. Details are also stressed in the military. The leader must adhere to the standard operating procedures and be sure there is every attention to detail. It is normally a matter of life and death.

Youth sports are a very effective training ground to be a leader in a less-stressful, less "life and death" situation. But handling the attitudes, performance, and teamwork of nine-year-olds and 14-year-olds provides the opportunity to see how to motivate and inspire people to achieve a common goal. The patience to endure failure is also enhanced.

S.S.: What do you see as the toughest challenge facing leads during a game-development project cycle or at a game-development company generally?

S.M.: The toughest challenge is balancing the Holy Trinity of Project Management: quality, time, and cost. This is best handled by adhering to a design-driven methodology. This helps keep the technology and art from taking over the ultimately important decision point: Do we have a fun game?

S.S.: What are some common mistakes you've seen leads make, be they new or experienced?

- **Territorial:** This shows a lack of confidence and collaboration. It leads to short-sighted results and a myopic approach to problems.

- **Too hands on:** Your subordinates do not get a sense of ownership, trust, or importance. They also do not develop their own skills and styles. It inhibits growth.

- **Managing, not leading:** Inspire and motivate your people to achieve results; don't just manage the specific process.

- **Ego:** Needing to appear as the smartest guy in the room. Needing to be stroked; needing public recognition.

These attitudes will not gain you one iota of respect from your peers or subordinates.

S.S.: How have you seen new leads best get support from directors or executives?

S.M.: The best support that directors give is facilitating communication by providing the opportunity for regular and continuing discussion or presentations, and by setting measurable milestones and demanding accountability to them.

S.S.: Do you think good leaders can be trained? Or is the essence of a good leader simply innate ability?

S.M.: I believe that leaders are born. I believe that certain character traits are inherent in your personality that draw someone to leadership. Those traits begin to show themselves as an individual grows from an adolescent to an adult, and are demonstrated throughout their life. Those traits are

- **Helping others achieve results.** We expect leaders to achieve success through a group. We expect them to help their subordinates grow and develop.

- **Being responsible for achieving objectives.** You can have a satisfying life without a results focus, but if you're going to lead successfully, you have to have the drive and willingness to be measured by the results of your leadership.

- **Willingness to make decisions.** Lots of people wake up every day and let the world happen to them. Leaders must be able and willing to make decisions that affect themselves and others.

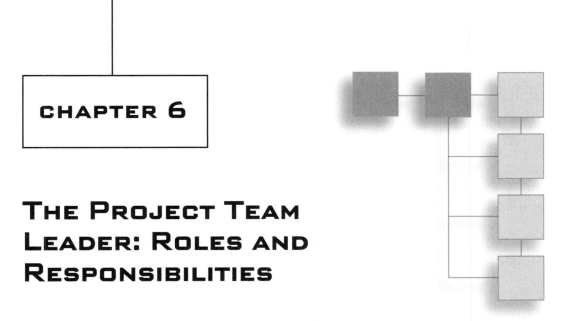

CHAPTER 6

THE PROJECT TEAM LEADER: ROLES AND RESPONSIBILITIES

Almost every leader in the game industry starts out not as a department or studio director, but rather as a project-based leader of some sort. It is therefore worthwhile to accurately define the scope of the various project lead roles and provide some guidance for approaching the responsibilities associated with the roles.

Establishing a job description—defining areas of responsibility and limits of authority—is an easy task This job description, at least in theory, serves as a roadmap for the daily functions of a lead. Detailing a job description does not, however, provide an ideal daily work model to follow any more than the building an organization chart builds a functioning organization. Nonetheless, establishing these descriptions is necessary.

Beyond the text definitions of the responsibilities comes the individual's approach to time management and task prioritization. Knowing what to do when, and having the self-discipline to not get distracted or commit to tasks that are not core to the lead responsibilities, comes with experience. New leads are sometimes shocked that they can be furiously busy all day long with ad hoc meetings, asset or code reviews, and staffing and personnel issues—and feel, at the end of the day, that they seem to have accomplished nothing. Maybe they haven't, but more likely, the new lead is not looking at the right things to evaluate his or her performance—that is, the accomplishments of the team and the advancement of the project at the end of the day.

The main project leadership positions include but are certainly not limited to the specialist lead; leads for the art, design, and programming departments; and the producer and assistant or associate producer in the production department. Additionally, many project teams include a position called "project lead" or "project manager," which, depending on the studio in question, may be the executive project lead who is responsible for overseeing the game as a whole. He or she may be the decision-maker on resource expenses and features, and may evaluate the quality and fun-factor of a game.

For the art and programming leads, the job responsibilities are largely the same:

- Coordinate scheduling

- Specify and assign tasks

- Coordinate resources

- Perform asset or code review

- Engage in some degree of personnel management

In contrast, producers focus on the following:

- Ensuring smooth, timely production of the game

- Facilitating communication

- Tracking progress

- Acting as the communication "point-person" for a parent company or external publisher's producer regarding day-to-day production issues.

Leads of all disciplines are expected further to be the vision holders for the project. They are the champions of the game to the rest of the team and company. Leads model the behavior and attitude they expect from the team.

The specific responsibilities of the lead role vary from studio to studio around the industry. Presented here is the unfiltered list compiled by attendees of the 2005 Art Director/Lead Artist Round Table at GDC when asked to name the traits of a great art lead:

- Is passionate about the project and can inspire the team

- Can effectively carry and enforce the project art vision

- Has no ego (i.e., is willing to delegate)

- Is organized

- Is able to handle inter-departmental diplomacy (i.e., is people oriented)

- Is able to give effective critiques

- Is detail oriented

- Has the trust and respect of the artists

- Is a good mentor/teacher

- Is first in and last out (i.e., works longer hours), and is ultimately responsible for all art on the project

- Is not always the best artist (you want the best artists to be actually creating art)

- Knows the process (i.e., is responsible for the creation or oversight of the pipeline documents)

The 2006 session offered a few additional traits:

- Delegates effectively

- Is a self-starter

- Is a problem solver (i.e., is solution driven)

- Maintains a holistic view of the project

- Is patient

- Communicates a vision and is decisive

- Is organized

You'll notice many words from this list—responsible, patient, decisive, mentor, delegates—feature prominently in, and were in fact lifted for, the "Build Your Ideal Lead" exercise in Chapter 4, "A Litmus Test for Leaders." While I don't completely embrace or encourage the adoption of every point on this list, it does provide a good starting point for determining what qualities will serve your particular studio well.

Note

Although this list of ideal traits was generated by a room of art people, few of the traits have anything to do with art. In fact, with a simple word-replace, you could probably build a decent programming lead list from what you see here.

Presented in this chapter are job descriptions for the specialist lead and lead positions. This comes from my own art department at Firaxis Games. The wording has been modified in only minor ways to make the descriptions more universal.

The Specialist Lead

The specialist lead's role is to manage and review a specific section of a development team. The specialist lead's ultimate goal is to reduce the load of direct reports coming to the lead and, in doing so, remove that communication bottleneck to the production group within that discipline.

Note

This position is sometimes called a "sub-lead" in the game industry, but, to me, the term "sub" connotes a lesser-valued position; I think the term "specialist" is more descriptive and more positive. Note, however, that credited titles should not, in most cases, read "specialist lead," but instead should directly reflect the nature of the specialization, such as animation lead, graphics lead, or multi-player lead.

Following is a sample list of roles, responsibilities, and qualifications for this position.

Role

Provide direction and production art for an area of specialization within a given discipline.

Responsibilities

- Accountable for leadership and the timely production of assets or code within his or her area of specialization. Scheduled production time should be considered as a percentage of overall time based on team size and capabilities.

- Performs all direct asset, code, or feature review tasks, aesthetic (if applicable) and technical, within area of specialization. (May coordinate with the designer for approval of an asset or feature.)

- Reports to the lead and is responsible for daily management of any personnel within the area of specialization.

- Meets with the lead at least once per week, or more frequently as dictated by project needs.

- Creates or directs the creation of any pipeline/processor coding standards docs as requested by the lead.

- Establishes task times and schedules tasks in area of specialization.

- Assists the lead artist in establishing overall project vision and is a champion for the game.

- Builds and maintains team morale.

Qualifications

- Displays or shows aptitude for developing great communication and leadership skills.

- Is considered a problem solver and self-starter.

- Always pushes the quality bar.

- Displays consistent, professional demeanor at all times.

- Reacts well under stressful situations.

- Is a positive force for company morale.

The Lead

The lead's role is to manage, lead, and review a specific discipline (art, programming, design) within a development team. The lead also establishes (or coordinates with senior team members or specialist leads to establish) all development pipelines.

Following is a sample list of roles, responsibilities, and qualifications for this position.

Role

Provides clear and consistent vision and team leadership within a given discipline.

Responsibilities

- Accountable for leadership and the timely production of all assets or components for the entire project within a given discipline. Scheduled production time, if any, should be considered as a percentage of overall time based on team size and capabilities.

- Establishes the overall project vision for his or her discipline and is a champion for the game.

- Is a strong advocate for his or her discipline but is able to maintain a holistic view of the project.

- Builds and maintains team morale.

- Reviews assets, code, and features, from an aesthetic (where appropriate) and technical viewpoint, to ensure high quality standards are met and style is consistent. (May coordinate with the designer for approval of an asset or feature.)

- Reports to the department director and is responsible for daily management of all personnel within the discipline not managed by a specialist lead.

- Coordinates and communicates well with the producer and other project leads to ensure efficient interdepartmental coordination.

- Directs the creation any pipeline documentation needed.

- Establishes task times and schedules tasks in area of specialization.

- Mentors other leads where appropriate.

Qualifications

- Displays great communication and leadership skills.

- Demonstrates compelling vision and passion for the project.

- Is considered a problem solver and self starter.

- Always pushes the quality bar.

- Displays consistent, professional demeanor at all times.

- Reacts well under stressful situations.

- Is an active and positive force for company morale.

Lead Responsibilities

The preceding descriptions are useful summaries of lead responsibilities, but more thought needs to go into the specific points in order to ensure that new leads in particular have a more detailed foundation.

Accountable for Leadership and the Timely Production of all Assets or Components for the Entire Project Within a Given Discipline

Perhaps the most basic and self-evident of the responsibilities, this one probably requires the least explanation and detail. For specialist leads, this is in their direct control. Full leads, while they frequently rely on specialist leads for large areas of game-asset or code production, must have the willingness and desire to be ultimately accountable for every facet of their discipline on the project.

Fulfilling this responsibility involves asking, "What are my tasks, what are my deadlines, and what are my resources?" Leads and managers typically work under an established deadline, may request resources (project personnel), and are empowered to largely define the scope of the work needed to complete a game. Different leads have different approaches to defining their tasks, but once scope and quality goals are set, the leads are responsible and accountable for them. This does not mean that leads are chained to their early estimations and specific schedules, but that they are responsible for the completion of the game to the expectations of their publisher or senior management. When reality rears its ugly head, as it always does in development, the leads are required to manage the crisis, communicate any problems to senior management and the team, and recommend and implement solutions as a group.

Establishes the Overall Project Vision for His or Her Discipline and Is a Champion for the Game

The leads group largely defines the project vision, and the individual leads are responsible for establishing the vision for their discipline. Each project should begin pre-production with overall goals and a mission statement. Following from that, the leads group should translate and interpret that vision to identify goals within their disciplines. Art, for example, may communicate its vision through concept art, prototype assets, and demo movies. Design and programming will do so by building a playable prototype and, to a lesser degree (at least in my opinion), through design and technical documentation. I say "to a lesser degree" because these purely written items, while important, are frequently too abstract, too removed from any context to effectively communicate a design or technical vision.

Each lead should be a champion for the game to the team and the company. No team can afford unenthusiastic team members, and an unenthusiastic lead is unacceptable. Does "enthusiastic" mean that the lead has a glued on smile and jumps around the office? No, but as a lead, you must maintain a positive outlook with the team. Your words carry added weight, and you need to acknowledge and accept that. Start making the Kool-Aid or hand the ladle to someone else.

Is a Strong Advocate for His or Her Discipline But Is Able to Maintain a Holistic View of the Project

The lead is in a competition of sorts with other leads and other projects for resources and project influence. Successful leads will strongly advocate for the resource needs of their discipline while not losing sight of the larger needs of the entire project team, and without deviating from the core goals and vision of the game itself.

Note

You may have heard about studios being "design driven," art driven," tech driven," and even "process driven." This unbalanced state of affairs generally comes about on account of a few strong personalities and high-level performers in one discipline, combined with relatively weaker influences in other areas. It's not necessarily a bad thing; great games come out of studios with these reputations. But establishing such a reputation or perception can result in a self-fulfilling prophecy if, for example, talented artists bypass studios that are known for and highlight their technical or design achievements.

Builds and Maintains Team Morale

Building morale is easier with some teams than others, and on some projects as compared to others. Universally, however, people respond positively when:

▪ Their contributions are solicited and included in planning and design.

- They feel they are learning valuable job skills.

- Their efforts are personally noted and verbally appreciated, and their leads care about them and their professional development.

- They feel like they are part of a cohesive team moving toward a well-defined goal.

Teams with poor morale tend to be ones whose leaders present unfocused or unrealistic goals and close out team member participation in decision-making.

Be aware that the visible behavior and personal outlook of the leads also affects the team. Team members are free to gripe to each other in the break room or out of the office with their co-workers. Leads, however, are not—or at least they shouldn't be. That's not to say, however, that everyone—leads included—needs to vent their daily frustrations somewhere and to someone. Leads must have the discipline and the understanding of their role to vent their concerns *up* the reporting chain, not down or even across.

This is one of the difficulties with maintaining personal friendships with team members as a lead. It is important to consider that when a lead vents to team members, those team members have no avenue for action that is not open and more accessible than that which the lead has. So, upon hearing their trusted lead blow up, they ask themselves, why am I hearing this? The answer must be, they assume, that there are big problems higher up in the company that they don't know anything about and certainly can't do anything about if their boss can't. Now those employees have two new items on their to-do lists that afternoon:

- Discuss the issue with co-workers to see if they know anything about it.

- Polish up the resume.

In short, very bad things happen. Vent concerns and frustrations with your director or senior management.

Reviews Assets, Code, and Features, from an Aesthetic (Where Appropriate) and Technical Viewpoint, to Ensure High Quality Standards Are Met and Style Is Consistent

This responsibility typically occupies most of the leads' time in production. The lead or specialist lead will review and critique the work of every team member on the project at least a few times per week if not on a daily basis depending on the task. This is a lot of communication.

Like any communication, feedback occurs between at least two people—and regardless of the roles of the participants, each one has a responsibility to make the exchange successful. In my experience, one participant alone is rarely to blame when communication problems emerge within project teams.

Following are four "best-practices" that I try to impart to all leads to help them organize their approach to reviews and feedback. Each participant in the critique/review situation has a responsibility to adhere to each of these points.

Note

For the several years, my feedback rules were limited to the "three Cs" below—clear, complete, and consistent. It was a concise little acronym for presentations and workshops. Recently, however, I have been compelled to add a fourth, professional. This ruins the "Three C's" terms but, interestingly, now makes the acronym CCCP, which will be essentially meaningless to anyone born after the Cold War.

Feedback Should Be Clear

All communication should be in plain language, with the end result being an understanding and agreement among both parties. Some of the costliest mistakes I've made in my career stemmed from not making my feedback, instructions, and expectations for modification clear enough. Since then, I've learned to follow a good maxim I picked up from a co-worker: "Things that go without saying often go a lot better when said."

On the flip side, those being reviewed should ask themselves if there is anything that they do not completely understand and, if so, to ask for clarification from the lead.

Feedback Should Be Complete

All feedback should address as much of the asset or feature as possible. Very few things frustrate employees more than hearing incremental feedback on issues that could have been addressed in earlier review sessions and may, because of earlier omission, cause further rework. It requires some discipline to comment on lesser issues because, when making evaluations, lesser issues are "lesser" only relationally. For example, suppose that in reviewing a lighting implementation, the graphics lead sees that the main light is several times too strong, shadows are being cast as flat black and not aliased, and the rim light is not present. The fact that the rim light is missing is a minor issue in comparison and easily overlooked. But what if, for example, the programmer implementing the lighting solution did not know that a rim light was a required element? In leaving this point out of the critique the lead furthers the risk that the task will remain unimplemented.

The person whose work is being reviewed very often will not ask for clarification on every aspect that the lead did not comment on, assuming, hopefully correctly, that the lead addressed all problematic issues.

Feedback Should Be Consistent

Feedback should come from a consistent source. Inconsistent communication paths cause confused employees, reworked assets, and unnecessary slippage as a result. Artists working in open areas are particularly plagued by inconsistent feedback for the simple reason that their work is inherently easy to comment on (as opposed to lines of code on a screen). No doubt you've seen it happen: A concept artist working diligently to respond to feedback that his or her art lead gave 15 minutes ago by making a particular asset taller and skinnier, when the studio director—or worse, the art director—walks by and says, "Wow, that looks awesome, man. Hey, maybe you could make it shorter and fatter!"

Everyone in the studio needs to understand and respect the reporting structure. That said, rigid adherence to a reporting structure can never be the absolute rule. Directors will make "drive-by" comments, but these should be couched in terms that respect the reporting structure, such as, "Wow, that looks awesome man. It'd look really cool shorter and fatter, but don't do anything about that now, let me talk to the art lead about that." Additionally, individuals on the team, regardless of level, should always be encouraged and empowered to reinforce the reporting structure by saying things like, "Yeah, that's a really interesting idea, let me run that past my lead because I think there was a good reason why we want it taller." In practice, though remember that some employees are not going to want to say anything to a studio director except, "Right away!"

As a director, I encourage my peers—and personally strive—to withhold specific feedback until I talk to a lead. Giving feedback to team members is good practice, but I might frame the comment something like, "Hey, that looks awesome, man," and leave it at that until the next time I see the lead, who would be the beneficiary of my full opinion.

Feedback also needs to be consistent in theme as it relates to the overall goals of the game. This is particularly true for art. The act of making qualitative judgments regarding art assets will always have some degree of subjectivity, but the lead can ensure that an objective measure is available by using a style guide, either physical or digital, to evaluate new assets for overall consistency.

Feedback Should Be Professional

Reviews and feedback should always be professionally handled. By this I mean that the reviewer should approach either written or oral critiques with due respect to the person whose work is under review. Leads should avoid derogatory language and personal attacks of any nature and limit critiques to the work at hand. Again, art critiques are, by nature, more subjective than programming or some design critiques, and the lead should be prepared for this by referring to style guides or previously completed work to more objectively measure the asset under review.

The individual whose work is being reviewed is likewise expected to respond to the lead in a professional manner. That is not to say that the reviewee needs to agree 100 percent with the lead's assessment, simply that he or she must respond professionally to the feedback, rationally express any differing thoughts, and understand that, in the end, the lead has the final say. Critiques and reviews are how our work gets better, but some take even professionally delivered reviews very personally and react defensively. This attitude makes the lead less likely to provide detailed critiques to that person. As a result, the work that he or she does is likely to suffer over the long term—along with his or her reputation for being an effective (and enjoyable) team member.

It's good practice for the reviewee to take written notes during all critiques with the lead. If the nature of the feedback on the asset or feature is very complex, it greatly helps both parties for the note-taker to send a follow-up e-mail with the list of comments and agreed-upon actions to be taken. This gives the reviewer a chance to clarify any instructions and serves as a fix checklist for the reviewee.

Review Stage Guidelines

The stages at which assets or features are reviewed and feedback delivered should be established and communicated to all production personnel. These can be very loose or as detailed as needed, depending on the task in question. The important factor is that everyone understands the stages at which reviews occur, and what aspects will be covered at each stage. Using this information, production personnel can work more effectively with the lead to alert him or her when reviews are required. Following is a sample approval sequence for a few assets.

Concept Approval Schedule

1. Basic silhouette review—8 to 12 simple black and white silhouettes
   Aesthetic and functional quality
   Proportion and relative scale

2. Rough sketch of selected silhouettes from above
   Aesthetic review
   More detailed design function review
   Modeler/animator review for game functionality, if needed
   Rough color check

3. Review of final color work
   Aesthetic review
   Modeler/animator review for game functionality, if needed

Model Approval Schedule

1. Low poly model review
   Correct proportion and scale
   All functional elements included (design may have a part in this review)
   Tech checklist: poly count, auto-check run, no over-detailed areas

2. ZBrush model review
   Concept faithfulness, general aesthetic review
   All functional elements included

3. Unwrap review
   Intelligent use of texture space
   Appropriate pixel density across model

Each asset type, be it an animation sequence, concept art, level design, tool, or design feature, should have understood—preferably written—review guidelines. This may seem like an overly structured process, but it is important for both parties to understand task requirements and expectations as clearly as possible. The procedure becomes second nature very quickly during production.

Reports to the Department Director and Is Responsible for Daily Management of All Personnel Within the Discipline Not Managed by a Specialist Lead

This is a description of the expected reporting lines that the lead is required to maintain through development. The description is fairly straightforward, but the practice can be complex and time consuming if not planned properly.

Direct Reports

As detailed in Chapter 2, "The Anatomy of a Game-Development Company," the lead can become a bottleneck if there are too many team members directly reporting to him or her. How many is too many? It depends on the nature and frequency of the reports. I think 8–10 direct reports are about the limit that a lead can maintain through production and expect to adequately perform other duties. It should be noted that at that level, very little or no actual production work will be able to be assigned to the lead.

Indirect Reports

The lead also needs to communicate with every team member as frequently as possible. This may be difficult with team sizes of 30 or so, but it's not impossible. Personally delivered praise and recognition are enormously important to the morale of the people on the team. The effect is magnified when it is delivered by the lead, who is probably most familiar with the effort being made and most engaged with the entire project.

Reporting Up

There is a time-honored bit of Army advice for new officers that goes like this: "Keep your troops out of the sun and don't B.S. the old man."

You can go a long way in management just by following this one piece of advice. One of the worst mistakes a lead can make is not giving honest assessments to directors and senior managers. Significant problems can be hidden for a time on any project, and some leads are tempted to do so out of fear of being perceived to have failed. They do so in most instances with the well-intentioned rationalization that they can rectify the situation within the next milestone, and that reporting a given problem will just cause more headaches for them from their boss, which will ultimately delay the fix that they envision.

This is not a disaster waiting to happen, but a disaster actively occurring on the project. Mistakes, big and small, happen on all projects. Any experienced manager expects that, and needs to hear about difficulties as early as possible. The only way to prevent a potential reporting failure like this is to demonstrate that, as a senior management group, you welcome all challenges, you are open to hearing about any and all project concerns that leads have, and you work constructively with the team to arrive at a course of action.

Coordinates and Communicates Well with the Producer and Other Project Leads to Ensure Efficient Interdepartmental Coordination

The other communication channel the lead needs to focus on is that to and from his or her fellow project leads. Regular leads meetings should be held led by either the producer or project lead; in these meetings, the leads should discuss, debate, and even argue about project issues—but consistently present a unified message to the team. Additionally, I recommend off-site meetings at least once a month, such as lunch meetings. These offer the opportunity for team leads to learn each other's individual communication styles in a more social and relaxed setting. In my experience, social meetings like these take place with frequency in the early stages of projects, eventually taper off, and ultimately cease later in the production cycle as perceived production priorities mount. It should be incumbent upon the leads group to keep these going, however, because I've found that in their absence, the cohesion of the group can evaporate. Cohesion is an important factor of a successful leads group. The team needs to see its leads as speaking with one voice and moving in the same direction. If that lead unity is perceived to be suffering, the entire team may lose respect for the reporting/decision-making structure or, worse, factionalize around different leads.

Note

At one point, my company had an issue with the lack of team exposure to leads meetings, which was revealed through informal means to our studio director. The team was intensely curious and nervous about the content leads meetings, concerned that major decisions were being made without their input. In reality, that was not the case, but in situations like this, perception is reality. To counter this growing concern, the team leads decided to open up the process by publishing leads meeting notes to the team after each meeting and, prior to each meeting, making available an agenda item request list to the team for any and all input.

Directs the Creation of Any Pipeline Documentation Needed

The lead is responsible for establishing and enforcing a coherent and consistent work process for tasks within his or her discipline. This does not mean that, for example, the programming lead needs to personally establish the coding standards across the project, simply that he or she is responsible for at least delegating that task, approving the results, and enforcing the standards set throughout the project.

This latter point becomes complicated when major processes change in the middle of production—which happens with great regularity. The leads in these cases must work to establish a new pipeline or process and ensure that the revision is effectively communicated to all affected project personnel. Failure to accomplish this may lead to lost development time, as assets or features need to be redone. Additionally, the team may begin to feel that it or its leads are not fully aware or in control of the development picture.

Establishes Task Times and Schedules Tasks in Area of Specialization

The lead is responsible for coordinating with the producer and with team members to develop a task list for the project and to build a schedule that, in some form, maps a path for the completion of the project that all stakeholders agree upon.

Developing task-time estimates is one of the more difficult undertakings in game development. There are many different production approaches to this issue, and a work of this nature cannot hope to go into any sort of detail on the subject. But whatever methodology you adopt, it is imperative that the lead work with team members in pre-production to arrive at task times that leads and production personnel agree on. Following are some general thoughts, and some common issues that are known to cause blown estimates.

How Long Is a "Day," and What Does "Done" Mean?

Many production personnel look at a given task, think it will take a few hours to do X, two hours to do Y, and two hours to do Z, and will say something like, "That will take a day to get done." What has not been defined for them is how long a "day" is, and what the producer believes that "done" means.

Day   Employment research—and my own personal experience—has shown that between five and six hours of solid production work typically gets done at a game-development company each day. The discrepancy between hours present on site and hours of production work that is completed is strictly from scheduled meetings, ad-hoc work-related interruptions, time lost switching between tasks, and other office- or work-related issues. It does not consider long lunches, surfing the Web, fantasy football trash-talking, and other prevalent non–work related distractions.

Producers and senior managers also need to be aware that all employees know and respect the cost and time pressures associated with development and want to provide the most aggressive estimate because they know that that is precisely what schedulers want to hear. So, with the best of intentions, when many individuals are asked to estimate how long it will take them to complete a task, they will imagine how many days it would take if they cranked through it uninterrupted and without making the usual iteration cycles. The scheduling producers and leads need to remind those people providing estimates to think in terms of hours per task instead of days to help counter this instinct.

Done   When production personnel are asked to provide estimates, they frequently fail to include time to export an asset and iterate prior to an official review or, in the case of programmers, the time it will most likely take to debug a feature, review it with design or art, and iterate on it before the task is truly complete. The leads must agree what "done" means—usually, it means the asset or feature is working as designed in the game and not causing any unwanted secondary effects such as crashes or performance degradations.

Estimates are usually generated in pre-production by actually building one of a given asset type, doing coding research for a feature, or building a prototype to test game play. These are all recommended practices, but in the end they can only serve as a starting point for building a time estimate because pre-production itself does not mimic the realities, rigors, and vagaries of production. Pre-production is also a time when new techniques are explored and discarded as needed. Given that, it is crucial that the estimates that come out of pre-production are carefully considered. Will actual times be faster now that the process has been established? Probably. Might task times instead be slower, once we realize that several extra steps are needed to export into the actual game? Maybe.

Under Promise, Over Deliver

One approach is to under-promise and over-deliver. This works particularly well for third-party developers who are operationally beholden to their publisher for steady milestone approvals. This is the prudent approach when hitting the release date is a hard requirement or resources are limited. Also, it allows for more polish time, feature additions, and/or schedule slippage. That said, some may argue that "prudence" is, in this case, "lying," and that this approach is guaranteed to produce sub-par results because the team is not being pushed to its limits.

Damn the Torpedoes!

The other approach is to shoot the moon. Establish very aggressive quality and scope goals and push for maximum project resources. This is a riskier approach that works well when stakeholders embrace the outlook that the game is done when it's done, not at the end of a given fiscal year or another arbitrary date. In the "pro" column for this approach, everyone wants the opportunity to do great things. Games are a hit-driven business, and some argue that if you are not scheduling for a hit game, maybe you shouldn't be making the game at all. Others, however, maintain that this approach practically guarantees extended overtime and/or a blown release date. This approach allows for less polish time, feature additions, and/or schedule slippage.

Monitoring Scheduling and Resources Through the Production Cycle

Once an initial schedule has been created, the leads' job has only begun. At this point, task tracking and feature-addition monitoring become the major tasks of the scheduling leads. Task tracking is fairly basic in a static schedule, but game features, assets, and schedules are very rarely anything remotely resembling "static." In almost every case in my experience, game projects grow in scale or complexity from what was initially imagined. There are many cases in which the asset list may be reduced from an initially ambitious list, but game features and technical details tend to grow, with hitherto hidden complexities tending to emerge during the course of a development cycle.

The leads have a responsibility to address scale and resource changes effectively in development. There is a tendency in the game industry to react to scope increases with vague plans to increase outsourcing, trim other areas, to "find some time between alpha and beta" (my all-time personal favorite), or completely discount the addition because some other area of the game is running ahead of schedule.

All of these answers lead to problems, including failed features, rushed assets, and extensive overtime for the team. Leads must recognize, embrace, and champion a scale/quality and resource/ development cycle balance. "Resources" refers to the number of project personnel and investment in engines or middleware. This concept is illustrated in Figure 6.1, adopted from a 2007 GDC production presentation. The figure represents an initial development balance between scale/quality and resources/development cycle achieved by the leads.

As development proceeds, new features are added or existing planned features turn out to be more complex and require additional time or resources. In many cases, additional time is simply not an option and, frequently, additional resources are not either. So what happens, as shown in Figure 6.2, is that the overall quality of the title diminishes as teams attempt to complete more work in the same amount of time with the same resources.

Leads should instead fight for increased resources or an increased time commitment, as illustrated in Figure 6.3. Here, balance is restored by adding resources. Adding length to the development cycle is another way that this scope

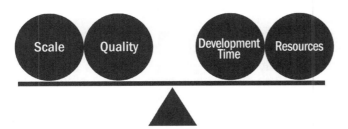

Figure 6.1
Initial scope/quality/resource/development cycle balance at the start of production.

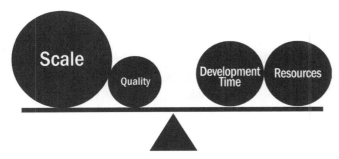

Figure 6.2
Quality shrinks due to increased scale requirements.

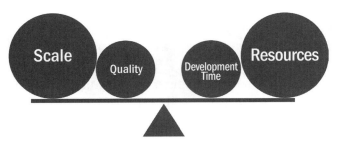

Figure 6.3
Balance is restored by increasing resources on the project.

expansion might be dealt with. Always fight to balance the addition of new features or recommend the trimming of existing features as appropriate with newfound development time or resource expansion.

Note

All these elements are subject to expansion and contraction for any number of reasons, including project slippage. Many years ago, I had the opportunity to visit a large and very successful West Coast developer that was in the final stage of development of an expansive role-playing game. The game world was on display in a concept area in the form of dozens of pieced-together sheets of graph paper covering an entire wall, floor-to-ceiling. After I had expressed my admiration of the sheer scale of the effort, the project producer confessed that they had had to shrink the world size "a bit" to complete development on schedule. When I asked how much smaller they had made it, he indicated an area on the wall that was about one quarter the size of initially designed world.

Mentors Other Leads Where Appropriate

A successful lead mentors other leads constantly, consciously or not, by modeling appropriate behavior as well as by providing observational feedback and making themselves available at all times for discussions regarding leadership and management challenges.

Consciously modeling behavior is one of the most important tools that mentoring leads can use. I think it's the way we teach and learn anything most effectively. Successfully doing this requires an openness to opportunities that present themselves to demonstrate the desired behavior to the individual in question.

Of course, it is not always possible to address a specific issue in a timely fashion, and that's where the lead should provide observational feedback and guidance. New leads should always be encouraged to seek advice on new situations. The chances are very good that a more senior lead has dealt with similar situations and can provide useful advice.

Lead Qualifications

Understanding lead qualifications is an important tool when evaluating potential leads or giving career guidance to someone who is seeking a lead role. In the latter case, having a list of qualifications to refer to and objectively apply to an individual is indispensable. That said, giving someone seeking a lead role the news that he or she won't be getting one anytime soon is awkward and disappointing. It helps greatly to be able to reiterate or introduce the concept of dual and equivalent career paths—but if the individual still wishes to pursue the lead track, you must detail the areas in which the individual must improve.

While there are certainly more qualifications that can and should be considered for every individual organization, following are a few I use regularly.

Displays Great Communication and Leadership Skills

Communication issues are some of the most difficult to address because they are so closely tied to an individual's personality. It greatly helps to be able to provide work-based examples of how the individual's poor communication affects others. The most obvious might be that he or she simply isn't vocal enough in team critiques or in one-on-one asset reviews. Other more challenging issues involve the communicator being too blunt to the point of being perceived as disrespectful to other team members, unclear, indecisive, or too defensive in response to critiques. In these cases, I bring up a few examples to the individual and suggest that he or she take time out to objectively evaluate interactions—specifically, their part in them—and how they feel such exchanges could be improved upon. Ideally, this exercise becomes a continuing dialog and provides many opportunities for specific and timely mentoring.

Demonstrates Compelling Vision and Passion for the Game

When I question whether someone is going to be able to be invested enough to take a lead role on a given product, I ask that person why he or she wants to be a lead? Usually the answer is that the person wants to advance his or her career, and feels that the project in question is the ideal fit. This can be evaluated very objectively by simply asking the person to follow-up in detail about what it is about the project that the person finds exciting and what is or her vision of it is. Sometimes during the course of this exchange, the candidate will come to the realization that he or she is not the right fit for the role.

Is Considered a Problem Solver and Self-Starter

Being a problem solver is one of those traits that separate senior contributors from other production personnel. Individuals who are not considered problem solvers are incapable of, or disinterested in, establishing workflow processes or working independently for long periods. Not being a problem solver is not necessarily a negative thing; I've worked with many valuable team members who were not known as problem solvers. But such a perception does limit one's contribution to the project and caps advancement within an organization. Obviously, leads need to be capable problem solvers. Again, they don't need to actually solve all the issues, but they need to define the problem, delegate the solution, and evaluate and approve the result.

Part of being a problem solver is being proactive with tasks—that is, being a self-starter. Leads must demonstrate individual initiative in order to be considered for the role because once in place, it is not likely that anyone is going to tell them what needs to be done and how to do it.

Always Pushes the Quality Bar

This is a trait that occurs in and is identifiable at all levels, even in the most junior members of a company. No software expertise or extensive development experience is needed to have a keen eye for quality and to not be satisfied with mediocre output from yourself or others on your team.

One cautionary note: There is a line between the relentless crusader for quality and the crusader for a subjective opinion who won't shut up about it. Don't be the latter. I've had the great pleasure to work with many individuals in my career who fall into the former category, and while I make the trait a qualifier for lead candidacy, it's every bit as—if not more—valuable as a trait in production personnel. Games are a team effort, and the larger the games get, and the larger the team sizes become, the harder it is for leads to focus on every single aspect of the game. Following from that fact, the more team members at all levels who are serious about investing time and effort into making their game the very best it can be, the better the final product will be.

Displays Consistent and Professional Demeanor at All Times

Project leads must demonstrate a consistent professional demeanor. This means they treat all project personnel in a manner consistent with company policy and consistent across the population of the team regardless of any potential personal differences or affinities. It also means that the lead should strive to be consistent in approach to project situations regardless of personal stress levels. This last point is rarely achieved in my direct experience, but should remain a goal.

Note

I once worked with a studio director outside the game industry who had two distinct professional manners. One we called Monday Ian, and the other was Regular Ian. Regular Ian was a rational, even relaxed manager who was an excellent communicator and skilled project manager. Monday Ian, in contrast, was a short-tempered, irrational manager who seemed to spend Saturday and Sunday stressing about projects, re-imagining them, and mentally reshuffling personnel and task priorities. He arrived at the studio every Monday morning personally checking on the staff to see where they were, arranging redundant meetings with senior personnel to discuss the crises he feared, and grilling senior members on project scheduling. By Tuesday, he would have transmogrified back into Regular Ian, with a state of imagined control, or at least studio awareness, that he was comfortable with, and we would move forward as a functioning team—until the next Monday.

Reacts Well under Stressful Situations

Game-development cycles are growing longer in most cases, but the content and the quality expectations always seem to rise a bit faster. This combination puts a great deal of stress on the development team—particularly on leads. It is important for leads to recognize that one of their roles is to keep the team focused on the task at hand and eliminate unnecessary distractions—especially being an unnecessarily distracting element themselves. Some people are simply better suited to remain calm under pressure than others. Most people attain greater composure with experience, but some never seem able to effectively deal with the cyclic pressures of game development. These latter people may well be very valuable team members who simply require more oversight during hectic periods, but they are not likely to be lead candidates. When addressing this issue, again, focus on the work result and the effect of the individual's behavior on the team environment.

Is an Active and Positive Force for Company Morale

This is related to an earlier point, in that positive-thinking people recognize that everyone contributes to the environment and culture of an organization and act accordingly. Having a positive attitude does not mean that one ignores concerns or looming problems, but that one directs those concerns appropriately— usually, upward. Individuals requesting consideration for a lead role who are not what you would consider positive influences need to be reminded that their words carry weight. Equally, their lack of vocal input—either critical or not—is also felt by the team.

Knowing What to Do When

We have established a template for leads' responsibilities and the qualifications they have been required to meet. But as Robert Martin said in his segment, one of the most difficult challenges he faced was "knowing what to do when." What we have so far established in this chapter is much like a list of ingredients for a soup. We know we need salt, stock, vegetables, chicken, and such, but we don't know how much of each in relation to each other, cooking time, or temperature. As with any good cook, though, understanding of these essential details comes with experience and, hopefully, a mentor—if only to prevent the kitchen from burning down.

A lead's first and foremost responsibility is to ensure that his or her team members have all the information, time, and resources to accomplish their tasks. As team sizes become larger, this task becomes more and more time consuming for the lead and specialist lead, but it remains the most essential. John Chowanec notes that, "It's not about you. The role of a leader is to lead, not necessarily to dictate. If you don't focus your efforts around those you are leading, you might find yourself with no one to lead any longer." In fact, most of the interview subjects spent some time underlining this point.

Almost every other specific task that leads perform falls from this first point. Establishing and monitoring schedules, building pipelines, communicating best practices and production expectations all serve the needs of the team. In this regard, the lead role is very much a selfless one.

In a practical and very physical sense, a leads' day often may look like a picture of chaos. Since the lead is ideally available to the team at all times, he or she is frequently in demand most of the day. So the idea of organizing your day in a meaningful way may seem like a far-fetched notion. In most cases, it is—and that's okay. There are, though, a few tools that leads use to prioritize their time. These include the following:

- Desktop computer software, such as Outlook, to schedule meetings and appointments.

- Personal digital assistants, phones, and BlackBerrys to manage personal schedules.

- Post-it notes. I find these to be most effective. Before I leave on a given day, when my unfinished business is clearest in my mind, I make a few hand-written notes and leave them on my keyboard. I don't consider myself a Luddite, but I find that, for simple task reminders, the immediacy of a hand-written note is superior to inserting another piece of technology into the process.

Team Morale and the Last Firewall

Leads, as a group and individually, set the tone for the project team. They also act as a buffer, or firewall, against external and internal distractions for the team. In the case of team leads, they are really the "last firewall" before the team. Other executive-level buffering may occur at the publisher producer or point-of-contact level, which typically center on higher-level issues—usually contracts—with the directors and senior management at the developer. Distractions of the kind from which a team needs to be shielded may include business difficulties with an external partner or personal feuds within the leads group itself, senior management, or an external publishing partner—basically, anything that does not relate to the continued development of the project but may be a source of concern and unneeded distraction for team members.

External Distractions

The project producer is usually in a unique role for exposure to this issue. The producer is typically the single point-of-contact person for the development team and an external publisher or parent company. As such, the producer is in a position to control and filter information to the team. The other leads are typically also privy to this information and, as much as possible, must contribute to the health of the team by limiting the flow of information to critical project-related issues.

An example of the importance of this might be a situation where an external producer is engaged in a fight on behalf of the developer over some game- or contract-related issue that the developer feels strongly about. The struggle over whatever feature or condition might last a while, with the result being that the feature or condition ends up being rejected by the publisher. If the team is exposed to the daily back-and-forth of the debate and the ultimate disappointment, the developer runs the risk of several bad outcomes. These include the following:

- The team feeling like its internal management failed to communicate the true importance of the issue.

- The team feeling like its external producer failed to persuade his or her company and is viewed as ineffective or incompetent for the remainder of the project.

- The team feeling that the external publishing partner is insensitive to its concerns.

- All of the above.

These feelings, once in place, will not be easily overcome, and will lead to lower morale in the team as long as the particular developer-publisher relationship exists. Only with a great deal of time and other positive experiences will this perception begin to change.

It is important to note that this does not mean that negative project feedback from the publisher should be kept from the team or even filtered. In fact, milestone or overall project feedback needs to communicated to the team using the feedback best practices cited earlier: clearly, completely, consistently, and professionally. Raw commentary from the publisher, like "This sucks," or the publisher's use of profanity can and probably should be worded professionally while preserving the intention. I have seen inexperienced producers soften publisher milestone feedback out of concern for the team's morale, leading to larger and continuing communication problems between the developer and publisher and, in one case, cancellation of the project by the publisher.

Note

Every organization has an "institutional memory." Institutional memory preserves experiences, both good and bad, and passes them along, either orally or written, to new employees who have no other context for the experience aside from whatever information is passed along. Good examples of institutional memory include the practice of preserving project post-mortem reporting, training documentation, and positive tales of personnel, company culture, or company practices. Negative aspects of institutional memory are almost always orally communicated and may concern pervasive negativity directed toward past or present employees or managers, bad blood between other local developers, poor practices of present or past publishers, and so on. It's helpful to take some time to consider the aspects of your company's institutional memory and discuss with other leaders how they perceive the issue and how specific concerns might be addressed.

Internal Distractions

Internal distractions in the form of lead disagreements or senior-management/lead friction are obviously harder to contain from the team, but are almost always more damaging than external distractions. This makes it all the more important to deal quickly and effectively with whatever the issue may be.

The leads, as a group, have the responsibility to handle interactions with each other and with senior management with professionalism. In times where this falters, leads or directors who are uninvolved in the conflict must step in quickly to get the parties in question together, state the problem that their conflict is causing on the team, and work with them to resolve the situation. In most cases, difficult situations can be defused when people have the chance to speak and listen to each other and recognize a common goal. As addressed in Chapter 3, "How Leaders Are Chosen, Are Supported, Perform, and Why," the worst thing leads can do in this situation is hope that the parties in question calm down on their own and get past whatever the point of conflict was. Time does not heal all wounds, and in the case of personnel difficulties, inaction, combined with the passage of time, deepens divides and can lead to truly intractable personality conflicts.

The Lead Role Versus the Lead Position

A question that frequently comes up in discussion about leads is, Should the lead in an organization be a continuing position or a role taken by senior artists on a per-project basis, with personnel rotating in and out as appropriate? There are advantages and disadvantages to both sides. On the "lead as a permanent position" side is the fact that good leads are in short supply, and the company should utilize them to their fullest and most useful potential. Also, the lead title is one that some leads simply prefer to retain. The opposing position holds that the hard skills that leads rely on to make sound estimates and that give them the ability to contribute to production discussions rapidly erode, becoming out of date even as the industry advances during a production cycle, and most do not want to see that happen. From a departmental standpoint, rotating leads generally allows greater flexibility, since more staff members are exposed to the role. This makes the department better prepared to staff for leadership positions in cases of personnel transition or company expansion.

My leaning currently is a theoretical preference for rotating the lead role, but in practical terms, it is not always possible. Good leads are rare and many of them prefer to hold on to the title and the role because they find it personally satisfying and professionally rewarding, and they are recognized as being good at it. In the end, the decision about rotation or permanence of the lead title will probably be largely determined by the size and composition of your company and the disposition of your lead or leads.

Interview: Brenda Brathwaite, Game Designer/Department Chair, Savannah College of Art and Design

Brenda Brathwaite is chair of and professor in the Interactive Design and Game Development department at the Savannah College of Art and Design, and she is also a freelance game designer. Brenda has an extensive video-gaming career that spans more than 25 years and 21 published products. Her contributions to the field include design on several top-selling games such as *Playboy: The Mansion*, *Dungeons & Dragons Heroes*, and *Wizardry 8*, which has received many accolades including numerous RPG of the Year awards. She is a frequent speaker at universities, colleges, and conferences, including the Game Developers Conference, MIT, and others.

Seth Spaulding: Describe your transition from a production position to a leadership position.

Brenda Brathwaite: I really had to think about this before remembering precisely where and when a transition happened—and there were many. Not all transitions are clean and obvious transitions like my move from a professor of game design to chair of the whole department. Getting that promotion was a fairly clear and obvious trajectory.

If I go way back to when I got into this industry, though, positions were still being defined and invented. I mean, we didn't really have game designers in the game industry back in the early days. We had programmers, and they did it all—art, programming, sound, and story. People like Dani Berry were "all in one" shows. In smaller companies even today, positions are still being invented and reinvented, and the transitions still aren't clear.

In my case, I apprenticed my way to my first leadership job. I began working in the industry in 1982 at Sir-tech Software, Inc. in Ogdensburg, NY. My initial job was to play the games, memorize the content, and then answer people's questions when they'd call to find out how to kill the Wizard on the 10th level. I guess I did a good job memorizing those things because I still remember it all today. [Author: She really does remember; I checked. See note at end of interview.] From that job, I went on to product development and worked with the various external developers we had. My official title was product development manager. That sounds a whole lot bigger today than it was back then. The industry was really a pretty small place, and my job consisted of reviewing software that others would send in for possible publishing as well as keeping track of the games currently in development. In a nutshell, I still got paid to play games, but a lot more was expected of me.

There are 18 years to this story, so I'll cut to the chase. In a nutshell, I worked my way up by apprenticing. I took the opportunity to learn from the best and worked with them. When they had too much work to do, I helped out, and eventually I found myself working as a designer on a project and ultimately as a lead.

The transition was slow—and I think that's necessary. In some fields, having an opportunity to work beside others to watch them do what they do, particularly through a massive role-playing game, is something that is invaluable when you're in a position to make those decisions yourself.

S.S.: What were some unexpected challenges or surprises?

B.B.: Having a week go smoothly—that would be unexpected and surprising. There are always things that happen, particularly as a lead, and some of those you can't anticipate—losing a member of your staff, having an employee in crisis, or having the marketing department randomly demand some absurd feature. You name it. I have held conversations with an employee who was under his desk absolutely freaking out because he couldn't fix some code. That he'd been up for 40+ hours straight didn't help, I'm sure. Being a lead means expecting the unexpected and making room in your schedule even if you have no idea at the time what will fill it.

There are some general truths about being a lead that I would not have expected. First off, being a leader doesn't mean that you get the last call on something. Some people are surprised to hear that. There have been three times in my career where I wanted to do something and had the support of the whole team, but ultimately, something else was done—and that call came from above my head. There wasn't a damned thing I could do about it. In particular, I remember this rather tragic game where they removed all the female characters from the game somewhere around alpha. It was a horrifying scramble to try to make it acceptable, let alone not embarrassing.

Another time, I recall being offered a rather large salary jump along with a particular promotion. I said I'd like to take some time to think about it, and when I returned to say "It sounds good" a couple days later, the offer had gone down by $20,000. I think I had some choice words to say, but I kept them to myself, and said I'd be glad to take the old offer were it to resurface.

S.S.: Looking back, are there any decisions or practices you would change, and if so, why?

B.B.: Absolutely, and I share this with anyone who will listen: Think hard before making anything more than a +1 jump. That means if you're a designer on a console RPG, it's a +1 to become a lead on a console RPG. If you're a hard-core RPG designer on a computer and you're planning to become a lead on an action console title, that adds up to a +3, and you're probably going to be either a) working your ass off, b) failing amazingly, or c) medicated inside of a year—and possibly all three. I know it's a simplistic formula, if you can even call it that, but there have been two times in my career where I either felt amazingly out of my element or didn't perform the way I would like to have performed, and in each, there was something more than a +1 going on. Opportunity is one thing, but taking advantage of that opportunity when it will burn you out or risk others' investment isn't cool.

I would have also stuck with programming, but I think that's less about leadership and more about being a game designer. I wish I could code now.

S.S.: What is the most important thing you would tell someone making that transition within their company?

B.B.: The first words that come to mind are probably not printable: "Don't be an asshole." When a promotion occurs, there are really three things that happen, and they may happen all at the same time:

- Other people find out they're not getting promoted.

- Other people find out it's you who got promoted.

- You find out it's you who got promoted.

So it's so important to recognize that along with your promotion, there could be some people who are feeling a bit sore about it. Why not me? In truth, they might be more qualified than you technically or artistically or even as a manager. However, the powers that be are looking for a particular person, a particular personality, in their lead. You also may not want your best coder dealing with lead stuff 40 percent or more of his or her time. I don't recall where I heard this, but I heard it early on in my career, and I've always remembered it: The job of a good lead is to make people who are better than the lead be as good as they can possibly be. I have felt that before. I had these two junior designers working with me who were really good at a number of things, but just amazing at others. It was their first serious game-industry gig, and at first, they were all over the place, overwhelmed with stuff we might take for granted (first-party submissions, TRC requirements, etc.). It took a while to figure out each designer's strengths, but man, once I got them working in their element? It was magic. I still work with one today, and the other's at Maxis. Without cheating, I pinged one of these guys and asked him if I had a good trait he would identify. Here's what he said: "Your greatest strength is empowerment. You're totally not afraid to let the people under you grow and flourish. Some leaders have this unnatural fear that the people under them will take their position away if they're given any leeway to make decisions on their own. You're totally not like that." Which is good, since I may need them to hire me someday.

Work *with* the people around you. Assume you are just the ambassador of your department, not the dictator. If you start to feel alone, you'll know how your people view you.

S.S.: Were there any people who helped, and if so, how?

B.B.: The Sirotek brothers, Rob and Norm. I joined their company, Sir-tech Software, Inc., when I was just 15, and they were so open with their knowledge. These are people who were there at the very beginning of the industry and ran a successful, private software company for 20 years. That's amazing, and I am so fortunate to have been there for all but two of those years.

Working with you [the author] was also quite helpful. As a lead and as a project lead, I had to watch you make some very difficult calls with some very difficult individuals, and never once did I detect anything but sincerity and respect in your voice. Because of that, even the disappointed and angry people respected you, and that was a great lesson to see.

In my present position, I have the tremendous support of the dean of the School of Film and Digital Media, Peter Weishar. That helps in all kinds of countless ways. I feel comfortable both professionally and creatively, and if either one of those were not true, I would not be as happy as I am.

In a more general sense, as a lead it's natural to become stressed at various times. It's during those times that your fellow leads, the project lead, and project producer can become invaluable. I'm a big believer in venting up. If you vent down, you just tear up morale.

I'm also pretty networked in the game industry. So, going to conferences and learning from similar experiences of my peers is helpful, too. Also, I've been greatly helped by watching leads throughout my career. I worked with some who were absolute tyrants, and they were as great an example as the really good ones.

S.S.: What are the most common traits shared by other effective leaders in your experience?

B.B.: Honesty. If you lie to your team members about the state of the project, they will remember it beyond the grave. Trust is the single most important thing you can develop with your team. If they trust you, it's gold.

Open-mindedness. Everyone has the freedom to be an idiot, including leads, and it's a wonderful thing. I've made catastrophically stupid design decisions in the past, and I'm still amused by them (because the game didn't ship with them). So, when people share thoughts that are contradictory to mine, I listen earnestly. You truly never know where a good idea is going to come from. And, if I disregard someone's opinion now, they become unlikely to share good ideas in the future. Also, pay attention to the quiet guy. There's a chance that he's been listening to everyone else while everyone else has been yapping away. Unlike everyone else, he has processed the information, and might actually have a good solution to whatever it is you're discussing. Open-mindedness also extends to being willing to admit when you're wrong, and apologize and make amends when necessary. I am sure I haven't always been the best lead I could be, but I'm also willing to apologize when that's the case.

Respect. This word is tossed about like a Wii controller, but next to honesty, it's the foundation of a good relationship with your peers. In my present job, I get that I'm working with some seriously amazing faculty members who are way better than I am in their respective areas. I feel like my number-one job as a chair is to give the students an awesome education, and I can't do that without happy, productive faculty. I respect them for what they do. I respect their families, and their personal time. I respect their different artistic needs and beliefs. I've been around people who class "game design" with "couldn't get a real job, eh?" so respecting the art of others has tremendous value to me. Also, by knowing what others do, it helps you to stay decently humble and avoid dictator-syndrome. At the chair level, I share the same floor with an Emmy winner, an Academy Award winner, and a BAFTA award winner, so it's not too hard. Respect also means that I'm willing to fight for things that I know are important to those who work under me. That just might be the Irish in me, though.

S.S.: Which traits do you feel are your strongest and how does knowledge of these traits affect how you approach leadership challenges?

B.B.: What a good question to follow up my humility comment. Well done on that.

Humor helps. I am also not at all afraid to say difficult things to people, provided that it's said in a kind way, it's necessary to say, and it's also true. Generally, I find that people who want to get better are receptive to critique, and as long as I welcome critique from them, it's good. Sometimes, you have to break up pretty tense situations, too.

In general, I try to be good to the people that I'm working with. If I have the ability to make their job a better job to be in—whether it's giving them a choice about assignment A or assignment B—I do it. In general, I find even discussing "leadership" things uncomfortable. While I am in a lead role and have been for a long time, I feel like one of the group, not the head of any particular group. I really just collate a whole bunch of desires, needs, and expectations, and try to make a balanced system. To think that I could do that well if the people who work with me weren't great, and if I weren't given the support from above to do, that is a misnomer.

I try to be clear about expectations. I make sure that people know exactly what I'm expecting, when I'm expecting it, and why it's expected. I don't know if one would consider that a trait, but I sure as hell know when it *doesn't* happen. I also really try to practice what I preach. I'm honest, open-minded (and if not, I'm told several times), and respect the people I work with.

One trait that I find very, very useful is game design. So many things are a game of territorial acquisition, territorial control, and resource management. I have spent my life studying that, and I know that it has given me the edge on numerous occasions. I don't roll the dice and hope things to go my way. I play to win, and design teaches me to study the systems and their interactions seriously.

S.S.: What are the worst traits a leader has exhibited in your experience?

B.B.: Disrespect and dishonesty. Once you lose either, you don't have enough time in a single project cycle to get them back.

For disrespect, it's pretty wide ranging, too. I have seen bad leaders who yelled at people (repeatedly and without reservation), didn't give them time to recoup with their families, trashed them to fellow workers thinking that they were somehow chumming someone up, and cut their work out of the project without at least giving a nod to how bad that might make someone feel. You don't have to put the level back, but at least you can acknowledge how it might make another person feel. Callousness is a classic hallmark of disrespect. You can also come in as the producer and play designer. That's lots of fun for designers. That said, I've worked with some producers who were seriously good designers, too. They just preferred production over design. We respected each other's work and enjoyed a great relationship.

Dishonesty doesn't need to be defined by anyone, I suppose, but something keeps coming to mind from my own experience. I recall working with a producer who told me well after a project had released that he knew something about it, but told the team something else. I never forgot that, and I would hesitate to work with him again on that basis. It was something that fundamentally affected the product, and the team should have known.

S.S.: How did these traits manifest themselves, and what was the result of their involvement in terms of the team, project, and/or company?

B.B.: Rather than looking at it individually, I take a more broad approach to it. You are literally one phone call away from everyone else in this industry. One. And we're tight knit as hell, too. So, people remember things, and they make phone calls when they're looking to hire. I know people who will struggle to get back into the industry, and others who can be dropped from their job today and get 20 offers tomorrow. The end result for their careers—good and bad—is the lasting thing.

I have worked with and worked beside people who struggled in a leadership role. I think very few people set out to be tragic leaders. They find themselves in over their heads, and they don't know how to handle it. With fear comes a lot of bad traits—dishonesty, anger, you name it. The stress only causes them to act worse. At that point, management needs to do something, or the other leads do.

The members of the team start to feel powerless, and then they don't even care, really. Only once have I seen what could be called a coup. A whole art team walked out. Things changed after that, but not a whole lot. I've also seen a revolt in which two EPs ousted the senior VP on the project. Not pretty, but I learned a lot during that process. I don't want that to be me.

S.S.: Are there any leadership traits you admire or perhaps aspire toward but don't feel you embody?

B.B.: Every day. This is a creative industry, and not a day goes by that I don't see someone doing something better than I do it—if I can even do it at all. So, I learn. The longer I am in this industry, the less I feel that I know, or the more I feel that I need to learn. I am a voracious reader, and I consume a lot of art stuff. I go to museums, architectural history lectures, and I watch documentaries on topics that are seemingly unrelated to what I do. I take a look at a guy like Sid Meier who has a pile of partly unboxed awards outside his door, and whose quiet humility and amazing design abilities consistently humble me. The best I *can* do is to learn and to practice what I learn a lot. I look for great people, and then I study them to find out what makes them great. So, to your original question, it's not so much a question of whether or not I have a trait, but how I view my skills in comparison to someone else I admire. It's a dynamic thing.

S.S.: How do you feel they would make you a better leader? Do you consciously try to develop them?

B.B.: I am always growing as a designer, a professor, the chair of the department and as an artist in general, and yes, I do consciously and openly work on my professional development. I regularly solicit feedback from those who work with me, and encourage them to let me know when something's not working for them. That's another thing, too. As a leader, you need to be good at receiving feedback. If you get defensive or start correcting people when they're pointing out something you could do better, you have just shut down many, many future opportunities to grow as a person. I've been in situations where I heard things that didn't particularly feel great to hear, but the comments were totally valid, and I'm a better person today because of it.

Being a lead is very much like being in a turn-based strategy game or a simulation, depending on your level of competitiveness. There are basic resources all of your people need, and then there are things that will make them even happier to be on your side.

S.S.: Do you mentor other leaders?

B.B.: Yes, all the time, and they return the favor. The game industry is such a small place that when one of us goes from one role to another, it's not uncommon to get e-mails asking questions about our past experience. Also, as a professor, I have a very direct role in mentoring leaders. Many of my students are going out there into roles as leaders or in positions that will eventually make them leaders. I am still in very active contact with many of them, and they know that door is always open.

S.S.: Do you have any training in leadership either formal or unstructured (e.g., armed forces experience)?

B.B.: No. I just started working at an early age, I guess. I was a DM for several years, but I don't know that that counts. I did once go to a management workshop organized by my employer. I don't think that I've ever felt like "This wasn't for me or the game industry" as much as I did that day. I do attend a lot of conferences, though, and network with others. Every little story helps.

S.S.: What do you see as the toughest challenge facing leads during a game-development project cycle or at a game-development company generally?

B.B.: Hmm. I think we create our own challenges. I've spent a good bit of time recently thinking about how I could have done better in past projects, even the award-winning ones. In so many cases, we're focused on *finishing* the game, and really, that's the player's job. Our job is to make a good game, and I am convinced now that this can happen in under most any circumstances, even tight schedules. Some things will clearly have to go, but games can be made within a set of minimum constraints, and we need to truly fit ourselves within those constraints.

I think many leads also lack perspective. I know I certainly have at times. When you're literally rushing from one project to the next and putting out fire after fire, do you have time to stop and think about what happened, what you could have done better? Do you have time to read some of the really excellent books out there like *Theory of Fun*? Do you play games beyond the digital realm? Are you exploring what's happening in the indie space? Learning about your field on a real atomic level makes you so much more adept an artist (and in this, I include programmers, who are certainly artists in their own medium). Are you trying to make a good game or finish a game?

The greatest natural threat to a lead designer (other than programmers) is what I call "lead's blindness." It develops as a result of lost perspective, and because your game is in your face all day, you start to think that things that aren't okay are okay just because you're so used to seeing them. Maybe nobody is playing the game because they're working on it, right? Or maybe it's because something is wrong with the game, and you need to fix it.

S.S.: How have you seen this handled most and least effectively?

B.B.: I love the way they do it at Google. Give people time and freedom to be creative on the schedule. Let them come up with stuff and explore neat ideas. Facilitate that on company time. You never know what kinds of stuff you might come up with.

The least effective way to handle these things is to ignore them; then you don't get very good games. Each member on the team has a responsibility to raise red flags and red mountains if necessary. I know that we work in a game "industry" and not a game "art movement," and that our goal is to get the product out and make money. At the same time, we trust other members on the team to truly work together toward this collaborative artistic thing we're making. A relationship with other leads is one of respect, and that means making our collaborative project as good as it can be.

S.S.: What are some common mistakes you've seen leads make, be they new or experienced?

B.B.: Never assume that everything is under control. It's not. If you think it is, you're not looking hard enough.

Experienced leads deliberately seek out critique because they know that it (whatever it is) could be done better. Inexperienced leads are happy when it's finished.

S.S.: Do you think good leaders can be trained? Or is the essence of a good leader simply innate ability?

B.B.: Honestly? I want to answer one thing, but I really believe the other. I think it's innate, and then you can train it. I don't believe everyone can be made to do stand-up comedy. I don't think everyone can perform. Likewise, not everyone can lead. However, if you have those key ingredients, whatever they may be, people will want to work with you, and you will enjoy working with them. I love that kind of environment.

Note

To kill the Wizard on Level 10, you take the elevator to the fourth floor. Go down the hall, through the door, and turn to your right. Go to the end of the hall and take the door on your right. After getting through the combat, there's a door at the far end of the room that contains the Blue Ribbon. This will give you access to the elevator that takes you to the ninth level. Take that. When you walk out, turn to your left and go through the door there. In the far corner of the room, there is a teleporter that takes you to the 10th level of the dungeon. Once there, there is a series of seven hallways, each connected to a room. In each room, you will find a teleporter that takes you to the next hallway in the series. At the end of the seventh, you will find Werdna the Wizard. You kill him through persistence. Having a couple Madi spells and a few Tiltowaits doesn't hurt.

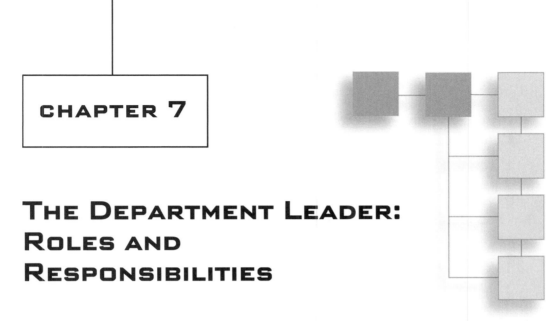

CHAPTER 7

THE DEPARTMENT LEADER: ROLES AND RESPONSIBILITIES

This book discusses the department director position as it applies to a multi-project development studio in which the director is associated with no specific project. Of course, many single-project studios have a separate director-level position above the art lead; in such instances, the job description for both the lead and the director may be very different. For example, I am familiar with large single-project studios that employ both a lead artist and an art director. In one case, the art director is responsible for artistic direction and communication with the executive level, while the lead artist is responsible for task tracking, daily team communication, and technical reviews.

Again, as with any role, it is important to establish a job description, and to define the areas of responsibility and limits of authority. As with any leadership role, this is the easy part. Knowing what to do when and having the self-discipline to avoid getting distracted or committing to tasks that are not core to the lead responsibilities comes with experience.

Directors of all disciplines are expected to set cross-project standards. They are the champions of their disciplines to the rest of the company, and are evangelists for the studio to the rest of the industry. Directors as much as leads model the behavior and attitude they expect from every studio employee.

The specific responsibilities of the director role vary from studio to studio. Presented here is a list that was compiled by the attendees of the 2006 Art

Director/Lead Artist Round Table at GDC when asked to list the responsibilities of a great art director. The list was edited to be inclusive of all director disciplines:

- Is responsible for creating the culture within the department across all projects—and hence, with the other directors—across the whole company

- Is responsible for reviewing all artwork, code, or feature functionality before milestone

- Is responsible for investigating (not necessarily personally) tools and applications for use in any or all project teams

- Is responsible for mentoring new leads

- Is responsible for career guidance for all department members

Arguably, the traits of a great director are similar to those of a great lead:

- Is comfortable pushing expectations for quality

- Delegates effectively

- Is a self-starter

- Is a problem solver (i.e., is solution driven)

- Maintains a holistic view of the studio and resource availability

- Is patient

- Communicates a vision and is decisive

- Is organized

You'll notice many words in this list—responsible, patient, decisive, mentor, delegates—feature prominently in, and were in fact lifted for, the "Build Your Ideal Lead" exercise in Chapter 4, "A Litmus Test for Leads."

Note

Although this list of ideal traits was generated by a room of all art people, few of the traits have anything to do with art. In fact, with a simple word-replace, you could probably build a decent programming lead list from what you see here.

Presented here is a sample job description for a department director position.

The Department Director

Following is a sample list of roles, responsibilities, and qualifications for this position.

Role

Provide leadership and management for a department composed of employees of a given discipline.

Responsibilities

- Responsible for departmental direction, leadership, and management.

- Responsible for resource allocation and departmental budgets.

- Reports to the studio head or senior executive and is responsible for daily management of any personnel not reporting to a lead within a project organizational structure.

- Supports the leads in establishing overall project vision; approves processes, assets, and features; and ensures that all project resource needs are appropriate and realized.

- Manages all performance reviews, hiring, firing, and personnel-management tasks above what the leads are responsible for.

- Coordinates and supports departmental training.

- Leads recruitment efforts and may give presentations to the department, company, or external groups regarding the direction of the department, project, or studio.

- Responsible for building and maintaining positive studio morale.

Qualifications

- Displays great communication, presentation, and leadership skills.

- Demonstrates compelling vision and passion for the discipline and projects that he or she represents, as well as for the studio.

- Is considered a problem solver and self-starter.

- Always pushes the quality bar.

- Displays consistent, professional demeanor at all times.

- Reacts well under stressful situations.

- Is an active and positive force for company morale.

Director Responsibilities

The preceding descriptions are useful summaries of director responsibilities, but more thought needs to go into the specific points in order to ensure that new directors in particular have a more detailed foundation.

Responsible for Departmental Direction, Leadership, and Management

The department director is responsible for the performance of employees in their discipline across all teams. The department director presents and champions a vision for how the department functions within the larger company and how members of the department function on each project team. This role description encompasses many specific duties, detailed in the following sections.

Responsible for Resource Allocation and Departmental Budgets

The department director is typically tasked by the studio head, COO, or CFO to develop operating budgets for the department and for individual projects. For new directors, this can be a challenging task, and failing to do this properly can lead to severe issues during the course of development. Important things to remember include the following:

- Outsourcer costs and estimated need. It's easiest to measure this in man-months, but difficult to predict the exact need at the start of development.

- Additional internal personnel and their associated infrastructure needs (software licenses, desks, computers, etc.).

- Middleware costs and contracts.

- Internal personnel assignments. These can and frequently do change during development.

It seems the safest course to over-budget in an initial plan; it is the rare project that actually turns out to be cheaper than originally thought. It's better to have and not need, than to need and not have. I've never in my career had to explain why a project came in *under* budget, but I have experienced—several times—the unfettered joy of having to ask my boss for more money or more personnel in the middle of a development cycle long after my budget has been requested and approved because of an oversight on my part.

While in general, it's wise policy to request a bit more than you think you will need, there are some caveats. If, in the course of reviewing your budget, the publisher or senior manager whittles down what are regarded as overly generous resource requests, that person will thereafter be wary of future resource requests, always be looking for the fat that you've added. On the other hand, if your padded resource request is approved, it is probably not what's best for the profitability of the project.

The safest and most accurate way to budget for a project is to make your estimates as fact-based as possible. You can do this best by looking at past projects for guidance. Even if the past projects were not on the same scale, using them as starting points is a better bet than simply going to the leads and asking how many people and how much money they imagine they might need.

Project leads are generally not given the task of considering project profitability in their resource requests. The department directors sit outside the individual project structures, which allows them to act with impartiality regarding company-wide resource planning. This also creates a natural state of tension between leads and directors. Leads will and should push for every resource that they feel is required to make the very best end product. Directors, however, need to consider overall project costs and also long-term staffing plans. Will there be enough work in the company to retain the personnel requested for one project team? If not, perhaps other means should be considered, such as reducing scope, extending the development cycle, or hiring contractors or outsource partners. The latter two solutions, while solving the important staffing dilemma, do raise the overall budget for the project, and that is of course a factor that senior executives or the publishing partner will be required to approve. Directors do not need to be aware of the complete financial picture in this model, but they should be given targets that allow them to plan for the entire project.

In short, to make project budgeting and allocations go smoothly, the needs of all roles must be understood and respected by all parties, including senior executives, directors, and leads.

Reports to the Studio Head or Senior Executive and Is Responsible for Daily Management of Any Personnel Not Reporting to a Lead Within a Project Organizational Structure

Directors report on the status of and future planning for their department to a senior executive or the studio head. They also receive direct reports from leads and directly manage those in their department who do not fall into an individual project. Examples in an art department might include an art outsource manager, assistant art director, or technical artist; in a tech department, such roles might include a tools lead or perhaps the IT manager.

Supports the Leads in Establishing Overall Project Vision; Approves Processes, Assets, and Features; and Ensures That All Project Resource Needs Are Appropriate and Realized

Note

This requirement is entirely for directors in multi-project studios; directors in single-project companies probably double as the lead for their discipline.

Directors must meet regularly with their leads. It is best practice to have some type of daily informal interaction and one formal meeting per week to review progress, give feedback, and discover any resource needs or personnel issues.

I make an effort not to critique assets for any non-direct reports, as such behavior creates inconsistent feedback loops and other communication problems. It is important, however, that directors review all work with their leads as often as appropriate for the project. I've found that weekly meetings work best for regularly scheduled reviews, but it is important that directors call for ad-hoc review meetings with leads whenever they see anything questionable going on within the project team. In most cases, the issue is only one of clarification, but the director, having an outside view of the project, can often spot issues such as the over-working assets or features, or the exclusion of some consideration.

The weekly meeting also offers an opportunity for leads to request any additional project resources. One of the director's jobs is to ensure that project resources are met and adequate to the task. As noted previously, some leads will over-request project resources (usually personnel) out of uncertainty about new features or incomplete design-scope specifics. These are difficult questions, and they continue on a project long after the initial budget is established. Directors need to ensure that emergent resource requests are justified. In most cases, this will require more planning work from the leads group to clarify the actual need. Once that is done, a meeting with the leads should be held to evaluate all possible avenues. Is a new hire the answer? Outsourcers? Middleware? Is additional time necessary? It's still not an enviable task to have to request more of whatever to get your project done, but the situation will go more smoothly if you have an answer for all of these scenarios before going to senior executives or your publisher with new requests.

Manages All Performance Reviews, Hiring, Firing, and Personnel-Management Tasks Above What the Leads Are Responsible For

Directors typically handle all personnel issues above the "front-line" management that leads and specialist leads perform. These duties include personnel reviews, career management, hiring, firing, and disciplinary action. All these involve coordinating closely with the Human Resources department, as they sometimes have very complex legal implications.

Performance Reviews

Directors typically handle performance-review tasks for their department, although in some larger studios, that task is given to project leads. Regardless of whether you are reviewing direct or indirect reports, it is important to gather feedback for the review from the subject's peers, subordinates, and other supervisors as appropriate. This will help build a more complete picture of the performance over the year and will provide a more objective overview.

Performance reviews, whether held annually, quarterly, or somewhere in between, offer the director and employees the opportunity to formally discuss and record a few very important subjects. The most obvious is the quality of work performance and level of contribution to the team. This recording of your assessment should never come as a surprise for the individual being reviewed. A great performer should probably know you think they are great by your and the lead's praise over their time on the project. If someone is surprised by your high opinion, that's a clue that you as a director should be more visible to the teams and more vocal with praise. Likewise, a poor performer should be aware of the director's perception through timely feedback during the production cycle, with inadequacies noted and addressed on the spot.

Another factor of performance reviews should be a discussion of long-term career-development goals. Many times, department members will seek out meetings with their managers during the year to discuss their career, but the review allows a formal time for this to be discussed. Discussions about career direction are vital to the retention of key employees. Most people in the course of their careers will want to explore some other branch related to what they do to expand their skill set or simply get out of a creative rut. If career development is never discussed formally, there is the possibility that these valuable employees will look elsewhere to make a change.

Note

I find it a good practice to separate the origin of the content of the review based on the message. If as a director you give reviews to indirect reports—that is, personnel who report to a lead or specialist lead on a project team—you may find it useful to present praise coming from you and the lead, and improvement recommendations or negative feedback as coming predominantly from you. This presents the review subject with a unified front among management in the event they feel compelled to dispute the review conclusions.

Hiring

Any director-level person with some experience has been through a hiring cycle and probably has a process that he or she employs to good effect. My process, loosely illustrated below, has evolved over the years due to suggestions from other leads and directors from around the industry. The subject of hiring was debated at the 2004 GDC Round Table, and the attendees and I learned that however bad we thought our hiring environments were, there simply didn't seem to be any happy scenarios anywhere. East-coast or mid-west developers felt they had a hard time recruiting top talent from the west coast, and west-coast developers were feeling intense competition from each other, which was causing job-hopping and inflating salaries in competitive market areas like Los Angeles and the Bay Area.

My own experience has been one of drought or flood, and each condition needs its own approach. But there are some common best practices:

- Always answer every applicant in a timely fashion.

- Make sure that viable candidates are vetted by key team members before proceeding to an interview. I send even marginal candidates out to my hiring group for review.

- Have your positions approved in advance through your corporate office, if applicable, before of the start of your search. A great candidate may come along on the first day, and great people don't last long in the market.

- Institute an art or coding test and administer it to candidates whose portfolio or experience leaves questions for your hiring group.

- If posting an ad for a U.S. studio, include a line reading, "Applicants must have U.S. current work authorization"—unless your studio has the time and money to devote to the lengthy H1-B process.

- If you reject a candidate after a phone interview, let him or her know by phone as well (as opposed to e-mail).

- Keep all candidates organized by ranking for future referral.

Hiring at large, well-known, and successful studios is not a job that can be done by the director alone. Many larger studios employ hiring managers as part of their HR department, either full time or on a contract basis, to assist with hiring administration and/or perform active recruiting work. Hiring managers may possibly be trained to evaluate programming skills from a candidate's resume or review portfolios to weed out unqualified candidates. The ratio of unqualified to qualified applicants for a given position varies with the type of position and the manner in which the search is advertised. In my experience, the typical Gamasutra ad route will yield about a ten-to-one ratio. The ratio gets worse if a wider net is cast. I recommend targeting position advertising as accurately as possible if not employing a recruiter to get the best candidate-viability ratios.

I divide the hiring process into three steps. After a candidate's information and portfolio have been sent to the hiring group and received a positive response, I start with a phone interview, then move to a personal interview at the studio, and finally convene the hiring group to discuss the candidate. The hiring group is composed of individuals on the team whom the director deems appropriate given the candidate and position in question. I personally keep the group to a manageable size of between five and seven. Lunch invitations are sent out to any additional people who I want to have an opportunity to meet and talk with a candidate.

Phone Interviews   You should begin phone interviews by giving the candidate an outline of the call and the position you are seeking to fill, and telling the candidate what it was about his or her work, skill set, or experience that interests you. I describe the duties of the position, and during the phone interview, try to get a sense of how the person communicates by asking one process question—i.e., how the candidate went about a certain task from his or her experience. Before going too deep into the call, also get an idea of what compensation the candidate is seeking. There are very few elegant ways to end what was a terrific hour-long phone interview with your dream candidate when you find out that the person on the other end of the phone wants double what you can afford.

Interviews   Assume that interviews will occupy the bulk of a day, as a potential employee meets the hiring group either individually or in pairs to save time. I begin interviews with a quick tour around the studio, and then give the candidate an outline of what he or she will be doing for the day. During the course of the "interview loop," I check in occasionally to make sure that the group is keeping to the schedule as well as to get feedback from those who have completed the session with the interviewee.

Keep in mind—and make clear to your hiring group—that the candidate is also interviewing the studio and its people. Does the studio look professional? Are the people generally relaxed and happy? Are the questions being asked appropriate? As an example, my wife was once asked in an interview, "How do you get along with difficult people?" What that question said to her was the place had more than one "difficult" person, and they weren't likely to be leaving.

Here are a few other things to look for in the interview:

- **How the person communicates a concept or approaches solving problems.** I usually ask a question like, "Describe a situation or task you were faced with where you didn't know how to proceed at first. What did you do? What was the outcome?" The answers I look for begin with language like, "I work with colleagues or locate experts who have done similar work in the past" or "I start with research." This question, and others like it, reveals the individual's ability to effectively communicate a process or state of condition. Answers that ramble into tangents or, conversely, are too brief and require follow-up questions to elicit important details indicate that the candidate may have difficulties communicating in a team environment. Another answer that reveals a potential problem might be, "Well, I've never been confronted with a situation that I couldn't work through." Honestly, though, it's hard to botch this question.

- **The person's true level of experience.** I've interviewed many people in the industry with very impressive resumes who have turned out to not have the practical skills that one would expect. The process of discovering true competence is not easy; given the increasing levels of skill specialization in the industry, the chance of a hiring manager having the knowledge to accurately assess all candidates in a given department is very low. This is where the hiring group becomes important. The chances that a group of specialists in the same field as the applicant will be able to accurately assess skill level are far higher. In this scenario, process questions can reveal a lot about how an individual works through a task, and also compels the interviewee to construct a narrative. The questions here are fairly basic, such as "Describe your modeling process on this piece in your portfolio. How did you approach this, from start to finish?" Beyond that, using an art or coding test can be the final measure of a candidate's real skill level. I recommend developing a standardized test for every discipline so that applicants can be comparatively evaluated.

- **The person's ability to react professionally to feedback.** This is a critical piece of information. One strategy I like to use in cases when this trait may be in question involves asking the candidate if there has ever been a time when he or she initially resisted feedback, but discovered that ultimately, implementing the suggested changes made the end result better in some way.

- **Whether the person has an interest in just any job or in the job I'm offering.** A couple questions can pull that out: "Why this company?" is a short one that most interviewees field well. Others include "Describe your ideal professional setting. What work are you doing? What kind of projects are you working on?" If you are concerned about this issue, ask this one early, before the interviewee has had time to polish his or her presentation. Good answers to these questions tell me that the candidate knows my studio's products and is interested in the specific position I have open. A notable fumble from my direct experience includes a junior modeling candidate telling me, "I see myself animating in a couple of years—or maybe concepting."

One manager colleague of mine likes starting with open-ended questions such as "What gets you excited, professionally speaking?" More specific probing questions can then be asked, depending on the interviewee's answer. Other open-ended questions directly address game-industry knowledge. For example, you might ask an artist, "What games have you played that most appealed to you visually and what aspects of them specifically drew you to them?" A question such as this can lead to a number of interesting tangential questions, again depending on the interviewee's answer. These sorts of questions are also very valuable to draw out the personality of a nervous interviewee or someone who simply isn't accustomed to as much verbal interaction as you expect in an interview.

At the end of the interview, the hiring manager should meet one-on-one with the interviewee and field any questions he or she might have. This can reveal a lot about how much the candidate has prepared for his or her visit, as well as the extent to which the candidate has been paying attention during the interview. Also, it is important to give the candidate as clear a picture as possible of what the next steps in the hiring process will be should things move forward, including a timeline.

Interview ''Don'ts''

Asking questions in an interview regarding ethnicity, marital status, religious practices, and certain other issues is considered discriminatory and can result in serious legal proceedings. If not in place already, have your HR department draft interview guidelines for the entire hiring group detailing in particular what is discriminatory and therefore illegal to bring up in an interview.

In addition to the legal no-no's, interviewers should not bad-mouth individuals or other departments within their company or the company in general. As odd as it may sound, this really happens. Sometimes it's an innocent slip or ill-considered remark prompted by a savvy interviewee question like, "What's the thing you like least about working here?" I get this one rarely, but it's a great opportunity to direct the focus to how your company solves problems rather than what the problems are. For instance, a bad answer would be, "Well, communication between art and programming is really bad sometimes." A better answer goes, "We had problems with intradepartmental communication on our last dev cycle, which came up in postmortem feedback. We're addressing that this time around by having weekly leads meetings to make sure that each discipline is staying on the same page." And of course, always sincerely highlight the positives of your studio.

Along the same lines, don't speak ill of any competitor's studio in an interview, either. You never know who has friends where, and that sort of information gets passed around quickly.

Always end interviews personally and ask if the candidate has any questions either about the position or the hiring process, or that were triggered by the earlier interviews. Give the candidate an idea of what the next steps in the process are, and give as accurate a timeline as possible for your next communication.

The Wrap-up   After the interview, assemble the hiring group to discuss the candidate. Negative perceptions of one person in the hiring group should not immediately doom a candidate (unless that person unearthed something terrifying in his or her session), but a general unease in the group should result in a "no-hire" decision.

This exercise can be very useful for simply spreading around information and insights to the other members of the hiring group. On occasion, the group will come to the conclusion, through discussion, that the candidate is solid but the role is wrong, and recommend him or her for another position.

The decision to hire is an extremely significant one, since dealing with problem employees is such a drain on you as a manager as well as your team and company. To that point, a GDC attendee added his own hiring philosophy: "If you or your team has any questions about a candidate, it's far better to not hire someone who might be a good employee than hire someone who turns out to be a bad one."

Reference Checks   There is a great deal of debate concerning the usefulness of reference checks, although candidate-supplied references are valuable in cases of experienced personnel.

Disciplinary Action and Firing

Directors have the responsibility of taking disciplinary action when necessary, up to and including termination of employment for those in their department. Again, this is an area where it is a good idea to coordinate closely with the HR department to ensure that you and your company are not vulnerable to unfair-termination suits or other discrimination violations that may spring from the actions of the disciplinary process. Also, employment law varies from state to state in the U.S., and it's just as complex in the European Union. (Actually, it may be *less* complex, but I usually can't understand what they're saying, and I figure better safe than sorry.) Employees are in an "at-will" status in most states in the U.S. This means that an employee may be fired for any reason, including no reason at all. However, many states have amendments to this doctrine, and your HR manager will be thrilled to go into specific detail on the complexity and the current condition of the issue for your location.

Progressive Discipline   There are many reasons that an individual may not be performing well. Progressive discipline attempts to address poor performance in a way that seeks a positive resolution for the employee and at the same creates documentation of underperformance in case the specific situation should lead to more severe measures such as termination. This is a very detailed topic and will be discussed more fully in Chapter 8, "Difficult Employees, Underperformers, and Bad Leads."

In my experience, progressive discipline is effective in cases where the individual in question is talented, has a genuine desire to be a part of your team, but perhaps has found himself or herself in the wrong role, needs additional training, or simply needs to be made aware of an issue requiring correction, such as a drop in quality of work for no visible reason. As might be inferred, I find the concept of progressive discipline to be less effective in cases where the individual has an inherent lack of talent or skills that do not improve significantly with additional training.

One of the problems with progressive discipline is that it is invisible to the rest of the team, which sometimes will perceive that no action is being taken by management to deal with a performance situation. For this reason, it frequently appears to those not involved in the disciplinary process that the decision to end the employment of an individual occurs much later than it should. This is important to keep in mind for directors because a major cause of poor morale and a feeling of mistrust of management can stem from the team feeling like they are being weighed down by poor performers and their leaders are blind to the problem or choose not to act.

Termination   Hopefully, the individual in question will have some idea that termination is coming, but regardless, you should be prepared for a lot emotion. Be sympathetic, but do not waver from your message. Messages such as the following are effective: "We're sincerely sorry this situation didn't work out, but our decision is final."

Just as with other employee-related actions, it is important to coordinate the act of termination with the HR director. Your HR manager may or may not want to take over from the point that the message is given. In any case, the fired individual should be told to gather a few things and leave the building, and should return at a later time to clean out the rest of his or her work area. This gives the individual time to cool down and time for the director to inform the team and the company of the action taken. The action itself might be done in the morning or late afternoon, on a Monday or a Friday—arguments may be made for either day. Some say the company can make a cleaner break on a Friday, but others maintain that a Monday termination affords the employee the opportunity to immediately begin a new search rather than spending the weekend dwelling on the negative situation.

Termination of employment is the director's last resort for poorly performing employees. It is on the one hand important to try to avoid firing due to the expense involved in hiring someone new and the potential disruption of work on a team. It is equally important, however, to consider that termination of a poorly performing member may be the best answer for the team.

Resignation   We all strive for low or no turnover in our departments, but people do of course leave of their own accord for any number of reasons. I firmly believe that managers and executives need be as proactive as possible in retaining key personnel, but to be prepared for turnover. They shouldn't overreact to it and certainly shouldn't take departures personally. A caveat is that a large number of departures in a single department or team should cause managers and executives to honestly evaluate their own performance.

So how can a director best handle employees who resign? Some companies employ a blanket policy that you leave the day you give notice. They of course pay salary over the period of a two-week "notice," but they prefer that people who have chosen to leave not linger. I recommend this approach when employees are leaving under questionable terms or have been particularly unhappy in their role. At best, their continued presence may lower company morale due to what amounts to a protracted goodbye; at worst, they might maliciously cause damage.

On the other hand, I tend to be very respectful of employees who approach me with their resignation but state their desire to leave on good terms and to train others in their tasks to ensure a smooth transition, or who offer extended notice to enable them to take their current tasks to completion. In these cases, I think it's best to permit the individual to stay on—but at the same time ask that they treat their departure professionally and respect continuing production schedules.

Coordinates and Supports Departmental Training

Few industries change as rapidly and continuously as the game industry. Change occurs not just in scope and complexity but also in process and coding expertise. The skills that I had when I entered the game industry most likely would not have gotten me an interview less than five years later. It is the responsibility of directors to ensure that the skills and expertise of their departments remain current and relevant.

There are a few common components to departmental training:

- **Self-directed training.** This occurs spontaneously among staff who seek to improve their craft independently. Directors can and should support this by setting up a portion of their department budget for training resources such as books, DVDs, and downloadable training videos.

- **Individual mentoring.** One-on-one mentoring should be set up by leads or directors according to project needs. This can also be spontaneous and should be encouraged by directors as project needs permit.

- **Department-wide tutorial sessions.** These should be held when training in a specific skill or process is desired for the entire department or discipline group such as animation or modeling. I've found these sessions to be most valuable when combined with easily accessible training videos.

- **Professional training classes.** These are a valuable resource when you have no internal expertise in a given specialty skill or development practice. Implementation of a licensed engine, complex piece of middleware, or new content creation-software are situations that might call for professional training.

In all cases, training is most effective when supported by persistent and accessible training media.

Leads Recruitment Efforts and May Give Presentations to the Department, Company, or External Groups Regarding the Direction of the Department, Project, or Studio

Directors are responsible for initiating and supervising recruitment efforts in their company. They determine need, draft job postings, review submissions, coordinate interviews, and make the final decision to hire or not. Prior to the hiring of any one individual comes a great deal of work building connections and focusing on making their company a preferred employer in their area.

There are many ways to work toward becoming a preferred employer. For the game industry, the best way is to make hit games. If you put out blockbuster games, your studio could sit on a landfill and be filled with asylum escapees and still attract top talent (at least for a while). For the vast majority of studios out there that have not yet built their signature game, there are other avenues for making your company stand out:

- **Highlight your location advantages.** Austin, Texas and Raleigh, North Carolina are two examples of advantageous locations. They have very active cultural environments combined with a relatively low cost of living. Many studios in more expensive regions emphasize the cultural advantages of their cities.

- **Develop a good reputation.** Become known for having an enjoyable working environment, effective practices, a rational leadership team, and equally sane production schedules. This can be a big factor when considering issues like the amount of overtime involved in a job—something that almost every interviewee asks about. Like any reputation, this one takes time to build, but once built may become second nature to those within the company.

- **Offer a superior benefits package.** Obviously, this will raise your operating expenses, but in a competitive market, offering superior benefits will help you attract senior personnel. These workers are more likely to have families, and thus more swayed by a robust benefits package.

- **Focus on your unique gaming genre.** In an area filled with shooter developers, for example, a role-playing game developer will have an advantage luring local talent.

Every studio is different, and each one has some unique aspect that can be exploited as competitive advantages in the hiring market.

Responsible for Building and Maintaining Positive Studio Morale

In order to help foster positive morale and energy, directors need to work every day to maintain contact with the people in their departments—particularly those who are not direct reports. Daily contact is the single most important thing that directors can do to help everyone in the company feel connected. People feel positive about coming to work when they know they personally are doing great work, they feel that their team is doing great work, and personally know that their creative contributions are being noticed. Daily contact does not need to be a sit-down meeting; it can be as simple as a hello—just something to establish contact and let the other person know that you're present and available if needed. Additionally, as much as possible, directors' doors need to be open to everyone in the company. Directors should not be isolated spatially in the office floor plan, and should strive to make their demeanor and environment one of approachability and accessibility.

Note

I asked the non-director attendees at the 2007 GDC Round Table if they had any recommenda-tions for improvements in this area for directors. Although there was a noticeable reticence to say anything with directors from Sony, Blizzard, and EA present, one brave attendee did finally break the ice. The number-one concern was that many participants felt that their director was not accessible to them due to the busy meeting schedules they maintained and a general unap-proachable nature. One participant from a very well-known and successful studio added that his director rarely met with him outside of a formal review, which left him and his co-workers feeling isolated.

Director Qualifications

All the qualifications that make for a good lead also apply to the director. Without enumerating them in detail again, directors need to be highly organized, capable of being decisive and making objective decisions, and able to consider issues from multiple perspectives. Also important is experience. It is extremely helpful to have directors who have led many game-development teams and shipped successful products. Directors must also excel at effective communica-tion and conflict resolution, should possess strong interpersonal skills, and have the ability to delegate well.

Note

One of the questions asked in the Build Your Ideal Lead exercise directly spoke to the issue of experience. As noted, almost every group picked the director who had led more projects rather than one highly successful project.

I've Gathered You All Here Today...

Meetings are an essential component of game development, but they tend to be one of the most maligned elements due in large part to mismanagement. In the development cycle of a game built by a team of any size, questions must be posed, different development approaches considered and debated, decisions made, and information disseminated to the team. All of this requires meetings—and during the preproduction phase, lots of meetings. Team leaders must become proficient at leading these meetings in order to get the most out of them. Indeed, running efficient and effective meetings actually helps team morale.

Meetings are expensive simply in terms of the salaries of the attendees. If a lead hosts a team meeting that runs an hour, it could easily cost several hundred dollars in salaries. If the meeting is run properly, that's a bargain; but if the meeting is ineffective, not only is that money and time wasted, but team members will quickly come to disparage the concept of meetings and be more likely to be disengaged during them—meaning, ultimately, that team leaders will have an increasingly difficult time achieving effective results.

Here's a quick list of why meetings fail:

- The meeting starts late.

- Too many non-essential participants or key participants are missing.

- The agenda or purpose of the meeting is not clear or perceived as unimportant.

- There is no clear meeting leader.

- The main focus of the meeting goes off-track, pursuing unrelated tangential issues.

- Only a few attendees participate vocally.

- The meeting runs long.

- No written record of the meeting is preserved or circulated to participants and stakeholders.

Knowing these points of failure, team and department leaders can easily put procedures in place to address them. It is important to remember that, like any communication situation, all parties share responsibility for successful and efficient meeting management. Anyone in a meeting should feel empowered to ask for an agenda, call out tangential topics, or call on less-vocal attendees to offer their thoughts. These actions are the primary responsibility of the meeting leader, but the meeting leader may not be focused on a specific problem in the meeting or, in fact, may be the cause of a tangential thread.

Start on Time

This sounds like the simplest thing in the world, but it's sometimes very difficult to do in practice. Team members may be away from their desk or distracted by a critical project or personnel issue, or may miss an automated reminder. When this happens, these people need to be tracked down and brought in—and in the meantime, a compelling debate about the merits of *Star Wars Episode II* versus *Episode III* will have eaten up ten minutes of your scheduled time.

The best way to avoid situations like this as a meeting leader is to arrive a few minutes early, call participants at the start of the meeting time (or even a minute prior), and end casual conversations to start on time. Late arrivals will still happen, but tardy employees will face the scrutiny of the other attendees; most likely, over time, better habits will emerge.

Have the Right Participants

Meeting attendees should be invited based on their necessity for input and/or decision-making authority. For example, suppose a project producer wants to evaluate whether to purchase a piece of engine middleware. As the meeting organizer, the producer might want to invite engineers who specialize in that area, as well as the technical director, who will ultimately make the decision.

Inviting additional participants should be based on whether they will contribute to the meeting. There will always be many more people *interested* in the outcome of a meeting than are appropriate to invite to *participate* in a meeting. Interested parties, as appropriate to their role, should have the meeting notes and decisions sent to them in a timely manner along with all the meeting participants.

Having a meeting that is overcrowded with non-participants will lead to a longer meeting than is necessary and result in more disengaged people around the table. By the same token, holding the same meeting without a key participant such as the tech director or a senior engineer from the team will probably result in the need for an additional gathering of the same group of people at a later time to accomplish the same goal. If key personnel are unavailable for a meeting, the meeting should usually be postponed.

Have a Written Agenda

The meeting agenda should be sent along with the meeting request to all participants. The meeting leader (at least) should always have a written agenda at the meeting. Agendas sent in advance help attendees be better prepared to discuss the subject and also help keep the meeting in focus. Meetings should be limited to addressing issues that are critical and capable of being addressed by the participants in a reasonable amount of time. Having a meeting with too many points can lead to an exhausting affair that will degrade participants' attention spans and judgments. Holding too many brief meetings with swift resolutions is simply an inefficient use of your staff's time.

Note

When visiting a large west-coast developer in the late 1990s, I observed a meeting-management initiative in progress. My small group was visiting the studio as a subcontracting company, and we were about to get a project briefing from the producer. He ushered us into a conference room and was about to begin our meeting when the studio president poked his head in the room and said he wanted to introduce himself and sit in on the meeting. Introductions were made and we sat down again, ready to proceed, when the studio president asked if he could have a copy of the agenda. The producer paused, and began to say something about this just being a quick project overview, but he didn't get to finish his sentence; the studio president abruptly got up and walked out of the room without saying a word. Obviously, this studio had some significant issues to work through around meetings, but this particular message was clear—no written agenda, no meeting.

Identify a Meeting Leader

The meeting leader is typically—but not always—the organizer of the meeting. In the preceding example, the meeting organizer might name the tech director as the meeting leader or perhaps even the tech lead for the project in question. Regardless, the meeting leader is responsible for organizing the discussion, keeping the group involved, and maintaining the agenda and duration of the meeting. The meeting leader is also responsible for bringing the meeting to a close, recapping decisions, identifying any actions called for, and clarifying the individuals responsible for them. It remains true, however, that all meeting participants are responsible for supporting the leader in all of the above responsibilities. Failure to identify a meeting leader or having a meeting leader who does not understand and effectively perform his or her role practically guarantees that the meeting will lack focus and probably end with few concrete and well-understood decisions.

Stay on Topic

Meeting discussions should remain focused on the agenda topics. Game development is a creative undertaking from start to finish, and that creativity brings with it a degree of organizational chaos. It is very common to have all sorts of meetings generate very significant but tangential or even totally unrelated issues in the course of discussions around the topics on the written agenda. These should not be completely brushed aside; rather, the meeting leader should acknowledge important issues, enter them into the meeting notes, and indicate that they require further discussion at a later time.

This is important for a few reasons: First, the mix of people at this particular meeting may not be the one needed to properly address the tangent. Second, research tasks may need to be completed before addressing the new topic. Finally, tangential discussions drag a meeting out. Often, only a subset of the meeting participants is engaged in the tangent, with the other participants swiftly becoming bored and disengaged by the proceedings.

Many times, the meeting leader is responsible for wandering from the agenda. I've seen many meetings stray far a field on account of the meeting leader getting bogged down by a departure from the agenda. Again, these are usually important and even critical topics, but anyone at the table should be able to say, "Hey, that subject is really important, but we'll need another meeting to properly address that." And as much as everyone chafes at a meeting that generates another meeting—or two—they will appreciate not having to be immediately involved in a long tangent.

Meeting Participation

One of the roles of the meeting leader—and, in fact, all participants—is to ensure that all attendees have a voice at the table. Everyone at a meeting table is there for a reason and needs to be represented, but people have different degrees of comfort speaking in meetings. Some may have a valid opinion and feel very strongly about it but be very shy speaking in public, while others may have profoundly idiotic opinions and won't shut up.

It is the job of the meeting leader to call on the quieter members of the group to extract their thoughts. Usually, it takes very little effort to say, "Henry, you've been pretty quiet, what are some networking issues that might come about if we adopt this middleware?" Note that the question is phrased to avoid a one word response.

Another participation-management task, which some find more difficult, is limiting a particularly outgoing and opinionated participant or group of participants. These people have a tendency to dominate in a group situation, offering their opinions on every topic and leaving little room or time for other voices. If there are two or three of them, they may hijack a meeting entirely. The meeting leader may try a subtle approach, such as summarizing the point of the over-talker and moving on. For example, the meeting leader might say something along the lines of, "Bob, in short, you point out that we need to be careful about over-committing to an unproven approach. I hear you, and we'll definitely monitor that as we move forward. Now, Jennifer, you mentioned . . . ." Essentially, you, as the meeting leader, are redirecting the conversation flow and reasserting your authority; from this point, you can move the meeting forward or involve other people in the issue. Sometimes, though, a more blunt approach is needed, such as "Bob, I understand you're concerns but I'd like to hear Jennifer's thoughts now."

End the Meeting on Time

Meeting leaders are responsible for ending meetings on time. By keeping discussions focused, meetings can usually close on time or early, but there are cases where, despite following best practices, the meeting topic proves to be more complex than can be accounted for in the meeting time originally set. The temptation to stay until the goal of the meeting is accomplished is very strong because no one wants to reconvene to discuss the same issue or issues, but there are good reasons to do just that. In most cases, meeting participants have busy days—sometimes with other meetings beginning as their current one is ending. Meetings that run long can cause delays and reshuffles elsewhere. However, more importantly, the attention span of the attendees will begin to wane after 60 to 90 minutes. When that happens, overall participation goes down and digressions become more common.

Take Notes

Every meeting should have a designated note-taker. If possible, the note-taker should not be the meeting leader, since the act of taking notes will stretch the meeting out or the act of leading the meeting will result in a poorer recording of the meeting. Entire discussions do not need to be preserved, of course, but notes should include the following:

- Any decisions made regarding agenda items and key points around the decision if appropriate

- Action items or assignments and the individual responsible for them

- Announcements that should be circulated to the team

Failure to do this will lead to a situation I personally experienced on a project, where all the leads and senior contributors were gathered in a meeting room to address a critical issue that had emerged halfway through production. This is not an unusual situation in itself; because game development is such an iterative process, change in the production process is inevitable. In this case, though, after working through the issue for an hour or so, one of the participants remembered that we had in fact discussed this same issue for about the same amount of time and had come to the same conclusion months ago—but nobody recorded it.

After this annoying experience, we instituted a policy of having a note-taker for every meeting who was also responsible for sending the notes out to relevant parties. We also decided to place laptops for note-taking in all conference rooms. This alleviated the need for the note-taker to have to type handwritten notes after the meeting. Some people initially found it distracting to have a person at the meeting table typing away, but it swiftly became just part of the meeting environment. Most importantly, it helped ensure that even ad-hoc meeting participants were reminded to record their sessions.

All That Being Said...

It's the game industry. People are going to behave insanely, crack jokes, draw funny pictures on the white board, make tangential comments, and generally try to have fun in an environment designed explicitly to not be enjoyable. All that can still happen—and should, to a degree, in order for your company to maintain its creative energy. Successful meetings can still be had without running them like a military operation.

Presentations

Directors as well as leads often are given the opportunity to make presentations. Good presentation and public-speaking skills are very important for any number of situations including pitching project concepts, recruiting, speaking at conferences and schools, and of course, effectively speaking to your own department or team. Successful presentations depend equally on the content of the message and the ability of the speaker to deliver that message. Entire books have been written on making presentations, and this one cannot hope to cover this topic in any great detail, but it is important that leaders be aware of some key points.

Content

The content piece is fairly straightforward. The content of your presentation must

- Have a theme and purpose that is relevant to your audience.

- Present new information.

- Maintain focus on the theme of the talk.

- Draw meaningful and compelling conclusions from the information.

I use the word "fairly" because, while this is straightforward, it isn't easy. Presentations should speak to the level of the audience. A presentation on the history of the games industry, why it's great, and the skills needed to enter it works well for high school–level and even college-level students, but a presentation to a GDC audience obviously needs to have a more detailed focus and different purpose.

There is little point to a presentation that does not present new information, yet I've sat through my fair share of rehashed material organized in a slightly different order to draw the same rehashed conclusions. I've also sat through many presentations that end on the last bullet of the last PowerPoint slide; instead, at the end of a presentation, the theme should be reiterated and the (hopefully) meaningful conclusion stated clearly.

Presenting

Presentation ability can be taught, but like many leadership traits, there is an innate component to it. Some people are simply more comfortable standing up in front of a group of people and speaking. The best presentations generally are those whose presenter

- Is well-rehearsed.

- Is confident in demeanor.

- Engages the audience.

- Illustrates points through personal or professional experience.

- Includes relevant and interesting visual aids.

The number-one way to improve your presentation is to rehearse your material. Do dry runs in front of a test audience of co-workers, and remember to rehearse your slides or other accompanying media as well. A startling percentage of GDC presentations suffer from a lack of preparation by the speakers, much of which is evident in the coordination with their media. To that point, on the day of an important presentation, it is wise to test the room and your presentation media.

N o t e

I did just that at the 2007 GDC for a presentation that contained similar organization charts to those found in Chapter 2, "The Anatomy of a Game-Development Company." I wanted to make sure my smallest text was legible from the back of the room. I picked an empty presentation room on the day of my talk and the test was a success. What I didn't do was test it in the *actual* room I was given for the talk. The screen in *my* presentation room was about half the size of others and was made out of what looked like a bed sheet.

A key to a successful presentation is expressing confidence in your words and demeanor and engaging the audience. Following are a few basic tips:

- Speak to the back of the room in a meeting setting. This is critical to keeping the attention of your audience who are seated farthest away from you. Most of us have probably been in meetings where the speaker is muffled or inaudible at the back of the room; you're bored out of your mind and can't wait to leave. You may need to raise your voice somewhat, but if you need to yell to do this, then you need a sound system in place. In larger settings, where you are amplified to the entire room or hall, you should still make a point to look at the people in the back rows.

- Remember when your mom used to yell at you to stand up straight? Do that. It makes you appear more confident and professional.

- Pay attention to the pace of your speech. Most people who are uncomfortable talking to groups will unconsciously speed up their speech. Slow down and also look for natural points in your talk to pause for a breath.

- Read from your notes as little as possible. After doing a few dry runs, you should have a few sections of your talk committed to memory. The more you can speak to your audience without reading from your notes, the better.

- Don't read your PowerPoint slides verbatim. Nothing will cause an audience to check for the exits more quickly. Your supporting visuals should be just that: supporting. You are the presenter, not your slides. PowerPoint is a tool. Like any tool—say, a nail gun—it can be used for good (i.e., to build a house) or for evil (i.e., to painfully blind someone).

- Enunciate. Speak clearly and at a consistent and audible volume. Be aware that most verbal behavior, such as inserting "umms" or "rights" or trailing off at the ends of sentences, may be inaudible to you. Ask your audience during dry runs if they notice any of these. Some are very hard to break, but it's at least helpful to know about them in advance.

■ Eye contact is a powerful method of keeping people's attention. Keep as much of the room involved with you as possible. You can't look at everyone in a large meeting hall, but you can divide the audience into sections and pick out a few people in each section to make eye contact with during your talk.

Becoming comfortable speaking in front of a group of people is a different ability entirely. There are public-speaking courses available through universities and community colleges, which can help—if only by providing the opportunity to practice.

Project Staffing Exercise: Selecting a Lead

In this exercise, you will select two art leads from four candidates for two games. As noted in several preceding chapters, we are often asked to select project leads swiftly from the pool of candidates who are local and immediately available or from a pool of candidates currently within the organization. This is a situation faced by all multi-project studio directors at some point and is actually a better situation than having few or no personnel interested in lead roles. While the following example is from an art perspective, the basic traits and leadership issues are very similar across all disciplines.

Developer: LotsaFun Games Inc.

LotsaFun Games is an independent developer that has been in business about seven years with three PC titles plus three expansion packs completed. Recently, they decided to move their core franchise, *Spears of Doom* (*SoD*), to next-gen consoles and to add a small Xbox Live Arcade team. Their second project, *Thunder of Doom* (*ToD*), is a smaller-scale title.

Project 1

■ *Spears of Doom III*

■ Genre: fantasy role playing

■ *SoD* platforms: Xbox 360 and PC simultaneous release and maybe a PS3 or Wii port down the road (the publisher hasn't decided yet)

- Engine technology: update of *Spears II* engine

- Dev cycle: 22 months

- Budgeted art staff: 17, plus outsourcers

Project 2

- *Thunder of Doom*

- Genre: arcade-style adventure

- *ToD* platforms: Xbox Live Arcade, PSP port (outsourced); maybe a full project after that

- Engine technology: New engine

- Dev cycle: 12 months

- Budgeted art staff: 7

Both projects go into preproduction simultaneously in two weeks, after the staff takes a break from the *SoD II* crunch.

Mission: Choose an Art Lead for Each Product

Art department lead candidates are as follows:

- **Jack:** Jack has been with LotsaFun since it was founded and has led three projects during his tenure. He is a very capable project planner, but not the most skilled artist on staff, and his production skills are not as current as many others'. He is a quiet and reserved guy who is well respected by most of the staff. Some find him to be perhaps too relaxed and averse to confrontation or giving negative critiques. He is aware of this perception and has expressed a desire to improve in this area.

- **Wes:** Wes is one of the most experienced and skilled artists on staff. He led a very successful large art team previously (*Spears of Destiny II*, which was reviewed very highly), but has expressed reservations about doing so again due to the amount of overtime he experienced on *SoD II*. He is well respected by everyone in the department but is perceived by some as abrasive to team members in his pursuit of quality game art.

- **Sue:** A very talented and experienced 3D modeler and very capable concept artist, Sue has no lead experience, but she is passionate about the franchise and would be a very enthusiastic leader on *SoD III*. She is very well liked and respected by everyone in the department and close friends with some in the department. In sub-lead roles, she has shown a tendency to take over art assets from underperformers and complete them herself.

- **Karl:** Your newest senior artist, Karl has great skills, has four years of experience as a lead at another company, and seems very well organized. References indicate that he was an excellent lead, albeit on smaller-scale projects. He is somewhat well respected by the department but has only been with your company for four months. He is performing well as an individual contributor but has repeatedly expressed a strong desire to be a lead again.

There are many more traits that become apparent over time, but for the purposes of this exercise, assume that you are a new director in this company and this is all the information you have to make a decision.

- Who do you select for the two lead spots and why?

- Who, outside of the lead candidates themselves, would you wish to be involved in this decision?

- What do you say to the two you did not choose?

- What roles do you recommend for them instead?

- Would you consider looking outside the company for either position?

- What sorts of performance issues should you keep an eye on with each lead during the course of development?

Additionally, as you get into fully staffing these projects, consider what sort of clarifying questions you need to ask about them from the following people:

- The president or studio manager

- The technical director

- The hiring manager

There are not necessarily any right answers to these questions. Like the Build Your Ideal Lead exercise, this one is best done in groups of three with presentations of decisions made by the sub-groups given to the larger group and discussed.

Time permitting, a second session may be conducted in which the moderator assigns a mid-production staffing crisis and each group must respond with its solution. For example:

- Karl turns out to be incapable of organizing such a large team. He wants to remain lead, though, or at least hold on to the title.

- Jack's confrontation-averse tendencies plague the project team. He remains committed to improving but does not see the problem as being as severe as it is.

- The company feels that Sue has appointed specialist leads based on their social relationship, or perhaps she is simply taking on too many production tasks herself.

- You convinced Wes to take the lead job, but halfway through production, he informs you that he hates his role and wants to go back to working as a senior contributor.

Many more complications are possible, and for those completing this exercise, a great deal of customization is encouraged.

Interview: Steve Meyer, Technical Director, Firaxis Games

Steve Meyer has been in the game business for over 25 years, starting as a programmer of coin-op games and moving from there to VP of product development for MicroProse in 1986. He has started several entertainment software companies and has filled positions such as VP of R&D, director of software development, president, and CEO. He has also been the president of one of the top toy-invention firms in the world, creating and licensing mass-market toy concepts to all of the major toy manufacturers.

Seth Spaulding: Describe your transition from a production position to a leadership position. What were some unexpected challenges or surprises?

Steve Meyer: I made a fairly abrupt move from production in my own two-person company to a leadership role as VP of Product Development for a very young MicroProse back in 1986. This was my first management role, so I needed to do quite a bit of research about things like interviewing, hiring, performance reviews, motivation, and leadership. I found that I had a pretty good understanding of the people aspects of leadership, but no specific experiences that could tell me whether my instincts were right or wrong.

My biggest challenge was learning to truly evaluate individual performance as well as team performance and know when and how to make corrections. When I was on my own, it was much easier; I knew what had to be done, and I also knew that I was the one who had to get it done. I had a much more accurate understanding of where my project was at any given moment.

I was fortunate to have several members of the management team at MicroProse whom I could go to for the traditional management questions. In addition, I found it very helpful to understand the informal nature of the production group and identify who were the "informal" thought leaders. These people were usually able to paint a very accurate picture of where we stood as a group, and what was working and not. I would say that in making the transition in one's own company, understanding the culture and politics of the group is key, and finding ways to influence the culture in a way that allows you to set the company up long term to achieve its goals is very important. Tools to help with this are other managers and peers as well as just spending time with the people who are getting the real work done. Look for opportunities for informal interactions with people where you may find more of the true picture. Also, there is a tremendous amount of good literature on leadership and management.

S.S.: What are the most common traits shared by other effective leaders in your experience?

S.M.: Here are a few:

- Good communication skills

- Good business sense

- Ability to motivate and see and explain the "big picture"

- A passion for what they are doing

- Ability to evaluate people

- Laser-like focus

I feel that I bring good communication skills and an ability to see the bigger picture and get people excited about what we are doing. These traits cause me to manage more on an informal basis, in an "MBWA" sense (management by walking around). I also feel like I can connect with people to get a feel for what particular state they and the organization may be in and look for ways to move things in a positive direction.

S.S.: What are the worst traits a leader has exhibited in your experience?

S.M.: The following are among the worst traits:

- Defensiveness

- Insecurity

- Incompetence

- Poor communication

- Greed

- Narcissism

People who are in leadership roles with some of these traits, in my experience, have a difficult time gaining the trust and confidence of their team. Many times this creates a politically charged atmosphere where there are no clear common goals for the team and no understanding of what the company's and individual's objectives are and when they have been met. Often this leads to a demoralized team that is just not having any fun doing what should be a very rewarding and satisfying job (making games).

S.S.: Are there any leadership traits you admire or perhaps aspire toward but don't feel you embody?

S.M.: I admire a leader who can articulately focus the company or an individual on a company goal and build the excitement, enthusiasm, and respect to allow the team to achieve great results—results in fact beyond what anyone expected they could achieve. I admire a leader who gives people the opportunity to be as good as they can be and shows them how to get there, so, yes, I do enjoy mentoring other leaders. One of the most rewarding aspects of my career has been watching people whom I have worked with move on to become industry leaders.

S.S.: What do you see as the toughest challenge facing leads during a game-development project cycle or at a game-development company generally?

S.M.: One of the toughest challenges is leading enough. What I mean by that is that many times, very good engineers move up in their career paths and at a certain point "lead" is the next rung on the ladder. In order to advance, that person feels he or she must take this next step. Well it turns out that this step includes a sizable management component for which that engineer may or may not be qualified or ready. This problem can show up in the game-development cycle as a lead with a directionless team who believes that he or she must get it all done himself or herself, the associated lack of communication with the team, and the additional engineering workload taken on by the engineer, causing a downward spiral in moral and productivity that is hard to recover from. A solution to this is to make sure that a new lead understands that his actual engineering contributions will need to be reduced drastically and that his management tasks will need to be a specific and defined portion of his responsibility. Also, formal leadership training is a good thing. In addition, a dual career path, which rewards an engineer for being an engineer and allows that person to climb as high on the ladder as a lead, may be conducive to helping people find long-term career challenges within the same company, doing what they are best at.

S.S.: How have you seen new leads best get support from directors or executives?

S.M.: With the establishment of clear goals and regular meetings both formal and informal. In other words, great communication and a leader who has a vested interest in helping their leads be as good as they can be. Encourage your leads to talk through their problems with you. Walking through different solutions and allowing them to make the final decision. Most importantly, allowing them to make mistakes . . . that is how we all seem to learn best. Celebrating failures.

S.S.: Do you think good leaders can be trained? Or is the essence of a good leader simply innate ability?

S.M.: I think it is a combination of experience, ability, the right opportunities, and the right mentors. I believe that a deficiency in any one area can be compensated for by strength in the others, but ultimately, a good dose of all will lead to the best result.

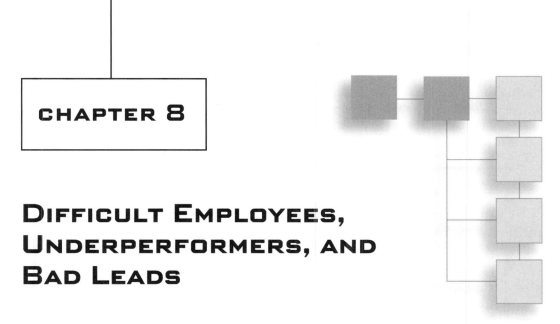

CHAPTER 8

DIFFICULT EMPLOYEES, UNDERPERFORMERS, AND BAD LEADS

At some point, every leader is confronted with people who are challenging to manage for any number of reasons. And every director or senior manager will eventually need to address a lead whose performance is poor and damaging to the company.

The dangers of these circumstances are obvious enough: Underperformers and difficult people cause others in the company to work harder than they should to pick up slack or find workarounds to avoid the problem team members. Eventually, this leads to lower morale across the company. Less obvious is the fact that ineffective handling of poor performers can actually do every bit as much damage as that wrought by the poor performers themselves, since the perception that arises is that ineffective managers are allowing ineffective people to remain in unsuitable roles, causing others to have to work harder.

Some of the biggest regrets I have as a manager involve failing to act quickly and decisively after becoming aware of difficulties. The temptation to wait out a situation—particularly in cases where the individual in question is a veteran and an otherwise well-liked and valuable team member—can be very strong. But as has already been stated, negative conditions rarely, if ever, resolve themselves independently.

Note

> The energy that managers must devote to dealing with underperformers and difficult employees is considerable. By my own experience and that of other directors, it can range anywhere from five to 30 percent of an average workday, depending on the size of the department and the number and level of problematic employees or relationships. This further highlights the importance of making good hiring decisions and of having a rigorous vetting process in place.

This chapter discusses some specific difficult behaviors I have encountered or been exposed to through discussions with other leads and directors. These include the following:

- Blamers

- Cynics, complainers, and surly folks

- Underperformers

- Bad leads

In all of these examples, you can assume that the hypothetical employees are talented individuals who may well be contributing to your projects at a very high level. The absence of this quality would obviously make these situations much easier to resolve—in the form of a rapid exit from the company. Also, these examples represent difficult cases that are correctable. The employee who creates a hostile work environment, sexually harasses, steals from the company, or commits actions of gross negligence or maliciousness does not qualify for consideration; these cases almost always call for immediate and clear removal.

Note

> I consider leads and specialist leads responsible for "front-line" review and feedback, but for not disciplinary measures (unless they want to be).

General Thoughts

Difficult employees, underperformers, and bad leads require immediate attention from managers and directors, not least of which because the effect of their presence is usually visible—and irritating—to the team well before it comes to the attention of senior management. "Immediate attention" does not imply disciplinary action without careful review of the facts of the matter—and "disciplinary action," when necessary, does not imply eventual termination.

Note

Some of the most rewarding moments of my career have come from intervening in a personnel matter in a way that brought about a positive change for an individual and, eventually, his or her project team.

Approaching any situation with a difficult employee involves tying the disruptive behavior to an effect on the workplace or on those in the workplace. If there is to be any hope for improvement, it is important—indeed, critical—to give the individual in question a concrete, business-specific example of why his or her behavior is unacceptable. For example, if an employee is excessively defensive when his work is reviewed, a director should relate that behavior to a negative effect on the team such as leads becoming more reluctant to spend time with him to develop their work—which, in turn, leads to the project, as well as the individual's work, suffering in quality.

Tips for New Managers

Situations requiring direct confrontation or some sort of personal intervention in the office setting may seem very unfamiliar to new managers. As individuals rise through the ranks of production to the status of lead or senior contributor, the art of "getting along with others" is not emphasized heavily beyond the basics; individuals simply need to be able to communicate well enough and work together as a part of a team to achieve a goal. Managers and leaders, however, need another set of interpersonal problem-solving skills to deal with situations that they probably have been hitherto encouraged to avoid.

Most management seminars, unless they are designed to address this specific issue, do not adequately provide new managers or leads with the strategies and language needed to handle these issues, which can be some of the toughest to deal with and the most critical to the success of your projects and company. But getting comfortable with addressing these issues simply involves practice. Absent that, books such as *Lifescripts: What to Say to Get What You Want in Life's Toughest Situations* by Stephen M. Pollan and Mark Levine and *A Survival Guide to Managing Employees from Hell: Handling Idiots, Whiners, Slackers, and Other Workplace Demons* by Gini Graham Scott can give a new manager some helpful language to consider. These resources are not cure-alls by any means, but they offer some helpful starting points.

Blamers

Blamers are a very dangerous element on a project. Their effect on the team includes an erosion of trust and morale as a result of real or perceived backbiting. Blamers themselves are one issue; left unchecked, their presence may lead to a culture of blaming.

Case Studies

A common blame scenario occurs when an employee attempts to turn negative performance-review feedback into a defensive affair by deflecting criticism onto other team members.

Another scenario, which I witnessed, involved a developer who allowed a culture of blame to flourish, mistaking blame for friendly competition. In time, the art and programming teams had been physically divided in the studio, and the two groups rarely spoke outside of meetings. Privately, many on the art team complained that they received no support from the programmers, who were viewed as passively antagonistic to them. The programmers in turn felt that the artists were not capable of creating efficient assets without the most restrictive tools possible.

Approaches

In both these cases, leaders must bring issues out into the open and find the underlying causes. Almost every action or reaction has an understandable source—although it may not necessarily be reasonable or logical. The only way to improve the situation is to be direct and honest about your observations and assessments and encourage the other party to be equally forthcoming. Once issues are understood from both sides, the manager must explain the negative consequences of the employee's actions or words and clearly communicate that the behavior must cease.

In my experience, blaming is often the result of feelings of insecurity—about one's company or, more frequently, about one's job skills or how one's efforts are perceived by management or fellow employees. Managers can and should work to mitigate this by making sure that praise is spread around the team as often as is appropriate. Someone who is reassured that his or her contributions are visible, validated, and appreciated will be more likely to come to his or her manager with issues than cast blame elsewhere.

Note

Do not involve the subject's peers in a disciplinary talk. When confronting a difficult employee, it's almost always better to say, "Bob, I've noticed a communication issue that we need to discuss" than it is to say, "Bob, a lot of your peers—especially Janet and Joe—have noticed a communication issue that we need to discuss." Even if most of your information about the situation comes from Janet and Joe, it's generally best not to draw them into your discussion. First, doing so will make the individual very uncomfortable around the office; second, Janet and Joe will probably not appreciate their appearance in your review. (Exceptions to this include people who want to be considered an information source for whatever reason.)

In the rare cases where two valuable employees are blaming each other for a particular circumstance, the manager needs to intercede individually with each party, determine the facts of the case to the extent it is possible, and do everything within his or her power to facilitate an understanding between the two parties. Trust in one's teammates is a vital component of a safe working environment; an office where an individual feels like his or her coworkers are vocally critical is not going to be a healthy environment conducive to retention.

Cynics, Complainers, and Surly Folks

This is a broad category of difficult employees who display a common set of behaviors that are detrimental to a studio. The common characteristic is a vocal dissatisfaction with some aspect of the studio, the project, or the person's role within the studio, and a penchant for expressing his or her unfiltered discontent to the wrong audience. The negative effect is greatly magnified when these behaviors are exhibited by leads or managers.

With respect to the cynic: There is a fine line between being cautious or conservative—i.e., raising a concern about an aspect of a game—and being cynical. Development concerns must be aired, and it is perfectly fine to be cautious. People are perceived as cynical, however, when they adopt a cynical attitude toward the challenges presented by said concerns. Cynical attitudes spread very quickly, particularly when the individual with the attitude is an outspoken "informal" leader in the company (that is, an individual who is not titled as a lead but who possesses a high degree of charisma or is well respected for his or her job skills).

Case Studies

The most common scenario occurs when an individual expresses generalized displeasure in front of team members. For example, production personnel or leads in a project meeting with team members present might say things like, "This project was a dumb idea and I don't think we should be doing it" or "The [other platform team] really dropped the ball and I know it's going to fall on us to fix it." These may well be honest and even valid opinions, but when aired in such a manner, they are toxic to morale.

Other scenarios are more subtle. One example is the individual who expresses needs or wants in a negative manner. For instance, upon recognizing that it would be a good practice to buy second monitors for programmers, this individual might say, "Why don't all programmers have second monitors? We should be doing that, and I don't understand why we haven't!" rather than using a more effective statement to accomplish the same goal, such as, "I think it would be a great idea to get the programmers a second monitor. The extra screen real estate really improves efficiency!"

Approaches

In most cases, other employees will be savvy enough to say to themselves, "That's just Angry Dave. Don't worry about him; that's just the way he is." Even so, Angry Dave needs to be alerted of the effect of his words or actions in a way that is tangible. The individual in question must also be reminded to share serious concerns with an appropriate audience—that is, one that is up the chain rather than across or down.

Note

There is no point to complaining anywhere but up. Otherwise, no goal will be accomplished, and the person or people to whom you are venting will suffer a morale hit.

A mentor of mine once confronted a chronic complainer over a specific incident by asking, "What did you think saying that would accomplish?" The individual had to admit that nothing could be accomplished by his actions, and resolved to improve the situation. Such a discussion can also be a good way to segue into one that addresses larger issues regarding why the employee might be unhappy. In some cases the chronic complainer is simply unhappy in his or her role in the company. As a manager, it is important to resolve this immediately by explaining why the employee is in his or her particular role and, where appropriate, what steps might be taken in the future to address the employee's complaints.

It's extremely important to deal with any cynics or complainers who are "informal leaders" in your company early and directly. Informal leaders are people whose job abilities or simply their personal charisma cause others to place a greater value on their opinions and actions. Informal leaders who are also complainers or cynics are very tough to deal with, but it's all the more important that they be addressed.

My advice to managers dealing with cynics or complainers on a team is to first point out to the person how his or her words and actions are perceived, note the effect of his or her comments on the team as you have observed it, and challenge him or her to bring realistic solutions to the team along with any concerns.

Underperformers

This is another broad category of difficult employees with a common set of behaviors that are detrimental to a studio. The problems that underperformers bring to a team make them the most damaging type of difficult employee when the condition is allowed to persist.

Underperformers may be identified variously as lazy, burned-out, or unskilled in some area of their job responsibility. Symptoms may include slow production pace and missed deadlines, late arrival or early departure, and/or work that suffers from poor aesthetic or technical quality and contains errors. The presence of an underperformer affects not only the quality of the final game but the morale of the entire team, since the work that the underperformer is not doing must eventually be done by someone else.

A potentially even more dangerous problem exists with a "legacy under-performer"—that is, someone who is not doing bad work, but whose skills have not advanced with the industry. He or she continues to fill niches on production teams doing more and more menial tasks while more junior individuals are charged with more critical and complex tasks. The problem, of course, is one of equity; the legacy underperformer is presumably compensated at a much higher level than is warranted for his or her current level of contribution to a project. This situation will not only breed resentment in the company as a whole, but will affect the ability of a company to succeed if left unchecked.

Case Studies

The question of underperformance and the problem of the legacy under-performer were topics of the 2006 Art Director/Lead Artist Round Table at GDC. Although the participants were initially reluctant to speak on the topic, after I detailed an example from my own experience—in which I was confronted with an individual in my department whose skills had not advanced in five years and who was ultimately proving to be a drag on the rest of the art department, and in which I failed to act to remove the individual because I never considered the impact of his underperformance on the team or our projects—one participant raised a hand to share a similar story, and then another, and then another.

Indeed, the group spent the remainder of the session on this one troubling topic, and would have gone on into the night if given the chance.

Many commentators pointed out the difficulties with simply removing employees whose work was not up to par but whose tenure at their company made them a part of its social fabric—a situation complicated by a kind of nepotism. When asked whether they would consider retaining an underperformer who did add a great deal to the social or cultural fabric of the company, the group was surprisingly divided, with a minority stating clearly that they felt that an employee's place in the company's social fabric should be given consideration to a degree. Other attendees, however, noted that over time, their company was unable to produce games using current practices and tools because so many of their staff lacked the skills to do so. When asked what plans they enacted to correct the situation, one attendee said, "Nothing. We went out of business. Legacy underperformers destroyed my company."

Approaches

Underperformers must be confronted and corrected very quickly, given the serious repercussions of their presence on a team. As with other problem employees, the most effective approach is to tie the behavior to a specific work effect. In this case, the work effect is usually very apparent: Work is not getting done on schedule, or the underperformer's skills have not advanced with current practices, making them unable to work to the level of their peers or in many cases even those junior to them.

Symptoms to be addressed may include

- Inferior production skills

- Slower-than-acceptable pace

- Late arrival/early departure

Helping an underperformer who is committed to improvement develop production skills is simply a matter of finding time for some mentoring from strong performers within the company. Managers should be aware, however, that in these cases, the underperformer (particularly the legacy underperformer) is usually a more senior individual than the one who is doing the mentoring—which can cause some feelings of resentment. Ideally, however, the underperformer will realize the seriousness of their situation and the value of the opportunity before them, and will make every effort to build the skills necessary to fulfill his or her job descriptions. Once this objective is achieved, managers must make sure that the skill development of those in question is given frequent attention to ensure that the situation does not reoccur down the road.

The problem can be more complex for the director if the individual in question possesses all the skills needed to do his or her job at an acceptable level of quality but works at a slower-than-acceptable pace. In such cases, the director or manager must first discover the root of the issue by talking to the individual using language such as, "I've noticed that over the past month, your production pace has really gone down" or "Your work has always been very solid, but your pace has not met expectations and has resulted in several blown dates," followed by "Your lead is concerned about the impact of this on the schedule, and I'm concerned that there may be some underlying cause for this."

Responses to this message can vary. Often, the individual will respond by saying, "The tasks I had this month were very poorly defined, and they ended up taking a lot longer than expected. That's done with now, and I expect to be on track next month." While this is a frequent response, however, it's not always accurate (and besides, if it were completely true, then the lead would be aware of the task complications and you as a director or manager probably wouldn't be involved). In that case, an appropriate response might be, "That's great to hear, I look forward to seeing your work get back on schedule this milestone. If there's anything that you can think of that might be an impediment to meeting that goal, please let me know." This both acknowledges the employee's explanation and states your expectations, attaching a specific time horizon. In addition, you have empowered the employee to take responsibility for raising concerns about the schedule as they occur.

If the goal is met, then the issue may move to a resolution. If not, the individual must be confronted again in a more serious manner—for example, "We agreed that the goal was to get back on schedule for this milestone. That's not happening, and we need to know what's going on. Are you unable to meet the schedule due to other duties? Is there any personal issue I should know about?" Again, responses here can vary widely. A frequent response is, "I thought that by working more hours I could get caught up, but it hasn't happened because I have these other tasks that are not scheduled but keep interrupting me." These "other tasks" might include mentoring others, handling outsourcers, or meeting unscheduled marketing requests—all very real and legitimate issues that should be dealt with proactively as early as possible. Beyond these legitimate examples, however, explanations can swiftly involve a pattern of excuses that often point to deeper problems. In some cases, the employee is simply in a rut professionally or personally and is having trouble staying focused on tasks in which he or she is no longer interested. In these instances, it may be possible to move the person into a different role where he or she may find more satisfaction—but the first step toward that resolution is discovering what the core issue is and, in some cases, getting the underperformer to admit or realize that there are some fundamental issues at play.

Unfortunately, some underperformers are people who have decided to pursue other career options and are actively looking elsewhere. During this period, they do everything they can to convince their manager that everything is fine; they don't want to deal with any disciplinary actions, as they leaving anyway. To combat this, I recommend encouraging people to be as open as possible about their career goals—even if pursuing those goals will take them away from your company. For example, you might say something like, "Bob, I understand that sometimes people need to move other places to satisfy their goals. You should know that I really want you to continue to be part of this team and this company—we really value your contribution—but if you feel you have to or just want to look around, I understand and support that. I can even help you with some of my connections in the industry if it should come to that." Although this approach often surprises people, I think it should be employed more. The fact is, employees are likely to leave my company at some point, even if it's after years of tenure, and I would rather know about it as far in advance as possible so that I can plan for succession. It is critical to communicate that if the employee decides to stay, no negative consequences will carry over in the form of reduced raises or merit promotions. Many assume that announcing to their boss that they are looking at other offers might damage their long-term prospects at their current company; it takes a good deal of trust to convince them to believe otherwise. But the positive morale and reciprocal trust that such a policy brings about make any efforts to earn that trust worthwhile.

Bad Leads

Sometimes, despite our best efforts, a lead situation simply does not work out. Bad leads, as discussed in Chapter 2, "The Anatomy of a Game-Development Company," are often the result of poor placement decisions, misguided judgment regarding the lead role and responsibilities, and simply the lack of a pool of capable candidates—The-Best-of-the-Bottom-of-the-Barrel syndrome.

Regardless of why a bad lead is in place, it is the responsibility of senior management to correct the situation in a timely manner—potentially a very delicate operation. On the one hand, teams need a lead who is capable of doing the job, and they need it quickly; on the other, the current lead is probably a highly valued member of your team who may be in the wrong role.

Depending on the individual and the point in the development cycle, it might be prudent to move the lead out of the role regardless of the consequences or possibly see him or her through to the end of the development cycle with increased support and supervision. Based purely on anecdotal experience, I recommend the former in almost every case. The move away from the lead spot will benefit the project immediately and will ultimately, if not immediately, be a benefit to the individual in question.

Note

These are cases in which it is determined that no amount of support or mentoring from peers or senior management will allow the individual to successfully lead the team to the completion of the product.

Following are three case studies from the game industry of leads who simply were not appropriate for the role and whose tenure ended before completion of the development cycle. There are of course many, many more stories of poor leads who fail in their role for any number of reasons. I've included these three because they reflect some of the more common situations I've encountered in the industry.

Case Study: Doug

As the best artist in his company, Doug was chosen by management as the art lead. Although he was a highly skilled artist who preferred, in most cases, to simply do art, Doug did recognize that as a lead, he needed to provide guidance to the team. Unfortunately, he did so on his own schedule, and without coordinating with any specialist leads. This led to daily miscommunications, as Doug was reviewing and giving feedback to the art team in a very random manner. In many cases, he gave several team members feedback that directly contradicted the animation lead's or modeling lead's review from a few minutes previously. When confronted with this by his specialist leads, he remained resolute in his right, as lead, to give anyone on the team feedback whenever he wanted. The specialist leads attempted to resolve the situation by inviting him to their daily reviews of the team's work so he could give feedback with the specialist lead present; unfortunately, he was not vocally participative in these sessions and maintained his previous behavior. At this point, the leads approached senior management—who were uninterested in the problem. Regrettably, the specialist leads discovered that their art lead was a "legacy lead" whose position was not going to be questioned. As a result, morale on the team steadily declined; some employees left after a time, while others stayed on and witnessed the team's performance degrade along with their morale. A couple years later, the company folded.

Approach

The lesson here is for both leads and senior management. Had Doug been mature enough to understand the importance of clarity of communication and had a proper understanding of the role of the specialist lead, the problem would not have occurred. Even given that, he had ample opportunities to listen to the needs of his specialist leads and respond in a meaningful way. Absent those qualities in the lead, much of this situation could still have been avoided if senior management had demonstrated some ability to listen to their staff and had then approached Doug with a request to adopt a few very sensible communication practices. As it was, the combination of an oddly stubborn senior-management group and a passive-aggressive art lead led to this intractable and very unhappy situation.

Case Study: Evan

Evan was approached to become a design lead on an upcoming project at a company that had recently experienced the departure of one experienced lead designer and whose only other solid lead candidate was halfway into production on another critical title. Although it was well known that Evan's communication skills had some shortcomings, he was experienced, and it was felt that with support from other leads, his experience alone would make him a capable lead—not a fantastic one, but capable.

As it happened, however, his development experience—while valuable in development—did not significantly aid him in the completion of his new duties. Additionally, it became clear that despite his desire to be a lead, he lacked the emotional stability needed to handle the additional responsibility and to colla-borate effectively with fellow leads and his own junior design team. As a result, discussions of development approaches tended to turn into shouting matches.

After the first blow-up, the art lead and programming lead confronted Evan, told him his behavior was inappropriate, and asked him to explain his position in detail. The result was few days of peace—but another outburst soon occurred. At that point, the company creative director stepped in and delivered an ultimatum that Evan improve his temper or a new lead would be found. In time, the decision was made by the creative director to remove Evan as the lead. He remained part of the team, but in a specialist lead capacity, doing strictly level-design work. Although he was initially upset about the decision, Evan came to realize after a week or so that it was personally and professionally the best outcome. The junior designer who replaced him was not a perfect fit either, but the project was able to regain its footing and finish on schedule. Management was, of course, criticized for putting Evan in the lead spot to start with, but was praised for taking the best approach in a bad situation.

Approach

This is a tough and certainly unenviable situation, but it is critical that if a lead does need to be removed, the removal occurs swiftly and in such a way that the team will have the best leadership possible. The removal should also be con-ducted in a manner that is respectful to the lead in question, who presumably remains a very valuable member of the team.

Case Study: Fiona

Fiona was named programming lead based on her desire to "see the game done right" and on her well-respected technical prowess. At the end of pre-produc-tion, as Fiona's team began to grow in size, she approached the programming department director and expressed her concern that she was no longer enjoying a job that, until now, she had loved. She was self-aware enough to realize that the cause was the lead role itself. As more people were brought to the team, she saw her management load increasing, and saw herself enjoying her job less and less.

Initially, the programming department director encouraged her to stay on and consider the reasons she had wanted to be lead in the first place. At the same time, he assured her that if she ultimately decided it wasn't the right fit, then a suitable specialist lead role would be found for her. Behind the scenes, he used this time to consider others for the role.

When Fiona announced her preference to find another role on the team, the department director was prepared to approach his choice for the lead spot that day and to coordinate the switch with the project leads and senior management.

After the transition, Fiona and the new lead, who previously had been the networking specialist lead under Fiona, encountered difficulties in their new dynamic. Fiona felt micromanaged, and the new lead felt that Fiona was acting far too independently and failing to fulfill the communication responsibilities of her position. Ultimately, the situation was resolved.

Approach

In any lead transition, even the peaceful ones, it is important to keep the entire team well informed about both the timeline for the change and the reasons behind it. One missed opportunity in this specific case that caused some difficulty on the team was that the director did not inform the entire programming staff of the change simultaneously, which led to some confusion during the transition.

When new roles are adopted mid-project, power struggles may occur as new and ex-leads define the scope of their responsibilities as they see them. The director—and the other parties, for that matter—needs to be vigilant but understanding during this transition. Problems can and will occur, and need to be confronted and resolved in a timely fashion. Monitoring of the situation by the director and his or her involvement in clarifying roles and responsibilities may be necessary at first.

Resolving Disputes—Before They Enter the Fistfight Stage

Resolution of disputes and dealing with feuding employees can be one of the more frustrating features of a manager's or director's job. Disputes in the office can be divided into two categories:

- **Work-related disputes.** Common work-related disputes center around proper approaches to development, project or office organization, confusion and disagreement around limits of authority, and extent of individual responsibility.

- **Personal disputes.** Specific variations of personal disputes are far too numerous to list, but most are rooted in the perception that one party has a low opinion or lack of respect for another party.

Both types of disputes require immediate attention from a manager, as they seldom resolve, and frequently intensify, with the passage of time.

A vast number of personal and work-related disputes have their genesis in some form of miscommunication—and as more communication tools become available (namely cell phones, PDAs, and e-mail), ostensibly to make communication "easier," the more miscommunications occur. E-mail is by far the most common office-communication tool, and hence the source of a large number of disputes and misunderstandings. Using e-mail to deliver a critique of some sort is very tricky—so many aspects of normal human communication, such as body language and voice inflection, are stripped away. E-mail shields the user from the social cues that we all employ and react to as a part of face-to-face communication. So to the degree it is possible, you should deliver messages requiring any level of nuance in person, and take extra care when crafting such messages that cannot be delivered in person.

Note

As far as conflict resolution goes, e-mail does have one silver lining: Everything said is in written form. As a manager, you have an objective record of the origin of the dispute.

Another frequent source of disputes is a misunderstanding of roles and responsibilities. Sometimes this can be a situation where an individual's understanding of his or her scope of responsibility is too narrow, meaning that certain issues are not addressed. Other times, the individual's understanding of the scope of his or her role is too broad and causes conflict with others on the team who feel encroached upon. The best way for managers to address this issue is to carefully clarify roles and responsibilities and define the decision-making structure very early in development. This early framework will be a valuable stepping-off point even if other structures and working relationships form during production.

The job of the manager or director in resolving disputes is to:

- **Gather information.** Most disputes are presented to a manager in a highly subjective and emotionally charged manner. The initial job of the manager is to investigate the issue and construct an accurate and objective view of the dispute. This is sometimes much harder than it sounds, since a large percentage of the information that can be gathered tends to be subjective and emotional.

- **Present this objective assessment to each party separately, explaining the effect of their continued disagreement on the team.** Where the assessment is disputed by one party, the manager should feel free to say things like, "Look, the details of this are not so relevant to me. Understand that the other party in this has a very different perception, and I need you to recognize that if we are to move on."

- **Meet with the two parties to reiterate your expectations.** Hopefully, you will see the beginning of some real acknowledgement of the problem from the individuals and a resolution to improve. Not everyone is going to be best friends with every co-worker, but all employees are expected to be 100-percent professional in their communications with one another.

- **Follow up.** Meet with each party separately to measure progress or to make sure that the relationship is indeed functional.

Interview: David Silverman, Director of Art, WB Games

David Silverman got his start in the interactive media industry in 1992, as a computer graphics artist. In 1995, Silverman graduated from Massachusetts College of Art with a Bachelor's Degree in Media and Performing Arts. During the course of his career, Silverman has served across a range of disciplines including art, game design, engineering, project management, studio management, and business development.

Silverman joined WBG as the company's director of art in January of 2008. Prior to moving to that, Silverman worked at Monolith Productions as technical art director, and at Cyberlore Studios as art department director. Prior to that, Silverman worked with a number of other game companies over the years, including Harmonix, Black Isle, and Floodgate Entertainment.

Seth Spaulding: Explain what a lead is from your perspective.

David Silverman: Leads are accountable for work completed in specific development disciplines. Some leads are managers, some are leaders/visionaries, and some are simply discipline experts/specialists. Depending on the number of approvals and direct reports a lead has, they may or may not be responsible for production work.

For example, a lead character artist running a team of four character artists, including himself, may have enough bandwidth to also do some character artwork, fitting it in amidst content reviews and personnel issues. In contrast, a project's art lead, managing each of the leads under art (and therefore all the project's artists), probably won't have much production work on his plate, but will have a ton of responsibilities including personnel, process/pipeline, scheduling, tasking, and project vision.

S.S: Describe your transition from a production position to a leadership position.

D.S.: Early in my career I worked on projects that ran about six months long with only a few people dedicated to them. Upper management gave us almost total autonomy concerning the end product, so every decision we made and every action we took affected our projects profoundly.

This small-project dynamic provided me with a solid foundation for my career in management. Being an integral part of a small team meant that anytime we misestimated the scope of some feature, didn't clearly communicate with our peers, overlooked some dependencies, or simply spent too much time trying to figure out the perfect solution to a problem, the whole team could get screwed. Our personal pain was directly proportional to the quality of our decisions, our ability to recover from bad ideas and dead ends, and our ability to collaborate effectively with the engineer or artists we happened to be working with.

We screwed up a lot, but we communicated constantly and were brutally honest about everything, so we failed pretty gracefully most of the time. We didn't have any formal project training at this point; we just tried to make the best decisions possible, given the information we had at any given time.

During this same period, I also worked on the side as an art contractor, which taught me valuable lessons about working to strict requirements and time tables, establishing clear expectations and outcomes between multiple parties, and small business finance (like getting people to pay on time and taxes). Also, I've always been very inquisitive about things outside my discipline, and spent a great deal of my free time learning about marketing and general business concepts on the side, by reading up on trade journals that one of my coworkers in marketing subscribed to and hanging out with him to talk shop.

So in the years preceding my move into management, I developed a very broad range of skills and interests that provided me a holistic view that served me well. In many ways, I was naturally a very broad-based generalist.

My eventual transition into management came a couple years later (at another company), and the experience was equal parts humbling and enlightening. I got promoted when upper management changed hands and they realized that I was essentially doing the job of my immediate boss. I took over the department officially while my immediate supervisor got phased out.

A couple of the employees that transitioned under me were long-time friends of mine that I actually helped get hired. This presented a unique learning opportunity during my formative time as a manager. I made a lot mistakes. I didn't respect the manager/employee boundaries, treating my friends like friends (not employees), while expecting them to treat me like a boss. I gave them tasks without clearly defined outcomes and then would personally redo their work when they failed to meet my poorly communicated outcomes. I was fortunate, in a way, that my friends were brutally honest with me, and that I wasn't too wrapped up in my pride to listen. I was modeling unprofessional behavior, and they reciprocated. We eventually identified it after some difficult discussions, and called a truce since neither party was happy with where the relationship was going. I focused on acting professionally with them, they focused on acting professionally with me, and we mutually agreed to police each other should either party slip up. This turned something negative into something positive, and we all were the better for it.

S.S.: What were some unexpected challenges or surprises?

D.S.: There were three in particular:

- **Confronting difficult people:** I tend to be a pretty laid-back person, so confronting difficult employees goes against my grain. It was something I had to learn to overcome. I have a legacy of failed attempts at letting stuff just blow over, but it rarely does. I learned that when someone exhibits unacceptable behavior consistently, they are likely to fall into a pattern of it. You can break the pattern, but it will probably return. You have to be persistent with keeping these folks on track and consistent with your approach.

- **Firing someone (a case study):** I had an employee who needed to be fired due to his inability to manage the rigors of his job. Our other artists were able to meet our project's scheduling requirements, but this employee simply couldn't keep up. He constantly needed reminding of the basics of his job (often draining valuable production time from our best performers in the process). The stress and the workload forced him to work through lunch and lose sleep, which eventually affected his health. We tried to hand-feed him work and reduce his overall workload, but the work didn't disappear since there was only so much content that could be cut. So we began piling what he couldn't do onto our best performers who were ahead of schedule, which essentially amounted to rewarding a weak employee by penalizing the strong.

  Firing this employee was a good thing. We had a clear plan that was well considered, and I want to believe that we followed it well, but I was too removed from the process to know if the right messages were getting across. He was surprised when I went to fire him. That's the part that still gets me to this day. How could he be surprised? I believe this was because any words of encouragement were escalated in his mind. Encouragement didn't mean that he was off the hook, but it meant he was making progress. His pace of progress, however, was too slow, and we knew he'd have to go. Firing him was hard because it was such a shock to him. I've let people go in the past, and that process was quite easy. It wasn't a comment on their capacity, but the company's finances. Firing is different—by it's nature, its a humiliating slap in the face that says "You're not good enough." How do you do this, and also make it a positive thing, and not so shocking? It's a difficult issue that I'll continue to struggle with given that I rarely have the occasion to fire someone.

▪ **Dealing with the law:** I didn't realize how much legal stuff I'd have to learn. The law touches on so many things these days that ignorance can be dangerous. You have to possess some measure of awareness of certain laws to be safe. They cover things like what you can and cannot say to a candidate during an interview, how to deal with difficult employees, fair usage laws as they pertain to the content you're building for your games—the list goes on and on.

S.S.: Looking back, are there any decisions or practices you would change, and if so, why?

D.S.: I think great managers constantly analyze their actions and the implications these actions have on their teams. I don't think it's healthy to have regrets. My prior experience, good and bad, has made me a better manager, so it's hard for me to look back and say "What if?" This is especially true considering that the biggest blunders of my career have also been turning points in my growth.

S.S.: What is the most important thing you would tell someone making that transition within their company?

D.S.: Managing isn't about being the boss. Instead:

▪ It's about coordinating and facilitating the efforts of the various disciplines of the team.

▪ It's about laying down the overall planning and ground work for a project, and ensuring a clear plan to success lies ahead.

▪ It's about acting as the advocate for and representing the team to external groups and upper management.

- It's about mentoring your people to be better professionals, and helping them develop their careers.

- It's about getting your people to focus on priorities and holding them accountable for the results.

- It's about making decisions after weighing the pros and cons with your team's experts.

S.S.: Were there any people who helped, and if so how?

D.S.: The transition into management can be difficult without help from everyone you work with. I personally gained a lot of wisdom into how to do my job better by asking my employees, peers, and supervisors for feedback.

- Your employees can help you learn how people like to be managed, what motivates them, and get feedback concerning how you're progressing as a manager.

- Your peers are going through the same issues you are. Collaborate with them on devising new approaches and use them as a sounding board. Practice difficult conversations with them before confronting your under-achievers. It's great to have someone to sympathize with.

- Your supervisors can remind you of the company goals, visions, and values, and mentor you through difficult times. They've probably been through what you're going through now and may have unique insight.

S.S.: What are the most common traits shared by other effective leaders in your experience?

D.S.: Off the top of my head, the traits shared by the best managers I've worked with and observed are as follows:

- Possesses the ability to think at all levels (from abstract to detailed), creates new concepts from seemingly unrelated components, and clearly communicates these concepts to any party regardless of recipient's background.

- Possesses excellent judgment and acts according to strong core values.

- Exhibits very consistent behavior even under duress while exuding positivity tempered by honesty.

- Demonstrates the courage to be honest and direct.

- Possesses the ability to inspire respect in people by giving them respect.

- Provides clear expectations and holds his or her people to these expectations.

- Demonstrates disciplined thought and action.

- Encourages individual growth from his or her team.

- Promotes a culture of transparency and accountability.

- Possesses a strong ability to be introspective and has insight into the behavioral motivations of others.

- Promotes a culture that has a rare and healthy mix of collaboration and competition (a.k.a "coopertition").

- Puts the team's success above his or her own.

- Has a good sense of humor and doesn't take anything too seriously.

- Has a good sense of how to set achievable goals, requirements, and priorities for all work his or her team commits to.

- Understands when to focus on the practical over theoretical, and vice versa.

S.S.: Which traits do you feel are your strongest and how does knowledge of these traits affect how you approach leadership challenges?

D.S.: I think I possess each of these traits to some degree (though thinking I have good judgment means I'm drinking my own Kool-Aid, which I do). My strongest traits from the list above are my sense of humor and my combination of introspection and insight into other people's behavior.

S.S.: What are the worst traits a leader has exhibited in your experience? How did these traits manifest themselves, and what was the result of their involvement in terms of the team, project, and/or company?

D.S.: A leader's quality can be judged by whether he or she got the job done on time, on budget, at the desired quality level, and without burning through talent. Leaders are expected to possess the ability to influence a team and synthesize the practical from the theoretical through their efforts. This is no small task and there's a lot of ways they can fail. I'm not going to list traits; instead, I'm going to list the worst behaviors exhibited by leaders I've observed, and the outcomes that resulted:

Behavior #1: Failed to make decisions in a timely manner.
Outcome: Decisions got made by default, and/or the team's faith in the manager's abilities eroded.

Behavior #2: Made decisions without providing context to the team.
Outcome: The team continued to make daily micro-decisions and, lacking the proper context, made assumptions that got the project off course.

Behavior #3: Failed to set clear goals, requirements, and priorities.
Outcome: Similar outcomes to #2. The team had no basis upon which to make informed decisions. Individuals battled over implementation details, wasting precious project time and reducing team cohesion due to in-fighting.

Behavior #4: Neglected to establish vision and values.
Outcome: Similar outcomes to #2. The team had no basis upon which to make informed decisions. Each person then worked by his or her own individual interpretation of the project's vision and values, and the project lost cohesion and consistency.

Behavior #5: Failed to hold people accountable.
Outcome: Employees stopped seeing the manager as an authority figure, and employees began to refuse to be managed.

Behavior #6: Made decisions without including key employees in the process.
Outcome: The key employees became disenfranchised because the manager didn't have enough respect for their opinions to include them.

Behavior #7: Failed to delegate and hogged the coolest work.
Outcome: Similar outcomes to #6. Individuals on the team became disenfranchised because the manager didn't have enough respect in their abilities to give them desirable opportunities and responsibilities.

Behavior #8: Failed to promote honesty and visibility.
Outcome: The project lost predictability due to lack of honest and regular progress and status reporting, and the schedule unraveled as a result.

Behavior #9: Held people accountable for the impossible.
Outcome: Similar outcomes to #8. People stopped being honest about their status and progress, and with the reduced visibility the project floundered.

Behavior #10: Displayed too much pride and ego.
Outcome: Team members stopped wanting to work with their manager and would become argumentative or passive aggressive.

Behavior #11: Held people to false milestones.
Outcome: Team members eventually recognized the false milestones and real milestones lost importance in their minds (since any milestone could be false).

Behavior #12: Forced mandatory overtime.
Outcome: Team members get stress at home from their significant others due to lack of family time and offloaded responsibilities, and their morale takes a hit. This is especially the case for employees that are on time or ahead of schedule. If it's a particularly bad crunch, depending on the status of individuals on your team, it can lead to poisonous attitudes and even attrition.

S.S.: Are there any leadership traits you admire or perhaps aspire toward but feel you could improve upon?

D.S.: I've always prided myself on being a great collaborator, a team player—except I recently learned that I often present matters in absolute terms, which often shuts down opportunities for collaboration with people who aren't thick-skinned. This type of feedback is essential for any leader, experienced or not. In my case, I have a weekly one-on-one talk with my supervisor that is scheduled, but fairly informal in format. Every week is not necessarily an assessment, but because we make the time to meet, the opportunity exists to regularly pass on any necessary performance feedback. This feedback is a two-way street. He may reinforce goals and desired outcomes, and I provide feedback about the department, our process, or even his management style.

S.S.: If so, how do you feel embodying these traits would make you a better leader?

D.S.: A great collaborator puts people at ease. If people don't find you threatening, they'll open up to you. If they open up to you, you can have more honest communication and trust.

S.S.: Do you consciously try to develop these traits?

D.S.: Yes, through regular practice, feedback from external observers, and introspection.

S.S.: Do you mentor other leaders?

D.S.: Yes. My job calls for mentoring leaders directly and indirectly. Typically this goes through our standard process, which follows a formal write-up that's presented by the project's producer, and sometimes it's hands-on when the feedback loop needs to be tight with the developer.

S.S.: Do you have any training in leadership, either formal or unstructured (e.g., armed forces experience)?

D.S.: I've taken the SkillPath Training Seminars course "Dealing Effectively with Unacceptable Employee Behavior," and the Rockhurst Seminar "Motivate a Team."

S.S.: If relevant, in what ways do you apply that training to challenges in your job?

D.S.: The course "Dealing Effectively with Unacceptable Employee Behavior" was a good one because it provided formalization of some skills and practices I've followed for a while, and it verified that I was on the right track with my own insights. Even better, though—one of my senior employees took the same course and used it to benchmark his own behavior. He found opportunities to improve himself and took advantage of them. Months after the course, he would remind me of key approaches to dealing with various situations, guided by the course. It was awesome to see the transformation and have him guide me with his new-found insights.

S.S.: What do you see as the toughest challenge facing leads during a game-development project cycle or at a game-development company generally?

D.S.: Preproduction is such a vital phase of any project, and is often the one developers utilize most poorly since they only do it once every couple of years. There are a number of key challenges that developers face during preproduction, which include the following:

- Establishing the concrete vision and values for each discipline, as well as the project as a whole

- Defining the core experience and previsualizing it to align all parties (both internal to the developer and at the publisher) and get them excited about the project

- Planning out all the resources, processes, and pipelines that will be required for the remainder of the project

- Building playable prototypes and probably a vertical slice (which is required for the green-light process at many publishers)

- Defining clear rules of engagement and procedures with the publisher independent of contractual obligations including things like change control, risk management, milestone definitions, outsourcing, legal requirements, localization, QA, marketing/PR/community, market research, approvals, and build deliveries

- Feeding a team of developers with work while getting everything else figured out

S.S.: How have you seen this handled most and least effectively?

D.S.: Companies that start with the core experience and work outward are the most successful because this gives them something tangible to base all future decisions and priorities on. Most developers fall apart when implementing their high-level concepts because they start off in the details before they've defined the big picture, or they don't correlate dependencies between disciplines adequately. Some developers want to explore their way to making a fun game, but this can be expensive and used as an excuse to avoid planning (which is a skill that many developers don't possess).

Something that hits most independent developers is dealing with all the extra production people during the foundational period of the project. They often see this as unwanted overhead. I've personally felt this way as well. Some companies, however, are very good at utilizing these people for brainstorming. These companies know that utilizing the "wisdom of crowds" approach (when done right) can be a massively successful process. It can improve individual investment in the project, gel the team, and it puts leaders more in a facilitator and moderator role (rather than making leads the guys who get to come up with all the cool ideas).

S.S.: What are some common mistakes you've seen leads make, be they new or experienced?

D.S.: One is that leads load up on too much production work and put themselves in the critical path. This typically results in reduced quality and/or schedule slippage, which leads to overtime for the entire team. Another is that leads hog all the good work. This typically reduces employee investment in a project because the lead didn't demonstrate enough trust or pride in his or her team's abilities.

S.S.: How could these missteps have been avoided?

D.S.: Leads should only take on production tasks that aren't in the critical path, act as a floating resource to address issues, define outcomes, feed their team with work though scheduling and tasking, and review their team's efforts. They should delegate, and use work as an opportunity to develop their employees' skills, and in some cases, even as a reward.

S.S.: How have you seen new leads best get support from directors or executives?

D.S.: A company's vision and values ideally start from the top, and all decisions should descend from this. It's probably expecting too much for the average manager to be able to recite the company's core tenets verbatim. Directors and executives should support their management through coaching to the vision and values of the company.

For example, let's say that visibility and openness are among your company's core values. As a new manager it may not be readily apparent how to embody these ideals or how to get your employees to act according to them. The company's upper management should clarify how these ideals are achieved. They might recommend that your team adopt a status-reporting process, with team-wide daily updates on progress and morning stand-ups. Perhaps they would recommend you maintain an open-door policy, walk the floor for informal discussions and troubleshooting, and have regular one-on-one meetings with individuals to discuss their career development, issues, and aspirations.

If you had issues with a troubled employee, upper management can also provide insight as to how to best approach the situation. For example, suppose the employee in question was often regarded as belligerent and trite. His contributions to the team were significant and unique, but he wanted to take on some more production responsibilities in a different discipline. He's demonstrated some skill in this area in the past, but his time away has caused his skills to atrophy, and the schedule is now built around specialists (not guys who pick it up once in a blue moon). His belligerence may have been the reason his participation in these production tasks were minimized, but the lack of production tasks in an area he considers desirable may be contributing to his belligerence. A new lead may not understand how to deal with this. Management could coach you through it, maybe make themselves available for some basic role playing to try out different approaches, or they might have scripts for certain situations that you could work from. It's a complex issue, and one that you shouldn't have to face alone. It's also a great learning opportunity. You could screw up, even with some advice from upper management, but these are the challenges you regularly encounter in management.

S.S.: Do you think good leaders can be trained? Or is the essence of a good leader simply innate ability?

D.S.: The best leaders I've seen in action have a combination of natural talent and training. Leadership is a complex skill set, and like any complex skill set, you don't gain mastery through talent or training alone.

This can be demonstrated by looking at the traits and skills of an artist. Could an artist with no talent and lots of training become great? I've worked with plenty of artists with moderate to low talent but tons of drive, but they weren't great artists. No amount of skill-based training was going to help them overcome fundamental problems such as their aesthetic judgment.

What about a highly talented artist who never trained or practiced? I've similarly worked with talented artists who never apply their talent and they too never became great. Great artists train and hone their skills out of a desire to be better at their craft. Without that drive to excel, a highly talented artist will never want to devote the large amount of time and energy necessary for skill development.

The message here is that great leads need the same mix of natural talent and training the artists do.

Training a leader doesn't necessarily have to happen in a formal manner, but not everyone intuitively knows what they need to learn. A great way to teach a leader is to have them shadow a trained leader through each aspect of the position. They can then have a transitional period where the two are in tight communication while the new leader gets to apply their learned knowledge alongside anything they might have come up with on their own.

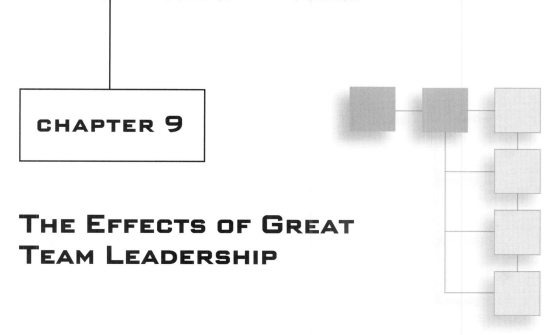

CHAPTER 9

THE EFFECTS OF GREAT TEAM LEADERSHIP

The most important goal of any game developer is to make great games. Having great team leadership, by itself, does not guarantee that a studio will make great games. Great games are made by great teams, not by great individuals in any area (including leaders), great technology, great marketing position, a great discipline group, or cutting-edge development practices. Team leaders, though, are uniquely influential components of a company. They greatly affect every individual in a studio for better or for worse, and shape every feature and perception of a studio.

Previous chapters have examined the consequences of poor leadership on individuals, teams, and companies. It really isn't enough to say that great leadership will prevent some of these horrible things from happening. So why should your studio pay more attention to leadership? Because investing in, and building great team leaders, brings about

- Reciprocal trust and loyalty

- Increased retention

- Improved external studio perception

- Greater company and team morale

- More-capable and supportive teams

- Healthier employees

- Improved succession outcomes

Note that this list still does not include "Make great games." That is the subject for another book—or several books. Solid team leaders, however, will probably make your games better, and will definitely allow your company to focus more on making a game great and less on simply getting a game through the development cycle.

A Foundation of Trust

Trust between an employer and employee is not easily gained in contemporary business settings, inside or outside the game-development world. Building trust requires commitment and consistent demonstration of the principles for which the company stands.

The word "trust" itself conjures many meanings, and some might ask why it is even particularly valuable. When trust is established, leaders can take a team in unfamiliar directions, and can make mistakes and be understood. For their part, employees can take risks and know that they will be supported rather than blamed. Game-development cycles are nothing if not filled with unknown challenges, costly mistakes, and risks. All these are, perhaps unfortunately, integral to making a great game—and may be richly rewarded if the game is successful. In studios where trust does not exist, however, no one is inclined to stray too far from accepted paths.

This pervasive sense of trust must start from the top. Senior management must give their leads not only support but a visible extension of trust. Senior management should avoid team meetings and allow leads to act unilaterally as they see fit. Oversight is necessary, but should be less visible to the team on a day-to-day basis. Leads should encourage—and even work to draw out—dissenting opinions and creative input from the team. The more ideas that are on the table, the better the result will be. Nothing kills morale on a team faster than a lead who has all the answers.

Increased Retention

Perhaps the greatest measure of high morale and loyalty to a studio is a high rate of retention. Great leaders encourage retention by demonstrating competence, and they help build an environment of trust that people naturally want to be a part of.

High retention is desirable for the following reasons:

- Employees who are familiar with your specific development environment and tools are increasingly more effective and efficient with each succeeding cycle.

- Engine technology and art tools benefit from development from a consistent source. Having new people cycle into a team inhibits the evolution of tools and processes as new arrivals must spend time—in the case of programmers, considerable time—simply learning and mastering the existing technology and processes.

- Teams familiar with each other are more effective communicating with each other with each succeeding cycle.

- Searches are expensive. Whether you employ recruiters, run ads, or work from employee referrals, searches can easily run into the thousands of dollars—and more if signing bonuses and relocation packages are considered. Added to that is the cost of time spent by senior employees, leads, and directors on the process of hiring.

- Even when you find and hire an ideal candidate, there is a period of inefficiency as members of the team devote a portion of their day to mentoring new arrivals.

There is no downside to a high retention rate as long as salaries are kept in line with the industry and remain appropriate to the level of contribution of the individual.

Improved External Perception

Studios that are well led and well managed enjoy at least a local reputation as being a good place to work. This can be an extremely valuable advantage in a competitive hiring market like Austin, Texas; the San Francisco Bay area; or Seattle/Vancouver. Even in smaller areas, which may have only two or three studios, you want yours to be known as the best place to work. Any positive studio feature can be leveraged to help make your studio a preferred employer, and having sound leadership is a major asset. Advertising this fact is not as easy as pointing to highly successful games or showing your on-site sauna in recruiting ads, however. Good reputations take time to build, and yet more time to travel through the industry—but they do travel, and they are effective.

The converse is also true. Poor reputations also travel—and generally more quickly. In one example, a west coast studio became known for having very poor senior management. The situation was so bad that employees were leaving at a rapid pace because of one particular legacy executive. That perception lingered around the studio for years, long after the upper-level management had cycled out of the studio and internal morale was, in fact, comparatively high.

Greater Company and Team Morale

As mentioned, good leadership helps build good morale in a studio. That this is desirable is a given, but it is important to consider the real impact of a team functioning with high morale. These teams approach challenges in a positive fashion, they take greater pride in the effort and results of their work, they inspire others in the company, and they work in a more focused and productive manner. This potentially equates to less overtime on development cycles—at least less mandatory overtime, since the team will be more self-motivated to achieve great results.

Good leadership does not guarantee high morale in the workplace, but it does do more for morale than any other factor. Game-development studios pride themselves on their various perks, designed to improve the atmosphere of their studio. These efforts include ping-pong tables, movie nights, extremely casual office dress codes, free pizza, on-site gyms—the list goes on. All of these are great, offering people the chance to unwind, refocus, and have fun as part of a sometimes time-intensive and personally stressful development process. I certainly endorse their usage as appropriate. But their positive effect on morale will amount to absolutely nothing if the day-to-day *work* experience for employees is not a pleasant and professional one due to the sub-par abilities of their direct supervisor or team lead.

More-Capable and Supportive Teams

More-capable and supportive teams arise from team members taking the initiative to mentor and lend assistance to their peers. Good leaders practice this and encourage it. In Stephen Martin's interview, he noted one trait of great leaders is that they shift the focus from themselves to others. It is certainly noticed by the team when a leader does this successfully and, as good leaders model the behavior and qualities they seek in their team, it follows that others will take their cue.

An example of this occurred at a developer whose tech director began a series of department-wide training sessions. These were popular, but excluded artists and designers by simple virtue of the subject matter. In response, an artist and programmer at the studio began planning and organizing a series of cross-disciplinary training sessions open to anyone in the company. These were held during lunchtime—the company contributed the ubiquitous free pizza—and were consistently filled to capacity.

Healthier Employees

It has always seemed intuitive to me that if your work is enjoyable, then you will have a healthier general outlook, and possibly be healthier physically. We spend a considerable portion of our waking adult lives pursuing our professions. If our professional experience is stressful or unhappy, it's bound to have an effect.

A study titled "Leadership, Job Well-Being, and Health Effects—A Systematic Review and a Meta-Analysis"—written by Jaana Kuoppala, MD, PhD; Anne Lamminpää, MD, PhD; Juha Liira, MD, PhD; and Harri Vainio, MD, PhD and published in the August 2008 issue of *The Journal of Occupational and Environmental Medicine*—examined the effects of leadership on employee's health as measured by job stress, anxiety levels, and depression. It found that employees whose workplace boasted good leadership (defined as respectful, professional, truthful, responsive to their needs, and provided intellectual stimulation, inspiration, and motivation) tested in the top 40 percent in all health-related categories that were measured. Additionally, it found a 27-percent reduction in the use of sick days and a 46-percent reduction in medical-disability claims. But there are significant benefits to having physically healthier employees, even outside of the obvious reduction in sick days. Healthier people are more alert and more capable of sustained focus and effort during work hours, and generally have a more positive attitude.

Improved Succession Outcomes

All companies experience personnel transitions at various levels at some point. While we strive to have great retention rates, people will leave due to changing career goals, various personal reasons, or simply retirement, and studios must be as well prepared for vacancies in key leadership spots as possible. Having an existing focus on leadership development, formal or informal, will help in times of transition because the internal pool of candidates for leadership positions should be correspondingly greater.

In cases where it is preferable to hire a lead externally or there is no suitable internal candidate, which forces an external search, having a greater focus on leadership means that the importance of solid team and departmental leadership is acknowledged and the skills, qualities, and experience that the studio is seeking in a lead are well understood by all who are involved in the search and hiring effort.

One specific case in the industry involved a studio who cycled through two design department directors in quick succession and decided to wait a while before initiating another search. In the interim, the studio head organized the senior designers into an advisory group to handle departmental issues like personnel management, hiring, and resource management. After a few months, it became clear that the arrangement was very inefficient for the studio head and that it had resulted in unclear departmental direction—which, in turn, lowered morale in the department and the studio. Despite this, the studio head remained reluctant to hire outside the company for such a critical position. The solution was found, in this case, by sharing the predicament with the senior designers and, with their unanimous consent, convincing one of their number to step into the leadership role. The individual chosen was not what might be considered a solid, well-rounded leader, but he had the clear support of his department and senior management, and performed quite well.

Creating a Successful Leadership Culture

Building a great company on a foundation of great leaders does not happen quickly or easily. In my experience, most studios do not boast a wealth of capable team leaders. So creating a studio with great leadership is a multi-pronged endeavor involving the following:

- Moving capable people into appropriate lead positions

- Hiring with an eye for leadership potential

- Developing leadership and management skills

By far the fastest way to improve leadership at your studio is to recognize when you have good leaders on your team and then move them, as fast as is appropriate, into lead roles. Smaller studios with more flexible leaders and less rigid procedures have a much easier time doing this. By way of example, I have seen a junior tester at a small studio rise to lead positions (design, then production) after one project cycle. In this particular example, the instincts of the senior executive were correct; the individual excelled in every lead role to which he was assigned over the succeeding years and had an extremely positive—even transformative—effect on the studio. If the studio management had decided to leave him in the testing department, even as a lead, many of his eventual contributions to the studio would never have occurred.

But suppose, like many studios—particularly those experiencing growth—that no individuals have the desire to take a lead position nor the necessary traits and skills to do so. In these cases, hiring from outside the studio is advisable.

Considering leadership potential in *any* new hire is always prudent, even when there are no lead roles available. I always consider leadership potential when conducting searches for senior personnel. Some portion of an interview is always spent evaluating the candidate's leadership interest and potential. While lack of or an abundance of either would not be a deciding factor, it is a compelling addition to a senior contributor's presentation.

Finally, studios should consciously develop new leads and mentor existing ones, even if only informally through modeled behavior. I do not believe that any individual can simply be trained to be an effective leader, but I do believe that those with the essential interpersonal skills *and* the desire to be a team lead can benefit from personal mentoring as well as targeted leadership training.

It is my hope that in the preceding text, a compelling case has been made for applying appropriate criteria to lead selections—ensuring, through the practice of dual and equivalent career paths, that the right people want to be leads for the right reasons. I hope, too, that team leads and aspiring team leads will have found a few bits of wisdom to improve their practice.

Interview: David Fifield—Lead Designer, Vicarious Visions/Activision

David Fifield has11 years of experience creating games for the PC and Xbox platforms in roles ranging from senior/lead designer to project leader/design director. He has delivered titles in the *Majesty*, *MechWarrior* and *MechAssault* series of games for Hasbro Interactive and Microsoft. Recent work includes a UFC fighting game for THQ Inc. and *Marvel Ultimate Alliance 2* for Activision.

Seth Spaulding: Describe your transition from a production position to a leadership position. What were some unexpected challenges or surprises?

David Fifield: I have yet to fully make a switch from production to leadership, I think because I have always had a balance of the two roles. While certainly some products saw me more and more in the trenches than others, there has always been a good amount of hands-on work involved even when in project-lead positions. While this dual focus is not always practical for the larger teams and responsibilities of next-generation titles, it has always been an integral part of teams in the 35- to 60-person range that everyone is "getting their hands dirty."

S.S.: Looking back, are there any decisions or practices you would change, and if so, why?

D.F.: Nothing jumps immediately to mind. So far I have worked at great companies with a good focus and culture on making the best games possible in a wide variety of circumstances. One thing I have observed repeatedly on teams and projects that struggle is a horizontal reporting tree and lack of proper delegation. I have always advocated leaders having fewer direct reports and a more vertical structure for both responsibility and authority to execute on all areas of a project.

S.S.: What are the most important things you would tell someone making that transition within their company?

D.F.: A few things:

- You have to delegate to be successful as a leader.

- You can never delegate responsibility to someone without giving him or her adequate authority to meet that responsibility.

- When you delegate responsibility and authority, you still retain full responsibility for the end result.

- Hire the best people possible and treat them like gold. You will only be as successful as the team you lead.

S.S.: Were there any people who helped, and if so, how?

D.F.: My first CEO, Joe Minton, was a key mentor in effective delegation and communication with team members. Additionally, he reinforced for me a strong ethical sense of "taking care of our people" beyond the surface level that most companies consider "good enough." With Joe, leadership came at an empathic level with a genuine care and concern for growing teams of quality people and not just finding cogs to fit our video-game machine.

S.S.: What are the most common traits shared by other effective leaders in your experience?

D.F.: Being able to see conflicts from more than one side and being able to effectively communicate their comprehension of the various points of view contributing to the conflict. Conflicts are often quickly settled when all parties feel they are being heard, understood, and given due consideration. From such a position, "correct" answers often become self-evident.

S.S.: Which traits do you feel are your strongest, and how does knowledge of these traits affect how you approach leadership challenges?

D.F.: Practicing empathy for all parties involved in a decision without compromising the end quality of the decision.

S.S.: What are the worst traits a leader has exhibited in your experience?

D.F.: Failure to delegate appropriately. Too often, this results in horizontal reporting structures where too many people are left waiting for feedback and direction from too few sources. This leads to employees feeling distrusted, undervalued, and ultimately becoming underproductive.

S.S.: Are there any leadership traits you admire or perhaps aspire toward but don't feel you embody?

D.F.: Sometimes I would like to have a better grasp on the core competencies of other people I have managed. It is difficult to effectively give direction when the subject matter (in my case, code and art) is beyond my personal proficiencies.

S.S.: How do you feel they would they make you a better leader?

D.F.: While this has provided excellent opportunity to build trust and practice delegation, I often would like to provide more practical problem-solving suggestions than I have been able to in those areas. It would also give artists and programmers a better sense that I knew what they are going through or what was being asked of them.

S.S.: Do you consciously try to develop them?

D.F.: Yes, I take whatever opportunities I can through professional training or available seminars and high-level documentation to understand the other departments in each company I have worked at.

S.S.: Do you mentor other leaders?

D.F.: Yes, most often at a very informal level of suggesting better ways to handle specific situations. First and foremost, I encourage seeing conflicts from the opposing point of view to better understand the problem that needs to be overcome. I also spend a lot of time encouraging team members to "manage up" in circumstances where they are frustrated with lack of direction or leadership. By "manage up" I am referring to a problem-solving strategy where you actively work to not only provide your boss with good answers to situations your group is facing, but anticipate reasons they will be hesitant to accept your suggestions and provide them with appropriate answers to those issues as well. Instead of simply being frustrated with answers or directions you are being given, work proactively to provide your leadership with better answers in a format that lets them buy into the proposal rather than see it as a challenge to their authority.

S.S.: Do you have any training in leadership, either formal or unstructured (e.g., armed forces experience)?

D.F.: I spent four years in the United States Army, from age 17 to 21, and learned a great deal about leadership there. The Army stresses clear and easily followed vertical reporting structures with a strong emphasis on authority and collective responsibility. They maintain their vertical reporting structures by following pretty tight guidelines for the numbers of specific direct reports the leader has. Company commanders have four platoon commanders, who have four squad leaders, etc. This prevents 16 people from all needing direct-report attention and not getting it.

As an overachieving private in a company of lower-achieving sergeants, I was also given ample opportunity to practice "managing up." Having ready answers for leaders who sometimes lacked answers to their own problems, and presenting them in such a way that let those leaders take credit for them and "make them their own," paid huge dividends. They would look to keep me close and available with helpful suggestions, often keeping me from less pleasant assignments a private might be sent on. The people they in turn were reporting too were smart enough to know many of the solutions were actually coming from me, so I didn't lack for recognition at the next level of command, and was quickly promoted through the ranks.

In a more unstructured sense, I have a very strong sense of right and wrong and tend to speak up when I think problems and especially people are being treated wrongly. Regardless of title, rank, or position, this behavior quickly attracts people to wanting advice, help, or simply to be on your team. Formal leadership is generally a foregone conclusion of building these types of relationships.

S.S.: What do you see as the toughest challenge facing leads during a game-development project cycle or at a game-development company generally?

D.F.: A common interview question I have heard over the years solicits an answer regarding managing team morale versus product quality. My answer is that product quality should be our bottom line and most always come first, but you need to build a culture in which high product quality equals high morale. Once your culture derives its satisfaction from the quality of the product you are making, achieving both high product quality and high morale is a natural occurrence. Falling into a mentality that says we have to take a hit on team morale in order to make a high-quality product most often results in failing at both. Achieving this culture shift is often difficult and comes through sacrifice from both management and the team.

Leaders in unproven or young companies are not often afforded budgets and time tables to achieve high product quality without a high level of overtime, iteration, and difficult cuts to product vision or original goals. In this "starting-out" situation, leaders need to emphasize their faith in the team's ability to deliver quality, set consistent goals for quality, and find the right balance of preaching both the need for quality and future rewards of quality.

Leaders in front-running companies with a strong history of quality face different challenges in establishing or maintaining this culture. Keeping egos (especially their own) checked at the door is paramount. So is quickly assimilating new hires into the culture of quality, avoiding the temptation to "make them pay dues" first, and perhaps most importantly spreading the wealth appropriately.

S.S.: What are some common mistakes you've seen leads make, be they new or experienced?

D.F.: Failure to delegate. See any of my references above. Also, excessive direction of their personal areas of interest. Most leaders were really good at some particular areas of the discipline they are now being asked to lead in. They don't stop being good at those things once they become leaders, and often have a hard time letting someone else do those specific tasks that they either did extremely well or simply enjoyed doing. Personally, as a designer, I always very much enjoyed writing dialog and story elements for the games I worked on. On a specific project where I was a project leader and lead designer, I should have delegated or outsourced the script and dialog writing, but instead retained that task for myself. On a later project where sheer volume of other tasks precluded me from writing dialog, I discovered a subordinate was even better at it than I was. Too bad he didn't have that shot on the previous title. Other times, this failure comes from the leader micromanaging an area unnecessarily, especially in situations where two methods are equally reasonable for solving a problem but the leader insists on his or her own method. Narrow-minded problem solving from leaders quickly erodes team morale and confidence.

S.S.: How have you seen new leads best get support from directors or executives?

D.F.: Trust. Also, not extending authority or responsibility beyond merit. It might seem obvious, but I often think leaders need to be reminded to set their people up for success, not to set them up to fail. I am not a fan of giving someone enough rope to hang himself. It is a cowardly and costly approach to dealing with subordinates.

S.S.: Do you think good leaders can be trained? Or is the essence of a good leader simply innate ability?

D.F.: I think good leaders have a large mix of traits that are both trainable and intrinsic or innate. I also think that it is sometimes possible to train or develop some the of the traits that I list below as intrinsic, but it is not always possible, nor is it ever simple.

Trained leadership traits such as punctuality, organization, and specific job proficiency are valuable in a candidate, but being more readily trainable they are not as important as the intrinsic traits that we more often think of as making somebody "who they are."

Intrinsic traits I consider important in good leadership are largely moral or ethical ones. Character, integrity, compassion, vision, and self-sacrifice come to mind when I think of the leaders I have the most respect for.

In closing, I think the best leaders are also the ones who pursue the role for the best motives and that at their core those motives are focused on the benefit of others. Someone who wants to be a leader because he or she is sick of other people screwing things up is not necessarily a person I'd want to follow. Someone who feels he or she should take on more responsibility in order to improve product quality by getting the best from everyone and then leveraging that quality product into quality of life for all who contributed to it is very much the type of person I would follow.

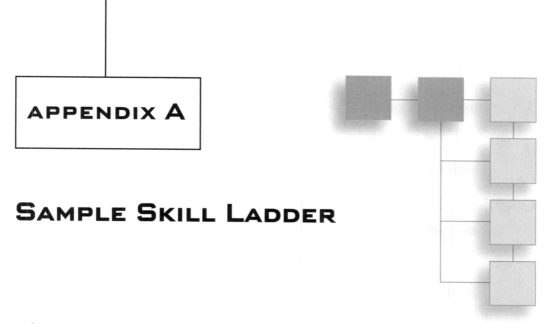

APPENDIX A

SAMPLE SKILL LADDER

Below is a sample skill ladder for an art department. Team leaders from other disciplines interested in this system can and should edit the entries, add or delete steps—whatever. The only critical component is the stepped skill progression concept with enough detail in each step for clarity.

While I do not employ a skill ladder in any formal fashion currently, I think it remains a very valuable tool for comparative evaluation when analyzing an existing department as a new manager. The primary disadvantage of a skill ladder is that it is not as helpful when comparatively evaluating people with different project roles and skill sets—i.e., concept artists versus animators.

Art Skill Ladder
Core Values

- Has a strong passion for creating great art

- Works well in a team environment

- Understands the need for and gives and receives criticism well

- Self-motivated, always learning and striving for improvement

- Dedicated, honest, and loyal

- Respectful to co-workers

- Hard-working, takes pride in one's work

- Enthusiastic, positive, embraces critiques

- Understands the audience and appreciates games

Level 10: Intern
Qualifications

- Embodies all core values and shows aptitude in one area of production art needed for the project (modeling, texturing, etc.)

- Shows promise of developing more advanced skills with the potential for becoming a full-time hire

Responsibilities

- Produce art assets as directed by an art lead or the art director on any of a variety of production tasks depending on the artist's area(s) of specialization

- Follow workflow pipelines and organize assets according to established guidelines

Level 20: Artist I
Qualifications

- Should have college-level organization and communication skills—both written and verbal

- Understands the general fundamentals of at least one 3D application, preferably 3DS Max

- Understands the general fundamentals of at least one 2D art application, preferably Photoshop

- Shows an aptitude for learning new tools quickly

- Must have capability in some traditional art skills, such as concept sketch ability

Responsibilities

- Produce art assets as directed by an art lead or the art director on any of a variety of production tasks depending on the artist's area(s) of specialization

- Follow workflow pipelines and organize assets according to established guidelines

- Responsible for understanding and following updates on documents and processes in area of specialization

- Approval of personal task time estimates

- Solicits peer review for initial feedback on art assets when appropriate

Level 25: Artist II
Qualifications

All of Level 20, plus:

- Understands the general fundamentals of 3DS Max.

- Understands the general fundamentals of Photoshop.

- Is able to thrive in a team environment supervised by a more senior artist.

- Creates game art that consistently meets expectations expressed in the concept art.

- Concept artist goal: Possesses a focused visual language that allows for timely creation of compelling and creative production-level concept art. Concept work conforms to guidelines provided by team leads.

- Concept artist goal: All modeling and texturing questions are answered clearly by the concept work.

Responsibilities

All of Level 20, plus:

- Proficient with basic functionality of source control, task tracking, and bug database software

- Can be relied upon by leads to meet production task times with acceptable quality level

- Understands the importance of and accurately employs established asset organizational structures and naming conventions

Level 30: Artist III
Qualifications

All of Level 25, plus:

- Approximately three to five years of industry experience or two to three development cycles.

- Displays solid skills in 3DS Max, Photoshop, and any other tool commonly used for production of art assets in area(s) of specialization.

- Able to work in an unsupervised capacity for the duration of a given task list.

- Makes independent creative decisions that result in game assets that often surpass expectations expressed in the concept art.

- Concept artist goal: Ability to quickly develop large numbers of concept roughs to select from with the goal of later refinement.

Responsibilities

All of Level 25, plus:

- Accurately follows and may help develop workflow pipelines and asset organization guidelines

- Responsible for understanding and assisting in the creation of workflow documents and processes in area(s) of specialization

- Creates art assets with very few or no technical quality issues

- Self-starter

- Is able to provide very accurate task time estimates

- Is a positive force in company and team morale

- Proficient with advanced functionality of source control, task tracking and bug database software

- Participates significantly in team meetings, CSAs, and milestone reviews

Level 35: Artist IV

Is eligible and may be called upon for art lead, principal artist, or specialist lead positions. (Not a requirement for artist IV, but a marker for consideration.)

Qualifications

All of Level 30, plus:

- Displays solid general skills in 3DS Max and has developed at least one area of focus or specialization.

- Has working knowledge of the games industry and keeps up with innovative games and games that set high visual bars.

- Possesses skills, creativity, and proven performance traits that are consistently in demand by project teams.

- Concept artist goal: Able to produce high-quality preproduction concept work given minimal direction by team leads. May be considered for storyboard creation tasks if applicable.

Responsibilities

All of Level 30, plus:

- Is recognized by the team as being a strong contributor to the project

- Absolutely reliable for the timely creation of 100-percent technically solid art

- Can be relied upon to quickly learn new processes and software as dictated by project needs

- Is considered a problem solver

- Motivates peers toward excellence

- Can be considered to lead art workshops

Level 40: Senior Artist I
Qualifications

All of Level 35, plus:

- Approximately six to eight years of industry experience or five development cycles.

- Has in-depth knowledge of basic and advanced technology, terminology, and techniques of game art development, including an awareness of design and programming considerations.

- Is able to see the "big picture" of the project.

- Is recognized by the team for having at least one area of deep expertise in a core area of game art development (concept art, UI, character animation, modeling/texturing, FX, etc.).

- Has mastery in at least two areas of 3DS Max, Photoshop, and any other tool commonly used for production of art assets.

- Able to work unsupervised for long periods and able to supervise others.

- Concept artist goal: Able to bring a large measure of creativity and initiative to both preproduction and production concept tasks and adapt swiftly to new themes as directed by the team.

Responsibilities

All of Level 35, plus:

- Can be relied upon to innovate and instruct the team regarding new processes and software as dictated by project needs; strong independent problem-solving ability

- Often considered to lead art workshops

Level 45: Senior Artist II
Qualifications

All of Level 40, plus:

- Often recommends new tools and processes to the company

- Able to effectively communicate art issues to non-artists

Responsibilities

All of Level 40, plus:

- Understands team dynamics and is an active cohesive force in the team

- Understands some underlying programming issues as they relate to areas of 3D art and can recommend practices to create more efficient art

- Tracks state-of-the-art industry practices through Web sites and trade journals; regularly brings findings to the department

- Is able to establish procedures and build style guides as needed by team leads

- Concept artist goal: May create and assemble style guides as directed by project leads

Level 50: Senior Artist III
Qualifications

All of Level 40, plus:

- Approximately 12 years of industry experience or seven development cycles.

- Has mastery of art tools in at least two areas of art production including: 3DS Max (modeling, rigging, effects, texturing, and/or animation), Photoshop, and any other tool commonly used for production of art assets.

- Can work across multiple projects at the same time.

- Concept artist goal: Able to switch between a few distinct styles while creating compelling concepts.

Responsibilities

All of Level 40, plus:

- Is a force for innovation of workflow pipelines and asset organization guidelines

- Actively pushes the art quality bar across all projects

- Is a positive force in company and team morale; is considered a "go-to" person by management and artists alike

- Is a positive force for the company at trade events; frequently is invited to speak at industry conferences and events

- Advises management on emerging art tools and techniques

- May effectively function in "firefighter" mode as needed by any project in the company

Level 60: Senior Artist IV—Luminary
Qualifications

All of Level 50, plus:

- Approximately 20 years of industry experience or nine shipped games.

- Has attained guru-level status in at least two areas of art production including: 3DS Max (modeling, rigging, effects, texturing and/or animation), Photoshop, and any other tool commonly used for production of art assets.

- Has achieved a high level of industry recognition and top accolades for work in area of expertise.

- Concept artist goal: Achieved recognition in the industry for superior concept art, has concept work accepted into juried shows and publications.

Responsibilities

All of Level 50, plus:

- Contributions advance art quality and techniques throughout the industry

- Works to enhance the public and industry image of Firaxis as a leader in the game art field

Lead Qualifications and Responsibilities

Note: This section is not part of the overall skill ladder. This is merely an enumeration of some of the core traits of great leads.

Specialist Art Lead
Qualifications

All of Level 30, plus:

- Shows aptitude for developing great communication and leadership skills

- Always pushes the art quality bar

- Displays consistent, professional demeanor at all times

- Reacts well under stressful situations

- Is a positive force in company morale

Responsibilities

- Provides artistic vision for lead area, whether animation, modeling, or UI

- First asset review for technical and aesthetic checks

- May create and maintain process docs in area of specialization

- May establish task times and schedule tasks in area of specialization for the art lead

Art Lead
Qualifications

All of Level 30 and specialist art lead, plus:

- Has demonstrated great communication and leadership skills

- Displays consistent, professional demeanor at all times; is considered a "rock" by staff and management alike

- Demonstrates effective delegation ability

- Can give effective art critiques

Responsibilities

- Achieves and maintains artistic vision for the project

- Advocates for team resources for their project; pushes for greater art quality but also has a holistic view of the project and understands the need for compromise

- Reviews all milestone assets as well as the "big picture" look and feel

- Oversees tool spec creation and maintenance

- Strives to get the best work out of all team members

- Establishes and maintains schedule with the producer

- Must have a general knowledge of all art tasks on the project

- Effectively communicates with management, other leads, and staff

INDEX